Tobias Walter

Bridging Technological Spaces: Towards the Combination of Model-Driven Engineering and Ontology Technologies

July 25, 2011

Vom Promotionsausschuss des Fachbereichs 4: Informatik der Universität Koblenz-Landau zur Verleihung des akademischen Grades Doktor der Naturwissenschaften (Dr. rer. nat.) genehmigte Dissertation.

Vorsitzender des Promotionsausschusses:
Prof. Dr. Rüdiger Grimm

Promotionskommission

Vorsitzender: Prof. Dr. Felix Hampe
Berichterstatter: Prof. Dr. Jürgen Ebert
                       Prof. Dr. Steffen Staab
                       Prof. Dr. Gerti Kappel

Tag der wissenschaftlichen Aussprache: 29. Juni 2011

Bibliografische Information der Deutschen Nationalbibliothek

Die Deutsche Nationalbibliothek verzeichnet diese Publikation in der
Deutschen Nationalbibliografie; detaillierte bibliografische Daten sind
im Internet über http://dnb.d-nb.de abrufbar.

ISBN 978-3-8325-2936-9

Logos Verlag Berlin GmbH
Comeniushof, Gubener Str. 47,
10243 Berlin
Tel.: +49 (0)30 42 85 10 90
Fax: +49 (0)30 42 85 10 92
INTERNET: http://www.logos-verlag.de

Abstract

Model-Driven Engineering (MDE) aims to raise the level of abstraction in software system specifications and increase automation in software development. *Modelware technological spaces* contain the languages and tools for MDE that software developers take into consideration to model systems and domains.

Ontoware technological spaces contain ontology languages and technologies to design, query, and reason on knowledge. With the advent of the *Semantic Web*, ontologies are now being used within the field of software development, as well.

In this thesis, *bridging technologies* are developed to combine two technological spaces in general. Transformation bridges translate models between spaces, mapping bridges relate different models between two spaces, and, integration bridges merge spaces to new all-embracing technological spaces. API bridges establish interoperability between the tools used in the space.

In particular, this thesis focuses on the combination of modelware and ontoware technological spaces. Subsequent to a sound comparison of languages and tools in both spaces, the integration bridge is used to build a common technological space, which allows for the hybrid use of languages and the interoperable use of tools. The new space allows for language and domain engineering.

Ontology-based software languages may be designed in the new space where syntax and formal semantics are defined with the support of ontology languages, and the correctness of language models is ensured by the use of ontology reasoning technologies. These languages represent a core means for exploiting expressive ontology reasoning in the software modeling domain, while remaining flexible enough to accommodate varying needs of software modelers.

Application domains are conceptually described by languages that allow for defining domain instances and types within one domain model. Integrated ontology languages may provide formal semantics for *domain-specific languages* and ontology technologies allow for reasoning over types and instances in domain models.

A scenario in which configurations for network device families are modeled illustrates the approaches discussed in this thesis. Furthermore, the implementation of all bridging technologies for the combination of technological spaces and all tools for ontology-based language engineering and use is illustrated.

Zusammenfassung

Die *modellgetriebene Softwareentwicklung* beabsichtigt die Spezifikation von Softwaresystemen durch Modelle zu vereinfachen und die automatisierte Entwicklung zu verbessern. Die Modellierungssprachen und Werkzeuge, die zur Modellierung von Systemen und Anwendungsdomänen herangezogen werden, werden in *modellbasierten technologischen Räumen* zusammengefasst. *Ontologiebasierte technologische Räume* enthalten Ontologiesprachen und Technologien zum Entwurf, der Anfrage und dem Schlussfolgern von Wissen. Mit der Verbreitung des *semantischen Webs* werden Ontologien in der Entwicklung von Software zunehmend eingesetzt.

In dieser Arbeit werden zur Kombination von technologischen Räumen *Brückentechnologien* vorgestellt. Transformationsbrücken übersetzen Modelle, Abbildungsbrücken stellen Beziehungen zwischen Modellen verschiedener technologischer Räume her und Integrationsbrücken verschmelzen Räume zu neuen allumfassenden technologischen Räumen. API Brücken erschaffen Interoperabilität zwischen Werkzeugen.

Diese Arbeit beschäftigt sich insbesondere mit der Kombination von modellbasierten und ontologiebasierten technologischen Räumen. Nach einem Vergleich zwischen Sprachen und Werkzeugen der einzelnen Räume wird die Integrationsbrücke herangezogen um einen neuen gemeinsamen technologischen Raum zu erstellen, der den hybriden Gebrauch von Sprachen und den interoperablen Einsatz von Werkzeugen ermöglicht.

Die Syntax und Semantik von Modellierungssprachen kann mit Hilfe von Ontologiesprachen spezifiziert werden. Die Korrektheit von Modellen wird durch den Einsatz von Ontologietechnologien gewährleistet. *Ontologiebasierte Modellierungssprachen* erlauben den Nutzen von Anfrage- und Schlussfolgerungstechnologien. Sie sind darüber hinaus so flexibel um verschiedene Anforderungen von Softwareentwicklern zu erfüllen.

Domänenspezifische Sprachen unterstützen neben der Spezifikation von Systemen auch die konzeptionelle Beschreibung von Domänen durch Modelle, die aus möglichen Laufzeitinstanzen und deren Typen bestehen. Integrierte Ontologiesprachen helfen eine formale Semantik für Domänenmodellierungssprachen zu definieren und Ontologietechnologien ermöglichen das Schlussfolgern über Typen und Instanzen.

Alle Ansätze in dieser Arbeit werden mit Hilfe eines Szenarios, in dem die Konfigurationen für Familien von Netzwerkgeräte modelliert werden, veranschaulicht. Ferner werden die Implementationen aller Brückentechnologien zur Kombination von technologischen Räumen und alle Werkzeuge für die ontologiebasierte Entwicklung von Modellierungssprachen illustriert.

Danksagung

An dieser Stelle möchte ich all jenen danken, die mir durch ihre fachliche und persönliche Unterstützung bei der Erarbeitung dieser Dissertation zur Seite standen.

Mein erster Dank geht an Prof. Dr. Jürgen Ebert und Prof. Dr. Steffen Staab. Sie haben mir ermöglicht in Koblenz zu promovieren und in einem internationalen Projekt zu arbeiten. Beide haben mit vielen spannenden Diskussionen und gezielter konstruktiver Kritik zur Entstehung dieser Arbeit beigetragen.

Prof. Dr. Gerti Kappel danke ich für das Interesse an meiner Arbeit und die Bereitschaft diese Dissertation zu begutachten.

Mit Gerd Gröner und Fernando Silva Parreiras habe ich das Büro geteilt und zusammen mit Hannes Schwarz viele interessante Diskussionen geführt. Für die vielen gemeinsamen Stunden in Koblenz und auf Dienstreisen bin ich allen sehr dankbar.

Auch meinem gesamten Kollegenkreis bin ich zu Dank verpflichtet. Obwohl ich jeweils ein halbes Mitglied des Instituts für *Web Science and Technologies* (WeST) und des *Instituts für Softwaretechnik* (IST) bin, werde ich stets von beiden als ein volles Mitglied akzeptiert.

Die zahlreichen Treffen im Rahmen des EU Forschungsprojekts *Marrying Ontology and Software Technology* (MOST) boten mir die Möglichkeit meine Ideen zu präsentieren und mit unseren Partnern Beispiele zu erarbeiten, die in dieser Arbeit zur Veranschaulichung meiner Ideen dienen.

Dankbar bin ich auch allen studentischen Hilfskräften, die im Rahmen des MOST und des TwoUse Projekts in den vergangenen drei Jahren halfen, die in dieser Arbeit vorgestellten Ansätze zu realisieren.

Mein letzter Dank geht an meine Familie und Freunde, die mich stets unterstützt haben und so auch ihren Beitrag zu dieser Arbeit geleistet haben.

Contents

Part IV Applications

Part I

Introduction and Motivation

1

Introduction

Nowadays *Model-Driven Engineering* (MDE) plays a key role in the description and engineering of software systems [Sch06]. Models are the central artifacts in model-driven engineering. They are designed using modeling languages and edited, queried, and transformed using corresponding tools during software development. Models describe views of the real world systems and applications.

Models may be defined by several modeling languages. *Modeling languages* are usually defined in their concrete syntax (the visual notation used), their abstract syntax (the structure behind the visualization), and their semantics (the intended meaning of given models). *Language designers* develop modeling languages which are applied by *language users*, who use the concrete syntax to build conforming models.

A prominent modeling language is UML - the *Unified Modeling Language* [OMG07b]. UML provides a visual notation and is a general-purpose modeling language since it provides concepts that are not dependent on any application domain. UML allows for modeling several views of a software system. Additionally to general-purpose modeling languages, *Domain-Specific Languages* (DSL) may be used. They focus on specific application domains and provide domain-specific abstractions and notations for the design of specific aspects of a system [KT07].

The concrete languages and tools used to develop the software depend on the technological spaces and modeling environments. A *technological space* is a working context with a set of associated modeling concepts and tools [KBA02]. A *modeling environment* provides all the software facilities, modeling languages, tools, and services for the development and support of software products [NE93].

A prominent technological space is the *Meta Object Facility* (MOF) technological space initiated by the *Object Management Group* (OMG) [OMG06]. In MOF the software development process is populated with a number of different models. They are described by different languages. The most popular is the UML.

We consider such UML/MOF-inspired technological spaces as *Modelware Technological Spaces*.

Besides modelware technological spaces other spaces can be easily identified, e.g., the *XML technological space* [W3C11], or the *grammarware technological space* [SW09]. The XML technological space is widely accepted as a standard for representation and exchange of structured and semi-structured data where XML documents are the central concept. The grammarware technological space is concerned with grammars, grammar-based description languages, and associated tools. A further space is the *ontoware technological space*, which is introduced below. In general, all spaces provide languages and tools, and they have advantages as well as drawbacks.

The heterogeneity of and the insufficient interoperability between technological spaces often hinders the simultaneous use of their respective languages, tools, and services. In this thesis we are going to tackle the interoperability between modelware technological spaces and other technological spaces. For the combination of technological spaces, appropriate techniques are required. We consider these techniques as *bridges*.

To define these bridges between technological spaces, their similarities (commonalities) and their dissimilarities (variabilities) must first be identified. The comparison leads to a mapping of the underlying concepts of spaces and is used as a basis for building concrete bridges.

Besides languages we must consider the tools and services. We will discover the technologies, which bring profit to the respective other spaces.

With the advent of the *Semantic Web* [AH08], ontologies are used in software modeling [WPS09, WPSE10], as well. Though in the stronger sense an ontology is *a formal explicit specification of a shared conceptualization for a domain of interest* [GOS09], the term ontology is actually being used for logical knowledge bases in a broader sense. Ontologies are based on description logics (DL) [BCM+03], and the term ontology is more and more used as a synonym for description logics knowledge bases in general.

Similar to software models, ontologies may be described by languages. A prominent example is the World Wide Web Consortium (W3C) standard *Web Ontology Language* (OWL) in its current version 2 [MPSH09]. OWL 2 allows for class based modeling. It provides a rich set of primitives used to formally conceptualize a domain. OWL 2 allows for defining classes representing the concepts of the domain. Class descriptions are extended by logical expressions on the properties that classes have. Axioms in OWL 2 ontologies define conditions on class memberships.

Given an ontology conceptualizing a domain, ontology reasoning tools and services may be used to check the correctness of logical expressions and derive relations between classes or its members. Information that is implicitly defined in an ontology can be made explicit by reasoning tools.

The OWL-based way of modeling together with reasoning and querying tools is summarized as *Ontoware Technological Space*, opposed to MOF/UML-like modeling and tooling in modelware technological spaces. To differentiate ontologies used as a shared conceptualization in the semantic world wide web and models described by OWL 2 representing a DL knowledge base, we introduce in this thesis the notion of *ontoware models*. Ontoware models are software models written in OWL 2 and represent a DL knowledge base.

In this thesis we concentrate on the combination of modelware and ontoware technological spaces. We will depict some challenges for modelware technological spaces, which may be tackled by ontoware technological spaces. We consider applications in the field of domain-specific modeling. We will show how the combinations of languages of the two spaces are used for domain-specific modeling and how different tools and services support the modeling tasks.

The remaining sections belonging to this chapter are structured as follows: In Section 1.1 we set up the key challenges for this thesis summarizing the requirements and shortcomings in model-driven engineering. We present the research contribution of this thesis by positioning research questions in Section 1.2. Answers to these research questions tackle the key challenges with the use of ontology languages and technologies. We illustrate the road map of this thesis providing guidance to the reader on how to read it in Section 1.3. In Section 1.4 we comment on the dissemination of the approaches presented in this thesis.

1.1 Challenges in Model-Driven Engineering

In this section we are going to present the shortcomings and requirements in *model-driven engineering* and *domain-specific modeling*. Given these shortcomings and requirements we set up four key challenges which are tackled in this thesis with the use of ontology languages and technologies.

1.1.1 Shortcomings in Model-Driven Engineering

Model-Driven Engineering (MDE) targets the improvement of software quality, reuse, and efficient software development [Béz06, MCF03]. The approach of model-driven engineering suggests to handle models as primary artefacts. In several steps they are transformed into executable models (e.g., source code).

France and Rumpe present in [FR07] a research road map for model-driven development of complex software. They present three categories of open challenges for MDE.

MDE 1: The *modeling language* challenge deals with the creation of problem-level abstractions using modeling languages. Modeling languages should provide abstractions of problems to be modeled and solved. This may be achieved by general purpose modeling languages. In addition, *language extension mechanisms* should allow for integrating suitable and domain-specific concepts abstracting a specific domain to one integrated modeling language.

MDE 2: The *separation of concerns* challenge arises from the problem that different views of one system are modeled using multiple languages. Modeling languages such as UML [OMG07b] support the design of systems from several fixed viewpoints. Nevertheless, concepts in one viewpoint may depend on those provided by other viewpoints. Modeling environments should provide mechanisms to integrate languages for separate views to one modeling language providing a consistent view to the complete system to be modeled.

MDE 3: The *model manipulation* challenge describes the design and use of model transformations. Typical model transformations define (binary) relations between two sets of models, where one set describes all source models, the other set describes the target models. A mechanism implementing the transformation considers a source model and produces a target model. Besides traditional transformations, modeling environments must support other forms becoming more widely used in MDE: (a) *Model compositions* take two source models representing different views and produce an integrated view. (b) *Model decomposition* is used to produce multiple target models for one integrated model. (c) *Model translations* transform a source model to a target model expressed in a different language better suited for some other purpose.

In addition to the problems described by France and Rumpe, Atkinson and Kühne describe in their papers [AK03, AK01] the foundations of infrastructures for model-driven engineering. An infrastructure for model-driven engineering must support the capabilities for language engineering and use. Much of their recent work on enhancing the infrastructure has focused on metamodeling as a method for engineering languages. Such infrastructures are supported by the traditional *4-layer metamodeling hierarchy*.

The 4-layer metamodeling hierarchy provided by OMG [OMG06] describes the specification and the use of modeling languages. At the *M3 layer* a metametamodel is defined. At the *M2 layer* the language is specified by defining a metamodel. Its elements are instances of elements in the metametamodel. At the *M1 layer* the specified language can be used for creating a model, which is an instance of the metamodel. All models at the M1 layer are representations of real world elements lying at the *M0 layer*.

Given the 4-layer metamodeling hierarchy, Atkinson and Kühne identify problems:

MDE 4: The metamodeling hierarchy implies that all instantiation relationships between types and instances are fundamentally of the same kind.
But different kinds of types exist. Types can *prescribe* instances to fulfill given properties, and types are used to *describe* sets of instances by
formulating the characteristics instances have.

MDE 5: A preference exists for using metalevel descriptions to provide predefined concepts. Besides metamodel designers, language users require the
capability to dynamically extend the set of types by specializing given
types or by adding new metatypes.

1.1.2 Shortcomings in Domain-Specific Modeling

Domain-specific modeling (DSM) aims for raising the level of abstraction be-
yond programming languages and source code by modeling the solution in a
language that directly uses concepts and rules from a specific problem domain. In the context of model-driven engineering, domain models, designed
using DSLs, may be combined with other models in standardized languages to
form a complete and consistent overall view to the system under development.

There is an agreement about the challenges faced by current DSL approaches [GFC+08]:

DSM 1: (*Tooling*) For many DSLs even basic tools such as debuggers or test-
ing engines are missing. Such tools are costly to build, but they are necessary because DSL tools must provide the abstraction and the assistance
for the domain to be modeled.
A typical activity in programming is debugging to find and repair defects
in programs. Domain models designed using domain-specific modeling languages may also have defects, e.g., models may not conform to language
specifications or elements in models may contradict each other. Debuggers
for domain models should identify the defects and suggest how to repair
them.

DSM 2: (*Interoperability*) Facilities for language interoperability are an improvement for domain-specific modeling. Domain modelers can shift freely
between domain-appropriate languages to model systems under different
aspects.
Different parts of the same system may be described by using different
DSLs. Thus, there must be a means to relate concepts across language
borders and a means to ensure consistency [FR07]. Therefore, France and
Rumpe require a sound integration approach of DSLs.

DSM 3: (*Formal semantics*) The design of DSLs is often concentrated on the
syntax. The abstract syntax, achieved by a metamodel, defines the domain
concepts available for domain modeling. The concrete syntax provides
notations for simplified modeling. Often a clear definition of semantics,
the meaning of domain concepts the language provides, is not achieved.
Formal semantics precisely describe the meaning of models in such a way

so that they do not remain open to different interpretations by different persons (or machines).

Formal semantics are required for validating domain models and evaluating well-formedness rules restricting the use of domain concepts. Usually domain models are validated and verified informally in design reviews. Such procedures might be error-prone. Proving properties about concepts and relationships in the domain is not possible due to the lack of formal semantics of DSLs. Given a formal semantic defined for a DSL, semantic analysis may help to validate the conformity of domain models with respect to language specifications.

1.1.3 Key Challenges of this Thesis

In the following we are going to set up *key challenges*, which summarize the problems, shortcomings, and requirements from the MDE and DSM community.

Challenge 1 (*Bridging Technologies*)

> *Since software systems to be built are modeled from different perspectives using several modeling languages, we must establish techniques that allow for combining modeling languages. We consider these techniques as bridges. Hence, the bridging technologies challenge discusses generic bridges used for the composition and the decomposition of modeling languages. For each bridge a sound procedure how to establish it for two given modeling languages and how to use it for respective conforming models must be developed.*
>
> *The approached shortcomings and requirements for this challenge are: MDE 2,3; DSM 2.*

Challenge 2 (*Formal Semantics and Correctness of Languages*)

> *The semantics of modeling languages is often not defined explicitly but hidden in modeling tools. To fix a specific formal semantics for models it should be defined declaratively in the metamodel. To make well-formedness constraints more explicit, they also should be defined declaratively in the metamodel specification.*
>
> *The approached shortcomings and requirements for this challenge are: MDE 1; DSM 3.*

Challenge 3 (*Tooling*)

> *Tooling is important for productive and error-free modeling. Model editors may be extended by integrated debugging and assistance services. A challenge is to develop a meta-tool infrastructure so that tools for DSLs can be created more easily [GFC+08, FR07]. Tools provide a set of services to users of DSLs [BGMR03]. Meta-tools also provide services, which*

> encapsulate basic functionalities and which are used by tool developers to implement the services for DSL users.
>
> The approached shortcomings and requirements for this challenge are: DSM 1.

Challenge 4 (*Domain Modeling*)

> Domain designers prefer the use of type descriptions to define concepts classifying domain instances in domain models. They require the capability to dynamically extend the set of types by specializing given types or by adding new metatypes. To design models consisting of several type layers, language users need appropriate languages. This challenge discusses the design of syntax and semantics of (domain-specific) modeling languages allowing for dynamically extending the set of domain types available for modeling.
>
> The approached shortcomings and requirements for this challenge are: MDE 4, 5.

1.2 Research Questions

In this thesis we are going to show how to tackle the key challenges listed in Section 1.1.3 with the combination of modelware technological spaces with ontoware technological spaces.

To combine modelware and ontoware languages and tools, we are going to ask *research questions*. These questions are stated at the beginning of each chapter in this thesis. In this section we are going to summarize these research questions to illustrate how they are arranged and related throughout the whole thesis.

Modelware and ontoware technological spaces provide the design of models using languages as well as providing tools and services. Before we start bridging them, we need a consistent view of both spaces. We must answer the question:

Question 1:   *What are the particular languages and tools in the respective spaces?*
(RQ1,2,3,4)

We must describe the syntax and semantics of languages used in the spaces and we must specify the tools and services the spaces provide.

Having a unique and consistent view of both technological spaces and their languages, tools, and services, we are going to answer the following question:

Question 2:   *What are the commonalities and variations of a modelware technological space and an ontoware technological space?*
(RQ5)

The goal is to find a mapping of language concepts that syntactically and semantically have similar properties in both spaces. Furthermore, variations of language concepts and tools must be indicated to outline benefits of technologies in the respective other space.

A mapping of concepts may help to establish bridges to combine both spaces. To realize and use bridges we must answer the question:

Question 3:   What are the techniques to bridge technological spaces?
    (RQ6)

We will develop bridges, indicate their respective advantages, and show how they are established and how they are used in a modeling environment. The goal is to present the bridges in a generic way such that they can be used for the combination of several spaces besides modelware and ontoware.

Having mechanisms to combine technological spaces, we are going to consider the combined use of modelware and ontoware languages and tools.

We target the engineering of new modeling languages in combination with ontology languages via bridges. Ontology languages with their rich set of primitives and their formal semantics may support the design of syntax and semantics of software modeling languages. We are going to answer the question:

Question 4:   How may the formal semantics of ontology languages be used for software modeling languages?
    (RQ7,9)

Answering this question, we target the engineering of new modeling languages in combination with ontology languages via bridges. Ontology languages may support the design of syntax and semantics in the software language engineering process. Having modeling languages designed and bridged with ontology languages, we must consider their use. Since ontology technologies allow for reasoning we must consider the question:

Question 5:   How do ontology technologies support the design and correctness of models?
    (RQ8,10)

The goal is to detect tools and services from the ontoware space that may help in using a modeling language. Besides editors, the users of languages are interested in the correctness of models and they require guidance through the modeling process. If defects in models are detected, the software modeler is guided in the deagnosis and handling of defects.

The techniques used to bridge modeling languages, the approaches of using ontology languages for software modeling, and, the detected ontology technologies supporting software modeling, may all be applied in domain-specific modeling. Therefore, we are going to tackle the following question:

Question 6:   How are integrated ontology technologies applied in domain-specific modeling?
    (RQ11,12)

To illustrate the use of ontology technologies in domain-specific modeling, we are going to consider the domain of *network routers*. Here domain-specific languages may be bridged with ontology languages and ontology technologies may be used for the correctness and support of designing domain models representing network routers.

1.3 Thesis Road Map

In Figure 1.1 we illustrate the road map of this thesis giving an overview of all chapters. It depicts the relations between chapters and the assignment of research questions.

Based on the requirements and shortcomings coming from the MDE community, we have established four key challenges that tackle these requirements and shortcomings with the use of ontology technologies.

In Part II we introduce the foundations for this thesis. We introduce a modelware technological space in Chapter 2 and an ontoware technological space in Chapter 3. The goal of these chapters is to specify the languages and services in a common framework making them comparable. Chapter 4 provides the comparison of both spaces comparing the languages and tools. Further, the chapter targets the establishment of a first mapping of language concepts between both spaces and figures out the potentials of modelware tools and ontoware tools.

In Part III of this thesis we show the combinations of modelware languages and technologies with ontoware technologies. In Chapter 5 we present the bridging technologies. We specify how they are established for two given languages and we show how they are used. The Chapters 6 and 7 consider these bridging technologies. Here we illustrate approaches that profit from ontology technologies in language engineering, use, and conceptual domain engineering.

Given several combinations of modelware and ontoware, we present in Part IV applications in the field of domain-specific modeling. In Chapter 8 we present a modeling environment for developing and using domain-specific modeling languages. In Chapter 9 we present the joint design of modeling languages for language engineering and domain engineering. In both chapters ontology languages are used to define the semantics of modeling languages and reasoning services are used for more productive modeling.

In Part V we conclude this thesis. In Chapter 10 we present the tools realizing the approaches discussed in this thesis. We furthermore review the key challenges set up in Section 1.1.3 and mention where in the thesis they are tackled and applied. Chapter 11 concludes this thesis and gives an outlook to future work.

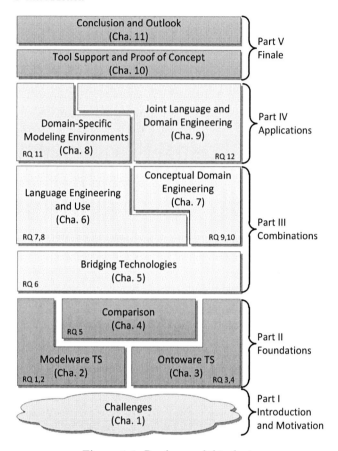

Figure 1.1. Road map of this thesis.

1.4 Dissemination and Publications

For the dissemination of the approaches discussed in this thesis, we have published several research papers at international conferences and workshops. The relevant ones and their contribution to the chapters are listed below.

Chapter 4: Walter, T., Schwarz, H., Ren, Y.: Establishing a Bridge from Graph-based Modeling Languages to Ontology Languages. In: Proceedings of the 3rd Workshop on Transforming and Weaving Ontologies in Model Driven Engineering (TWOMDE). Volume CEUR of 604, CEUR-WS.org (2010) [WSR10].

Chapter 5: Ebert, J., Walter, T.: Interoperability services for models and ontologies. In: Databases and Information Systems VI. Volume 224 of

Frontiers in Artificial Intelligence and Applications, IOSPress (2011) 19-36 [EW10].

Chapter 5: Walter, T., Ebert, J.: Combining DSLs and Ontologies Using Metamodel Integration. In: Proceedings of the IFIP Working Conference on Domain-Specific Languages. Volume 5658 of LNCS, Springer (2009) 148-169 [WE09].

Chapter 6: Staab, S., Walter, T., Gröner, G., Silva Parreiras, F.: Model Driven Engineering with Ontology Technologies. In: Reasoning Web. Volume 6325 of LNCS, Springer (2010) 62-98 [SWGP10].

Chapters 6, 8: Walter, T., Silva Parreiras, F., Staab, S.: OntoDSL: An Ontology-Based Framework for Domain-Specific Languages. In: Proceedings of the 12th International Conference on Model Driven Engineering Languages and Systems, (MoDELS). Volume 5795 of LNCS, Springer (2009) 408-422 [WPS09].

Chapters 7, 9: Walter, T., Silva Parreiras, F., Staab, S., Ebert, J.: Joint Language and Domain Engineering. In: Proceedings of the European Conference Modelling Foundations and Applications (ECMFA). Volume 6138 of LNCS, Springer (2010) 321-336 [WPSE10].

Besides conference talks for the respective publications above, we have given tutorials dealing with the combination of MDE and ontology technologies:

- Silva Parreiras, F., Walter, T., Wende, C., Thomas, E.: Model-Driven Software Development with Semantic Web Technologies. In: Tutorial at the 6th European Conference on Modelling Foundations and Applications, ECMFA 2010, Paris, France, June 15-18, 2010. (2010)
- Silva Parreiras, F., Walter, T., Wende, C., Thomas, E.: Bridging Software Languages and Ontology Technologies. In: SPLASH '10: Proceedings of the ACM international conference companion on Object oriented programming systems languages and applications companion, October 17, 2010, Reno/Tahoe, Nevada, USA., ACM (2010) 311-315
- Gasevic, D., Silva Parreiras, F., Walter, T.: Ontologies and Software Language Engineering. In: Tutorial at Generative Programming and Component Engineering (GPCE'10) co-located with Software Language Engineering (SLE 2010), October 10, 2010, Eindhoven, The Netherlands. (2010)

Part II

Foundations

2

A Modelware Technological Space

Modeling environments provide the capability for defining and using modeling languages. A *modeling language* is usually defined in its concrete syntax (the visual notation used), its abstract syntax (the structure behind the visualization) and its semantics (the intended meaning of given models).

The *concrete syntax* of a modeling language can be specified by textual or visual notations. A wide-spread approach to define the *abstract syntax* of modeling languages is to use UML class diagrams as so-called *metamodels* of the language. The *semantics* of modeling languages may be defined by a natural language specification or by set theory and predicate logics.

In modeling environments a given model is usually represented by its *abstract syntax graph*. This graph has to be conformant to its metamodel defining the abstract syntax of the language. Since this metamodel itself is also a model (designed with the modeling language for class diagrams), its abstract syntax graph has to be conformant to a further class diagram, called the *metametamodel* defining the language of these class diagrams.

To define bridging technologies interrelating modeling languages (Challenge 1) and to formally define the meaning of models (Challenge 2), we answer the following question in this chapter:

RQ1: *How are models and metamodels formally defined and how do they relate?*

Besides the aspect of designing models we consider their use. Given a modeling language, services are needed to create and manipulate models. Since models are becoming large, querying services help to retrieve elements. Changes to and evolution of modeling languages as well as interoperability with other tools require the manipulation of models, which is achieved by model transformations. In this chapter we exemplify services and tools provided by a modelware technological space. To support the usability and processing of models (Challenge 3) we answer the question:

RQ2: *Which services does a modelware technological space provide?*

2.1 Chapter Context

In this chapter we present a modelware technological space according to the definition given in [KBA02]:

A technological space is a working context with a set of associated concepts, body of knowledge, tools, required skills, and possibilities.

In the context of this chapter we concentrate on the *set of associated concepts* to model different kinds of modelware models and their relation. Furthermore, we concentrate on *tools*. Tools in a modelware technological space are composed of services.

2.1.1 Road Map

We describe the road map and structure of Section 2.2 along Figure 2.1, which depicts the metamodeling hierarchy of the *TGraph technological space* using the following concepts:

- The right column contains concrete models, i.e., an instance model, a schema, and a metaschema, the latter two being class diagrams.
- The left column contains the abstract syntax graphs of these models, i.e., an instance graph, a schema graph, and a metaschema graph.
- The vertical axis (*conformsTo*) depicts the conformance of the graphs/-models to those of the next higher level, i.e., it describes how models relate to metamodels.
- The horizontal dimension (*visualizes*) relates the models to their abstract syntax graph, i.e., it describes that the models are visualizations of their graphs.

Instance Layer. We start at the instance layer in Section 2.2.1 and present the definition of the concept of *TGraphs*, which are typed, attributed, and ordered directed graphs. In this thesis they are used as abstract syntax graphs to represent *models*. We use UML object diagrams [OMG07b] to depict TGraphs, but they may also be visualized by other more user-friendly visual or textual concrete notations if appropriate. Figure 2.2 illustrates the instance layer. It depicts a TGraph, which describes the abstract syntax representation of a state chart, and its visualization.

Schema Layer. For prescribing the structure of TGraphs and for assigning predefined types to their vertices and edges, we introduce *graph schemas* in Section 2.2.2. Graph schemas are depicted as UML class diagrams [OMG07b]. The subset of UML needed for defining the structure of TGraphs is called grUML (cf. Section 2.2.2). grUML diagrams are used to define the set of abstract syntax graphs of a given modeling language. Figure 2.2 illustrates the schema layer. It depicts a grUML diagram, which prescribes the structure of TGraphs representing a state chart model. To make the grUML diagrams amenable for a formal treatment, we initially translate them to an obvious *set notation* (cf. Section 2.2.2).

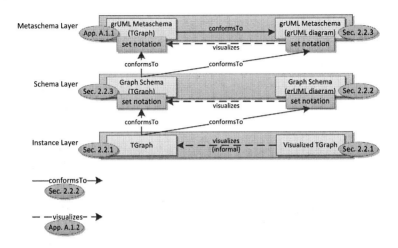

Figure 2.1. The TGraph metamodeling hierarchy.

conformsTo Relation. Based on the set notation of graph schemas, we define the *conformsTo* relation between TGraphs and schemas in Section 2.2.2. A TGraph conforms to a schema if its vertices conform to the vertex classes and its edges conform to the edge classes of the schema and all other properties of the schema are respected appropriately.

Metaschema Layer. Since graph schemas are models designed using the grUML language, every graph schema can also be represented by its own abstract syntax graph (cf. Section 2.2.3). Such as the prescription of TGraphs by graph schemas, we introduce a metaschema for prescribing the schema graphs in Section 2.2.3. This schema is called *grUML metaschema*, since it defines the abstract syntax of grUML precisely.

Visualizes Relation. Since we are tackling *any* kind of modeling language, the relation between the model and its abstract syntax graph is *not* formalized. In practice, this relation may be defined by some parser that extracts the abstract syntax from the model or (in the opposite direction) by some rendering procedure that generates the model from its abstract syntax graph. The relation may also be embodied in an editor that simultaneously holds the visualized model and its abstract syntax graph. grUML diagrams are visualizations of their abstract syntax graphs (ASGs). Since the visualization relationship is not used in this thesis, in Appendix A.1.2 we define the relation as a function on the set notation of a grUML diagram. The function returns for each grUML diagram element the element of the ASG, which is visualized by the given element.

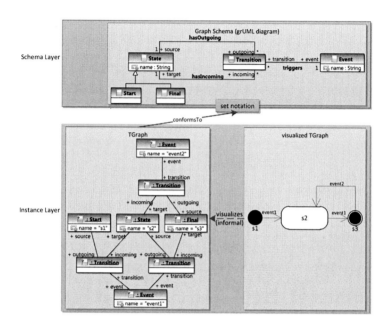

Figure 2.2. Example of a TGraph, its visualization and its conformance to a grUML diagram.

Self-Conformance. In Section 2.2.3 we present the grUML metaschema represented as grUML diagram (using the UML class diagram syntax). In Appendix A.1.1 we present the grUML metaschema as TGraph. Since the *conformsTo* relation relates TGraphs with graph schemas defined by the set notation, in Appendix A.1.1 we show how the grUML metaschema (as a TGraph) conforms to the grUML metaschema (as a grUML diagram).

Semantics. In Appendix A.1.3 we extend the semantics definition of modeling languages for designing TGraphs. We consider the relation between schemas and graphs where schemas represent the set of all possible graphs, which is called the extension of a given graph schema.

Since the visualizes relation, the grUML self-conformance, and the graph schema semantics are not relevant for this thesis but are needed for a complete view on the TGraph metamodeling hierarchy, they are presented in Appendix A.1.

2.1.2 Relation to OMGs Model Hierarchy

Table 2.1 relates the layers of the metamodeling hierarchy of the TGraph approach with the one proposed by OMG [OMG06].

As well as the TGraph approach, OMG suggests to separate models in different layers. Besides the *M0 layer* (representing the real world and not depicted in Table 2.1) the OMG model hierarchy differs between *M1 layer*, *M2 layer* and *M3 layer*. The direct counterparts in the TGraph approach are the *instance layer*, the *schema layer* and the *metaschema layer*.

At the M1 layer *models* are defined, which are comparable to TGraphs. Models in the OMG model hierarchy are described by *metamodels* lying at the M2 layer. Metamodels are comparable to graph schemas in the TGraph approach. To structure and prescribe metamodels OMG considers the MOF *metametamodel* at the M3 layer. In the TGraph metamodeling hierarchy, the grUML metaschema is used to prescribe the structure of graph schemas, which are the counterparts of metamodels in the TGraph approach.

OMG		TGraph Approach	
M3 layer	MOF Metametamodel	Metaschema layer	grUML Metaschema
M2 layer	Metamodel	Schema layer	Graph Schema
M1 layer	Model	Instance layer	TGraph

Table 2.1. Relation between the OMG's model hierarchy and the TGraph approach.

Since we are going to bridge modeling languages and to define its semantics and correctness, we need a well-defined understanding of the metamodel hierarchy and formal definitions of models, metamodels, and metametamodels. Hence, in this thesis we decide to consider the TGraph technological space as a formal basis for precise definitions of any kind of model. It is more powerful and formally defined compared to EMOF [OMG06].

Subsequent to the introduction of the TGraph approach, in Section 2.2.4 we comment on the mapping of concepts provided by the MOF metametamodel and the grUML metaschema.

2.2 The TGraph Approach

Since we need a formal description of a metamodel hierarchy, we present in this section precise definitions for TGraphs, the formal representations of models, graph schemas, the formal representation of metamodels, and its relations.

2.2.1 TGraphs

TGraphs are a powerful category of graphs, which is able to represent not only structural connections, but also all type and attribute information needed for an object-based view on the represented model.

Basic Definitions and Notations

TGraphs are typed, attributed, and ordered directed graphs, i.e., all graph elements (vertices and edges) are typed and may carry type-dependent attribute values. Furthermore, there are orderings of the vertex and the edge sets of the graph and of the incidences at all vertices. Lastly, all edges are directed.

Definition 1 (*TGraph*)

> *Let*
>
> - *Vertex be the universe of* vertices,
> - *Edge be the universe of* edges,
> - *TypeId be the universe of* type identifiers,
> - *AttrId be the universe of* attribute identifiers, *and*
> - *Value be the universe of* attribute values.
>
> *Assuming two finite sets*
>
> - a vertex set $V \subseteq Vertex$ *and*
> - an edge set $E \subseteq Edge$.
>
> $G = (Vseq, Eseq, Iseq, type, value)$ *is a TGraph iff*
>
> - $Vseq \in iseq\, V$ *is a permutation of* V,
> - $Eseq \in iseq\, E$ *is a permutation of* E,
> - $Iseq : V \rightarrow (iseq\, E \times \{in, out\})$ *is an incidence function where*
> $\forall e \in E : \exists! v, w \in V : (e, out) \in ran\, Iseq(v) \wedge (e, in) \in ran\, Iseq(w)$,
> - $type : V \cup E \rightarrow TypeId$ *is a type function, and*
> - $value : V \cup E \rightarrow (AttrId \nrightarrow Value)$ *is an attribute function where*
> $\forall x, y \in V \cup E : type(x) = type(y) \implies dom(value(x)) = dom(value(y))$.

Thus, a TGraph consists of an ordered vertex set V and an ordered edge set E, which are connected by the incidence function $Iseq$, which assigns the sequence of its incoming and outgoing edges to each vertex. Furthermore, all elements (i.e., vertices and edges) have a type and carry a type dependent set of attribute-value pairs.

Notations

Besides the notations for graphs below we introduce mathematical notations used in this thesis.

$A = B$ defines the equality of two sets and $a \in A$ states the membership of a in A. $\neg p$ states the negation of the predicate p, $p \wedge q$ and $p \vee q$ state the conjunction and disjunction of two predicates p and q. $\forall$ and $\exists$ are the universal and existential quantifiers. $p \Rightarrow q$ states the implication of q by p.

$X \leftrightarrow Y$ is a binary relation with $X \leftrightarrow Y = \mathcal{P}(X \times Y)$ where $\mathcal{P}$ is the power set. The maplet notation $x \mapsto y$ is a graphic way of expressing the ordered pair (x, y). $x \mapsto_R y$ expresses $(x, y) \in R$.

dom and ran define the domain and range of a binary relation. dom : $(X \leftrightarrow Y) \to \mathcal{P}(X)$ with dom $R = \{x \in X \mid \exists y \in Y : (x, y) \in R\}$ and ran : $(X \leftrightarrow Y) \to \mathcal{P}(Y)$ with ran $R = \{y \in Y \mid \exists x \in X : (x, y) \in R\}$

$X \nrightarrow Y$ is the set of partial functions with $\{f : X \leftrightarrow Y \mid \forall x \in X, y_1, y_2 \in Y : (x \mapsto y_1) \in f \land (x \mapsto y_2) \in f \Rightarrow y_1 = y_2\}$. $X \to Y$ is the set of total functions with $\{f : X \nrightarrow Y \mid \text{dom} f = X\}$.

In the following we give some simplified notation for easily accessing TGraphs.

The functions $\alpha : Edge \to Vertex$ and $\omega : Edge \to Vertex$ denote *start vertex* $\alpha(e)$ and *target vertex* $\omega(e)$ of some edge $e \in E$, respectively.

The relation $\to \subseteq Vertex \times Vertex$ with

$$\to = \{(v, w) \in Vertex \times Vertex \mid \exists e \in Edge : \alpha(e) = v \land \omega(e) = w\}$$

defines that there exists some edge $e \in Edge$ from vertex v to vertex w by writing $v \to w$ (here using an infix notation instead of $(v, w) \in \to$).

The relation $\to \subseteq Vertex \times Vertex \times \mathbb{F}(TypeId)$ with

$$\to = \{(v, w, \{t_1, \ldots, t_l\}) \in Vertex \times Vertex \times \mathbb{F}(TypeId) \mid$$
$$\exists e \in Edge : \alpha(e) = v \land \omega(e) = w \land type(e) \in \{t_1, \ldots, t_l\}\}$$

defines that there exists some edge $e \in Edge$ of type $t_1, t_2, \ldots, t_n$ from vertex $v \in V$ to vertex $w \in V$ by writing $v \to \{t_1, \ldots, t_n\}w$ (here using an infix notation instead of $(v, w, \{t_1, \ldots, t_n\}) \in \to$).

A path from v_0 to v_k in a TGraph G is an alternating sequence

$$P = \; <v_0, e_1, v_1, \ldots, e_k, v_k>, k \geq 0$$

of vertices and edges, where $\forall i \in \mathbb{N}$ with $1 \leq i \leq k$: $\alpha(e_i) = v_{i-1} \land \omega(e_i) = v_i$. The existence of a path between v_0 and v_k is denoted by $v_0 \to^* v_k$.

The set $\Gamma^+(v) = \{w \in Vertex \mid v \to w\}$ represents all direct successors of vertex v. The set $\Gamma^+(v, t) = \{w \in Vertex \mid v \to \{t\}w\}$ represents all direct successors of vertex $v \in V$ via some outgoing edge of type t.

The set $\Gamma^-(v) = \{w \in Vertex \mid w \to v\}$ represents all direct predecessors of vertex $v \in V$. The set $\Gamma^-(v, t) = \{w \in Vertex \mid w \to \{t\}v\}$ represents all direct predecessors of vertex $v \in V$ via some incoming edge of type t.

The function $\delta^+ : Vertex \to \mathbb{N}$ with $\delta(v) = \sharp\Gamma^+(v)$ returns the number of outgoing edges of vertex $v \in V$. The function $\delta^+ : Vertex \times TypeId \to \mathbb{N}$ with $\delta(v, t) = \sharp\Gamma^+(v, t)$ returns the number of outgoing edges of type t of vertex $v \in V$. The function $\delta^- : Vertex \to \mathbb{N}$ with $\delta(v) = \sharp\Gamma^-(v)$ returns the number of incoming edges of vertex $v \in V$. The function $\delta^- : Vertex \times TypeId \to \mathbb{N}$ with $\delta(v, t) = \sharp\Gamma^-(v, t)$ returns the number of incoming edges of type t of vertex $v \in V$.

All v, w denote vertices, all e edges, all t denote types for vertices or edges and all a attributes. x, y is used if it is not relevant, if the element is a vertex or edge. Functions, if not defined otherwise, are denoted by f.

Example of a TGraph

Figure 2.2 depicts at the instance layer in the left column a TGraph whose concrete syntax is similar to that of UML object diagrams [OMG07b]. A visualization of the same TGraph is depicted at the instance layer in the right column.

The TGraph describes a concrete state machine with three states s1, s2 and s3, three transitions, and two events event1 and event2. event1 triggers the transition that goes from s1 to s2 and the transition that goes from s2 to s3. event2 triggers the transitions that go from s3 to s2.

All vertices have a type (defined after : in the top of each vertex) and although it is not depicted in Figure 2.2 all edges also have a type (e.g., there are types of edges connecting states and transitions and other types of edges connecting transitions and events).

The model in the right column of Figure 2.2 depicts a possible visualization of the TGraph depicted in the left column. Here, the vertices of type Start, State, and Final are visualized by correspondent state elements. All vertices of type Transition are depicted by an arrow. Source and target of each transition are distinguished in the TGraph by edges, where the role of the edge beside the state is denoted with source or target. Each vertex of type Event is represented as an annotation. Events are assigned to those transitions, which are related by an edge in the TGraph.

Since we want to express more state machine graphs with the same structure of states, transitions, and events, where e.g., transitions have exactly one source and target state and where events are only able to trigger transitions, we are going to introduce graph schemas.

2.2.2 Graph Schemas

Graph schemas prescribe the structure of TGraphs and allow for assigning predefined types to vertices and edges of the TGraph. Types are arranged in a type hierarchy and have a set of predefined attributes. A graph schema describes which types of edges are incident with which types of vertices. In addition, types of edges can have multiplicities at both ends that allow a vertex only to be connected via edges of a given type with a predefined number of other vertices.

Example of a Graph Schema

Figure 2.2 depicts at the schema layer an example of a graph schema for state machine TGraphs. The syntax is similar to that of UML class diagrams [OMG07b]. The classes denote vertex types for states, transitions, and events. The associations between classes denote edge types for relations between states and incoming or outgoing transitions and for the relation between events and transitions. Thus class diagrams may be used to describe graph schemas. The subset of the UML-class diagrams that have a TGraph semantics is called *grUML* (*graph UML*). grUML is a metamodeling language that allows for describing graph schemas. In this case the graph schema can be called a *grUML diagram*. grUML is introduced in Section 2.2.3.

We consider a core of constructs that are sufficient for defining a valid graph schema. We will consider vertex classes and edge classes where both can be attributed. Vertex classes are represented by UML classes in a grUML diagram. Edge classes are represented by UML associations in a grUML diagram. If edge classes are attributed or have sub- or supertypes, they are then represented by UML association classes. Attributes may have the domains String, Integer, Double, and Boolean. The incidences of each edge class define constraints, since they restrict the types of the start and the end vertex of an edge. Furthermore, both incidences of an edge class define multiplicities, which restrict the number of vertices linked with some other vertex via an edge of a given edge class.

Graph Schemas in Concrete Syntax

Graph schemas are represented in *set notation*. Based on a given graph schema GS represented as a grUML diagram, we set up the sets and functions described in Definition 2.

Definition 2 (*Set Notation for a grUML Diagram*)

The set notation of a grUML diagram consists of the sets:

- V_{GS} *is the set of all classes in the grUML diagram.*
- E_{GS} *is the set of all associations in the grUML diagram.*
- *$Attr_{GS}$ is the set of attribute identifiers nested in classes of the grUML diagram.*
- *$Domain = \{Int, Double, String, Bool\}$ is the set of all possible domain identifiers for attributes.*

Furthermore, it provides the functions:

- *$typeDefinition : V_{GS} \cup E_{GS} \rightarrow (Attr_{GS} \nrightarrow Domain)$ represents the assignment of attributes to classes or associations in the grUML diagram.*
- *$isA : V_{GS} \cup E_{GS} \times V_{GS} \cup E_{GS}$ represents the relation of subtypes with supertypes as it is defined in the grUML diagram.*
- *$relates : E_{GS} \rightarrow V_{GS} \times V_{GS}$ represents the incidence relation of associations and classes in the grUML diagram.*
- *$multiplicity : E_{GS} \rightarrow Multiplicity \times Multiplicity$ with $Multiplicity = \{(min, max) \in \mathbb{N} \times \mathbb{N}_1 \mid min \leq max \leq \infty\}$ represents the assignment of multiplicities for both, association start and end.*

Conformance of TGraphs and Graph Schemas

Having a formal definition of TGraphs (cf. Definition 1) and grUML diagrams in set notations (cf. Definition 2), we can describe when and how a TGraph conforms to a graph schema.

In the TGraph Definition 1 the *type* function assigns a type identifier to each vertex and edge. These identifiers originate from the sets V_{GS} and E_{GS}, where GS is the graph schema, which prescribes the structure of the TGraph. However, the *type* function gives no information about which constraints a vertex or edge of the given type must fulfill and which attribute values may be allocated by values. In general, the *type* function does not suffice to describe the conformance of TGraphs to graph schemas.

Thus we introduce a *conformsTo* function in Definition 3, which describes the conformance of vertices and edges to classes and associations of a grUML diagram precisely.

Definition 3 (*Conformance of TGraphs*)

For a given TGraph $G = (Vseq, Eseq, Iseq, type, value)$ and a grUML diagram GS described by its set notation, the *conformsTo* function is declared as follows:

$$conformsTo : V \cup E \to \mathcal{P}(V_{GS}) \cup \mathcal{P}(E_{GS})$$

The *conformsTo* function assigns vertices and edges of a given TGraph G to sets of vertex classes and edge classes of a graph schema GS:

- All vertices in G conform to some class in the grUML diagram assigned by the *type* function and to the supertypes of this class:

$$\forall\, v \in V : conformsTo(v) = \{t \in V_{GS} \mid type(v)\ isA^*\ t\}$$

- All edges in G conform to some association assigned by the *type* function and to the supertypes of this association:

$$\forall\, e \in E : conformsTo(e) = \{t \in E_{GS} \mid type(e)\ isA^*\ t\}$$

Given Definition 3, a TGraph G, and a graph schema GS, all vertices and edges must fulfill constraints that are given by classes and incidences of associations.

Start and end vertex of an edge must conform to the corresponding classes, which are incident with the association in the grUML diagram[1]:

---

[1] Throughout this chapter, $first(relates(t))$ and $second(relates(t))$ return the source and target vertex classes of an edge class t. $first(multiplicity(t)).min$

$$\forall\, e \in E : \! first(relates(type(e))) \in conformsTo(\alpha(e))$$
$$\wedge second(relates(type(e))) \in conformsTo(\omega(e))$$

All vertices of a TGraph must fulfill the multiplicity restrictions for each association their type is incident with. Thus, each vertex must not have less or more outgoing or incoming edges as defined by the *multiplicity* function for each association in a grUML diagram:

$$\forall\, t \in E_{GS} : \! \forall\, e \in E : \forall\, v \in V : first(relates(t)) \in conformsTo(\alpha(e)) \Rightarrow$$
$$second(multiplicity(t)).min \le$$
$$\sharp\{e \in E \mid t \in conformsTo(e), (e, out) \in Iseq(v)\}$$
$$\le second(multiplicity(t)).max$$

$$\wedge$$

$$\forall\, e \in E : \forall\, v \in V : second(relates(t)) \in conformsTo(\omega(e)) \Rightarrow$$
$$first(multiplicity(t)).min \le$$
$$\sharp\{e \in E \mid t \in conformsTo(e), (e, in) \in Iseq(v)\}$$
$$\le first(multiplicity(t)).max$$

All vertices and edges exactly allocate those attributes with values, which are provided by the class or association, respectively, or one of their super-types:

$$\forall\, x \in V \cup E : \mathrm{dom}(value(x)) =$$
$$\{a \in Attr_{GS} \mid t \in conformsTo(x),$$
$$a \in \mathrm{dom}(typeDefinition(t)), t \in V_{GS} \cup E_{GS}\}$$

For all vertices and edges of the graph, all values assigned to an attribute must conform to the domain of the attribute. Therefore, we use the function $valueSet : Domain \rightarrow \mathcal{P}(Value)$, which assigns all natural numbers to the Int-domain ($valueSet(Int) = \mathbb{N}$), all real numbers to the $Double$-domain ($valueSet(Double) = \mathbb{R}$), all boolean values to the $Bool$-domain ($valueSet(Bool) = \{true, false\}$) and all character strings to the $String$-domain ($valueSet(String) = \{set\ of\ all\ possible\ strings\}$).

$$\forall\, x \in V \cup E : \! \forall\, a \in dom(value(x)), \forall\, t \in conformsTo(x) :$$
$$(value(x))(a) \in valueSet((typeDefinition(t))(a))$$

---

and $first(multiplicity(t)).max$ return the lower and upper multiplicity annotated at the edge class source. $second(multiplicity(t)).min$ and $second(multiplicity(t)).max$ return the lower and upper multiplicity annotated at the edge class target.

Now, since we have defined the *conforms To* function for vertices and edges, we can precisely set up a relation *conforms To*, which defines when a given TGraph G conforms to a graph schema GS (written G *conforms To* GS):

$$conforms\,To \subseteq \{G \mid G \text{ is a } TGraph\} \times \{GS \mid GS \text{ is a graph schema}\}$$

with

$$conforms\,To = \{(G, GS) \mid \forall\, v \in V : conforms\,To(v) \in V_{GS} \wedge$$
$$\forall\, e \in E : conforms\,To(e) \in E_{GS}\}$$

where the *conforms To* functions for vertices and edges ensure that required attribute implementations and multiplicity restrictions are fulfilled.

2.2.3 grUML

Since all graph schemas should contain classes to define sets of vertices and associations which in turn define sets of edges where both can be attributed and related by a specialization relationship, respectively, graph schemas are described by some metaschema. This schema is provided by grUML as the grUML-Metaschema.

grUML Metaschema

grUML (graph UML) is a sublanguage of UML and is based on TGraphs. grUML allows for defining graph schemas that represent classes of TGraphs.

Figure 2.3 depicts a part of the grUML metaschema. VertexClass describes types for vertices, which are represented in a grUML diagram by a UML class. Each vertex class can have several subclasses or superclasses via SpecializesVertexClass. EdgeClass describes types for edges, which are represented in a grUML diagram by a UML association. Each edge class can have several subclasses or superclasses via SpecializesEdgeClass. Each edge connects two vertex classes via some IncidenceClass. EdgeClass and VertexClass are specializations of GraphElementClass. Thus they can be part of a Package, which is contained by the Schema of the graph. Furthermore, GraphElementClass is a specialization of AttributedElementClass. Hence, all graph elements can be attributed.

Figure 2.4 depicts the excerpt of the grUML schema, which is responsible for defining domains. Here each attribute has a domain. Among others, grUML provides basic domains for Integer, Double, String, or Boolean values.

Graph Schemas in Abstract Syntax

After we have presented the grUML schema we are going to present the formalization of graph schemas in abstract syntax represented as a TGraph.

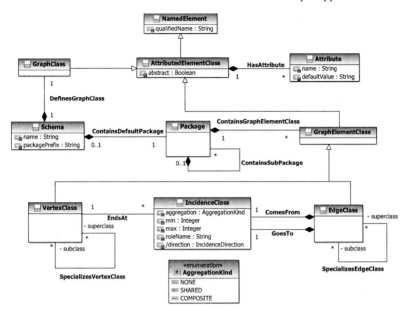

Figure 2.3. Simplified structure of the grUML schema.

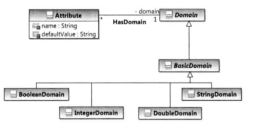

Figure 2.4. Excerpt of the domains provided by the grUML schema.

Example

Figure 2.5 depicts the graph, which is an instance graph of the grUML schema. A visualization of the instance graph in Figure 2.5 is the grUML diagram at the schema layer in Figure 2.2.

The graph consists of vertices of type VertexClass, which define concrete vertex classes for states, transitions, and events. It consists of vertices of type EdgeClass, which define concrete edge classes for linking states with other states via transitions and events with transitions. (The vertices of type Attribute representing the name attribute for states and events are not depicted.

They are linked with the vertex, which nests the attribute and with a vertex representing the String domain.)

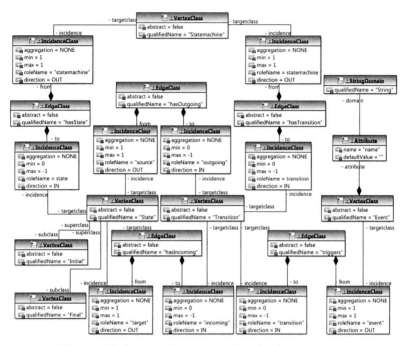

Figure 2.5. State machine graph schema in abstract syntax.

In Definition 2 we gave a formalization of grUML-diagrams (in concrete syntax) in set notation, which contains the sets V_{GS}, E_{GS}, $Attr_{GS}$ and $Domain$ and additional functions for attribute assignments ($typeDefinition$), type hierarchy definitions (isA), incidences ($relates$), and their multiplicities ($multiplicity$) (cf. Definition 2).

This formalization was used to define the $conformsTo$ relation between TGraphs and the graph schema (represented as grUML diagram).

Now we are going to repeat this formalization of a set notation with regard to graph schemas in abstract syntax, which are represented as a TGraph. In both ways, the $conformsTo$ relation with its constraints can be applied independently on a TGraph to prove that it conforms to a graph schema, either in abstract or concrete syntax form.

Definition 4 (*Set Notation for a Graph Schema as TGraph*)

For a given TGraph $G = (Vseq, Eseq, Iseq, type, value)$, which represents a graph schema in abstract syntax, the set notation of this graph schema consists of the sets:

- $V_{GS} = \{v \in V \mid type(v) = VertexClass\}$
- $E_{GS} = \{e \in V \mid type(e) = EdgeClass\}$
- $Attr_{GS} = \{a \in V \mid type(a) = Attribute\}$
- $Domain = \{Int, Double, String, Bool\}$ is the set of all possible domain identifiers for attributes.

Furthermore, the set notation has the functions:

- $typeDefinition : V_{GS} \cup E_{GS} \rightarrow (Attr_{GS} \nrightarrow Domain)$ represents the assignment of attributes to vertex classes or edge classes:

$$\forall\, t \in V_{GS} \cup E_{GS} : typeDefinition(t) = f_{as}$$
$$with\ f_{as} = A \rightarrow X\ where\ A = \Gamma^+(t, HasAttribute)$$
$$\wedge \forall\, a \in A : a \mapsto_{f_{as}} d, a \rightarrow \{HasDomain\}d$$

- $isA : V_{GS} \cup E_{GS} \times V_{GS} \cup E_{GS}$ represents the relation of subtypes:

$$isA =$$
$$\{(t_{sub}, t_{sup}) \mid t_{sub} \rightarrow \{SpecializesVertexClass, SpecializesEdgeClass\}t_{sup}\}$$

- $relates : E_{GS} \rightarrow V_{GS} \times V_{GS}$ represents the incidence relation of edge classes and vertex classes:

$$\forall\, e \in E_{GS} : relates(e) = (v, w),\ e \rightarrow \{ComesFrom\} \rightarrow \{EndsAt\}v$$
$$\wedge\ e \rightarrow \{GoesTo\} \rightarrow \{EndsAt\}w$$

- $multiplicity : E_{GS} \rightarrow Multiplicity \times Multiplicity$ with $Multiplicity = \{(min, max) \in \mathbb{N} \times \mathbb{N}_1 \mid min \leq max \leq \infty\}$ represents the assignment of multiplicities for both incidences:

$$\forall\, t \in E_{GS} : multiplicity(t) = ((min_s, max_s)(min_t, max_t))\ with :$$
$$\exists\, v_{i_1}, v_{i_2} \in V\ with\ type(v_{i_1}) = type(v_{i_2}) = IncidenceClass :$$
$$min_s = (value(v_{i_1}))(min),$$
$$max_s = (value(v_{i_1}))(max), t \rightarrow \{ComesFrom\}v_{i_1},$$
$$min_t = (value(v_{i_2}))(min),$$
$$max_t = (value(v_{i_2}))(max), t \rightarrow \{GoesTo\}v_{i_2}$$

In this Section 2.2.3 we have seen that graph schemas can be represented in abstract and in concrete syntax. In the case of abstract syntax, the schema represents a TGraph whose conforming schema is the grUML metaschema. In the case of concrete syntax, the graph schema is represented as a grUML diagram and is used to describe the structure of TGraphs. In Section 2.2.2 we have shown, that TGraphs conform to a graph schema if their vertices and edges fulfill the conditions of respective types.

2.2.4 Relation to MOF Metametamodels

Besides grUML and its TGraph approach there are some other metamodeling languages and approaches available. We consider the prominent approach of OMG with its metamodeling language MOF (Meta Object Facility) [OMG06]. The OMG approach provides the metamodeling language MOF with its subsets EMOF (Essential MOF) and CMOF (Complete MOF) (where EMOF is a subset of CMOF). We are going to compare both languages with grUML.

To simplify the MOF language and to facilitate ease of implementation and conformance, MOF 2 defines EMOF as a kernel metamodeling capability [OMG06]. The core of EMOF provides the capability to describe classes using the class Class in the metametamodel, which is similar to the grUML class VertexClass. The association superclass in the EMOF metametamodel allows for defining specialization hierarchies, which is provided by grUML using the SpecializesVertexClass association. EMOF allows for defining properties of classes (by creating instances of Property), which are used either for attributing the classes (here the property has a datatype) or to define references to other classes (here the property has as type a class). Since all graph elements in a TGraph can be attributed, grUML allows for defining attributes of vertex classes. In addition to EMOF, grUML allows for defining attributes of edge classes. References in metamodels can be described by grUML defining instances of EdgeClass together with two instances of IncidenceClass, which define the two ends of the TGraph edge. A difference of grUML compared to EMOF is the specialization of edge classes, which is not supported for properties. Similar to the EMOF Property, IncidenceClass allows for defining multiplicities. The opposite association in EMOF is realized by simple TGraph edges, which are navigable in both directions.

To support the attribution of associations and the relation of association types in hierarchies, MOF provides CMOF. In addition to EMOF, the CMOF metametamodel provides the concept Association. Associations in CMOF are classifiers, can be attributed, and have two ends that are described by the class Property. Since associations are classifiers, again they can be connected by associations. Such a construct is not available in grUML. Here, edge classes in a graph schema cannot be connected with other edge classes using an edge class. In addition to EMOF, CMOF allows for defining redefinitions and subsettings of properties (association ends). This is supported by grUML with regard to edge classes and is described in [Bil10].

In general we can state that the power of grUML lies between EMOF and CMOF.

2.3 Modelware Tools and Services

In this section we are going to introduce the tools and services a modelware technological space provides. In particular we focus on tools and services usable for the TGraph technological space where all models are represented by a graph.

In Section 2.3.1 we present the *Graph Repository Query Language* (GReQL) used to query TGraphs. In Section 2.3.2 we introduce the *Graph Repository Transformation Language* (GReTL) used to transform TGraphs according to a transformation definition to TGraph conforming to a given target graph schema. To complete the service specifications for modeling environments, in Appendix A.1.4 we introduce basic services, which allow for creating graphs. These services are used to either create a graph conforming to some graph schema, or to create a schema graph conforming to the grUML metaschema, which is visualized as a grUML diagram.

2.3.1 GReQL - Graph Repository Query Language

The *Graph Repository Query Language* is a declarative, expression-based query language for TGraphs [EB10, Bil08, Mar06]. It can be used to extract information from TGraphs, for example, attributes of vertices and edges or complete structures inside of graphs. Typical GReQL queries are the so-called *FWR expressions* and *quantified expressions.* One purpose of quantified expressions returning a boolean value in this work is the definition of constraints for graph schemas.

Regular Path Expressions

One feature of GReQL is its definition of regular path expressions over the graph structure defined in the graph schema. We are going to describe the main constructs to define regular path expressions.

Simple Path Description. In GReQL a simple path description consists of an edge symbol (--> (outgoing) , <-- (incoming), <-> (direction not important)) and optionally an edge type restriction in curly brackets. The following simple path descriptions check if v has an outgoing edge to w, if v and w are connected by some edge (where the direction is not important), or if w has an incoming edge of type hasIncoming from a vertex v:

```
v --> w
v <-> w
w <--{hasIncoming} v
```

Edge Path Description. In GReQL an edge path description --exp-> matches exactly one edge, given as expression exp. The following expression checks whether vertex v is connected via the outgoing edge e with the vertex w:

```
v --e-> w
```

Goal- and Start-restricted Path Description. In GReQL the start and end vertices of a path description can be restricted. A vertex class expression, which restricts the start or end vertex is separated from the path description with a &. The following expression ensures that a vertex t is connected via an outgoing edge with the vertex s of type State:

```
t −−> & {State} s
```

Sequential Path Description. GReQL supports the concatenation of path descriptions to sequential path descriptions. The following expression ensures that the vertex i is connected via a sequence of two edges with the vertex v:

```
i −−>−−> v
```

Optional and Alternative Path Description. In GReQL a path description can be marked as optional by surrounding it with brackets. The following expression ensures that the vertex o has a path of length one or optionally two to the vertex v:

```
o −−>[−−>] v
```

In GReQL it is possible to define paths as alternatives by separating them with a pipe. The following expression ensures that the vertex i is connected via an outgoing edge with a vertex of type State or alternatively a vertex of type Final:

```
i −−> &{State}| −−> &{Final}
```

Exponentiated and Iterated Path Description. Exponentiated path descriptions are defined by some path description followed by a given natural number. The following expressions ensures that the vertex i has an outgoing path of length 2 to the vertex v:

```
i −−>^2 v
```

GReQL supports the iteration of path descriptions by the use of Kleene operators * and +. The following expression ensures that i and f are connected by a path of arbitrary length (at least one edge):

```
i −−>+ f
```

Quantified Expressions

GReQL supports the use of quantifications, which specify whether all (universal quantification) or at least one (existential quantification) element of a given set of elements must fulfill a given condition.

The universal quantification in GReQL is realized by using the forall keyword. The following expression defines that all vertices s of vertex class State must fulfill the condition after @, i.e., the name-attribute may not be the empty string:

---

forall s:**V**{State} **@ not**(n.name = "")

The existential quantification is realized by using the **exists** keyword. The expression below defines that for each vertex f of vertex class **Final**, at least one vertex t of vertex class **Transition** exists, which is connected to f via a hasIncoming edge:

---

forall f:**V**{Final} **@ exists** t:**V**{Transition} **@** t − −>{hasIncoming} f

---

From-With-Report Expressions

FWR-expressions consist of the three clauses **from**, **with** and **report**. The from-clause declares variables for concerned elements (e.g., vertices and edges) in the graph. The domains of variables can be taken from the types defined in the graph schema. The optional **with**-clause summarizes predicates, which have to be fulfilled by the variables. These predicates can include powerful graph-oriented expressions such as regular path expressions. Finally, the **report**-clause determines the result structure of the query.

The following query exemplifies the FWR-expressions. It queries over all pairs of vertices i and f of type **Initial** and **Final** and reports a bag of pairs of vertices, which are linked via an iteration of a sequence of **hasOutgoing** and hasIncoming edges.

---

from i:**V**{Initial}, f:**V**{Final}
with i (− −>{hasOutgoing}− −>{hasIncoming})+ f
report i, f **end**

GReQL Querying Service

In Table 2.2 we specify a querying service, which gets a TGraph as input and a GReQL query and returns an answer set.

Name	GReQL Query Answering
Signature	ResultSet greqlQuery(Graph g, Greql2 q)
Pattern	a=Modelware.greqlQuery(g, q)
Description	evaluates the GReQL query q on the TGraph g and computes the answer a. If there is no answer a is null.

Table 2.2. GReQL querying service.

Relation to OCL

The result of a comparison in [SE10] of GReQL with the Object Constraint Language [WK03] (OCL) is that they are similar to a great extent, so that expressions in one language can in most cases be translated to the other one. OCL features, which are not present in GReQL are the capability to define contexts for expressions and an operation to iterate over collections with the capability to store the result of an expression involving the current element and to reuse this result in the next iteration. The advantages of GReQL are its graph orientation with the ability to efficiently handle graph structures and the support of regular path expressions to describe the structure of paths. In particular, the computation of the transitive closure is not possible with OCL.

2.3.2 GReTL - Graph Repository Transformation Language

GReTL [HE11], the *Graph Repository Transformation Language*, is a language for transforming TGraphs and graph schemas. In contrast to other transformation languages, the target schema of a GReTL transformation does not need to be predefined, but can be created in the course of the transformations.

We introduce GReTL by giving an overview of the GReTL framework, which is implemented in Java and by describing the elementary transformation operations used in this work.

GReTL Framework

The GReTL transformation framework is based on Java and is integrated with the *JGraLab* library for handling TGraphs. The central components of the GReTL transformation framework are the abstract class Transformation and the class Context. The Transformation class provides the set of transformation operations (where three operations are described below). They are used to create elements in the target schema and instances in the target graph. By subclassing the Transformation class, concrete transformations are implemented. The method transform(), which is provide by the Transformation class as abstract method, is overwritten and uses the elementary transformation operations. When instantiating a Transformation subclass, an instance of the class Context has to be passed to the constructor. It specifies the source schema and graphs and contains a reference to the target graph after the execution of the transformation.

GReTL Transformation Operations

To describe the transformation of models represented as TGraph to other models, three GReTL transformation operations are presented that allow for creating vertices, edges, and defining attribute values. All transformation operations are encapsulated by a Transformation object t.

Table 2.3 specifies the operation used to instantiate vertices of a given type for all elements described by a semantic expression.

Name	Instantiate Vertices
Signature	void instantiateVertices(VertexClass c, String semanticExpression)
Pattern	t.instantiateVertices(c, s)
Description	instantiates vertices of type c for each element in the set described by the semantic expression s. t is the Transformation object.

Table 2.3. Basic transformation operation: instantiateVertices.

The example given below illustrates the use of the instantiateVertices operation. The first use of the operation instantiates for all vertices of type State and reported by the semantic expression a new vertex of type Class. The second use of the operation instantiates for all vertices of type State and reported by the semantic expression a new vertex of type IRI.

```
t.instantiateVertices("Class", "from v:V{State} reportSet v end");
t.instantiateVertices("IRI", "from v:V{State} reportSet v end");
```

Table 2.4 specifies the operation used to instantiate edges of a given type for all elements described by a semantic expression. The semantic expression reports a triple, which describes the elements being the archetypes and the archetypes for source and target element of the new edge to be instantiated.

Name	Instantiate Edges
Signature	void instantiateEdges(EdgeClass c, String semanticExpression)
Pattern	o.instantiateEdges(c, s)
Description	instantiates edges of type c for each element in the set described by the semantic expression s. t is the Transformation object.

Table 2.4. Basic transformation operation: instantiateEdges.

The example given below illustrates the use of the instantiateEdges operation. The use of the operation instantiates for all pairs v and w of vertices belonging to the archetypes of vertices of type Class and IRI a new edge if v and w are the same. The edge connects those two vertices in the target graph having the archetype v and w.

```
t.instantiateEdges("HasEntityIRI", "from v:keySet(img_Class), w:keySet(img_IRI) with v=w reportSet v, v
    , w end");
```

Table 2.5 specifies the operation used to instantiate attributes in a given graph element class for all elements described by a semantic expression. The semantic expression reports a map, which maps the elements being the archetypes for the new attributes to the value assigned to the instantiated attribute.

The example given below illustrates the use of the instantiateAttributeValues operation. The use of the operation assigns to the iri attribute of the vertex class IRI the value reported by the semantic expression, which is the name of the archetype of v.

Name	Instantiate Attribute Values
Signature	void instantiateAttributeValues(GraphElementClass t, Attribute a, String semanticExpression)
Pattern	t.instantiateAttributeValues(c, a, s)
Description	instantiates the attributes a in the graph element class c and maps its value to the value described in the semantic expression. t is the Transformation object.

Table 2.5. Basic transformation operation: instantiateAttributeValues.

---

t.**instantiateAttributeValues**("IRI", "iri", "**from** v:keySet(img_Class) **reportMap** v, v.name **end**");

2.4 Conclusion

In this chapter we presented the TGraph technological space as one modelware technological space and answered the two research questions RQ1 and RQ2 asking for the concepts and languages, and the tools and services in a technological space.

The TGraph technological space allows for graph-based modeling, i.e., all models are described as a graph and may be visualized by respective concrete syntaxes. An approach to prescribe the structure of graphs is to use UML class diagrams representing graph schemas (metamodels). A graph has to be conformant to its graph schema. Since a graph schema itself is also a model its abstract syntax graph has to be conformant to a further class diagram, representing the metaschema (metametamodel).

With respect to the tools and services we presented GReQL as a language to query TGraphs and GReTL to transform TGraphs.

3

An Ontoware Technological Space

In this chapter we present an *ontoware technological space*. In particular we describe the concepts associated with the technological space and the tools it provides. The ontoware technological space mainly allows for designing and processing ontoware models. To bridge modelware models and ontoware models, as targeted by Challenge 1, they must be formally described by a modeling language defined by its metamodel, at least one concrete syntax and formal semantics. The formal semantics of a modeling language for designing ontoware models will underpin Challenge 2. It promises the definition of constraints and formal semantics of modeling languages (cf. Chapter 6 to 7). The following research question arises for the ontoware technological space:

RQ3:   *What are the appropriate modeling languages to design ontoware models?*

Based on a software language to design ontoware models and based on formal semantics, reasoning tools provide services for inferring implicit facts for ontoware models and for querying them. These services are used to support the tooling (Challenge 3) in software modeling. In this chapter we specify these services:

RQ4:   *What are the services provided by an ontoware technological space?*

All services describe the basic functionalities of ontology technologies. They are subsumed by an *ontoware API*, which later is used to build more complex user services.

3.1 Chapter Context

In this chapter we follow the definition and representation of models and metamodels introduced in Chapter 2. Figure 3.1 schematically depicts an ontoware technological space and describes the road map belonging to this chapter.

First, in Section 3.2.1 we start with the foundations of description logics and knowledge bases. A knowledge base is a special kind of database holding facts for the knowledge of a special domain. Description logics (DL) are a family of formal knowledge representation languages. All facts in a description logics knowledge base are written in such a language.

Description logics knowledge bases underlay the open world assumption by default. In Section 3.2.3 we consider the differences between an open and closed world and show which additional facts are needed to close a knowledge base.

In Section 3.3.1 we show how to represent description logics knowledge bases as ontoware models, where ontoware models are represented by TGraphs in abstract syntax form. These TGraphs are described by a graph schema representing the metamodel of OWL 2. The metamodel of OWL 2 is completely depicted in the Appendix A.2.

Finally, in Section 3.4 we present services for reasoning and querying ontoware models.

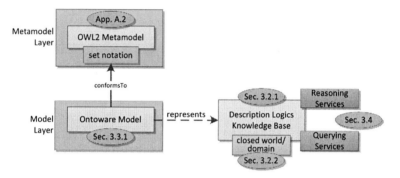

Figure 3.1. Ontoware technological space and road map of Chapter 3.

3.2 Description Logics

Description logics are a family of logics to represent structural knowledge [BCM+03]. A wide variety of description logics is developed with different expressive means. Thus, designers can choose the logic that is most suited for their goals.

A knowledge base containing the facts for the knowledge of a special domain consists of two main components: a terminological box (TBox) and an assertional box (ABox). In the TBox the domain to be modeled is described by using a concrete language coming from a description logics family. In the

ABox concrete knowledge is asserted by instances of concepts and roles, the latter defines relations between concepts in the TBox.

Description logics are based on formal model-theoretic semantics [Far03]. Once the knowledge is established by concepts and roles, separate as well as joint sound and complete reasoning about TBox and ABox is possible. Reasoning allows for inferring implicit knowledge in the knowledge base. Section 3.4 provides a list of reasoning services.

3.2.1 DL Families

Concepts and roles are the basic elements of a description logic (DL). A specific DL is defined by a specific set of atomic constructs it provides to form complex expressions over concepts and roles. Concepts describe sets of instances, where roles describe sets of relations between instances.

The following concept intuitively describes a set of models, which only contain entities, which in turn must have a reference or attribute as a feature.

$$Model \sqcap \forall\, containsModelEntity.(Entity \sqcap \exists\, hasFeature.(Reference \sqcup Attribute))$$

Different description logics have received specific names. $\mathcal{FL}$ [BL84] is the language with the basic syntactic elements - *concepts* and *roles*. In addition it allows for universal quantification, unqualified existential quantification and conjunction. An example in $\mathcal{FL}$ is the following one, which describes a model, where all entities have a feature (which is not qualified):

$$Model \sqcap \forall\, containsModelEntity.(Entity \sqcap \exists\, hasFeature.\top)$$

The description logic $\mathcal{AL}$ [MS91] extends $\mathcal{FL}$ with negation of atomic concepts, where $\mathcal{ALC}$ extends $\mathcal{AL}$ with full negation. An example for $\mathcal{ALC}$ is the following one, which describes those entities, which have at least one reference feature:

$$Entity \sqcap \exists\, hasFeature.Reference$$

Below, we give a precise definition of $\mathcal{ALC}$, *concept inclusion axioms*, *TBox* and *ABox*, and *interpretations*. In Tables 3.1 to 3.4 we show a summary of the most commonly used constructs and their semantics, which are based on the interpretation definition.

Definition 5 (*[Sat03]*)

Let $\boldsymbol{C}$ and $\boldsymbol{R}$ be disjoint sets of concept and role names. The set of $\mathcal{ALC}$-concepts is the smallest set such that each concept name $A \in \boldsymbol{C}$ is an $\mathcal{ALC}$-concept and, if C and D are $\mathcal{ALC}$-concepts and r is a role name, then

$\neg C, C \sqcap D, C \sqcup D, \exists\, r.C,$ and $\forall\, r.C$ are also $\mathcal{ALC}$-concepts.

A general concept inclusion axiom (GCI) is of the form $C \sqsubseteq D$ for C, D $\mathcal{ALC}$-concepts. A TBox is a finite set of GCIs. An interpretation $\mathcal{I} = (\Delta^{\mathcal{I}}, \cdot^{\mathcal{I}})$ consists of a non-empty set $\Delta^{\mathcal{I}}$, the interpretation domain, and a mapping $\cdot^{\mathcal{I}}$, which associates with each concept name A, a set $A^{\mathcal{I}} \subseteq \Delta^{\mathcal{I}}$, and, with each role name r, a binary relation $r^{\mathcal{I}} \subseteq \Delta^{\mathcal{I}} \times \Delta^{\mathcal{I}}$.

The interpretation of complex constructs is defined in Tables 3.1 to 3.4.

An interpretation $\mathcal{I}$ satisfies a GCI $C \sqsubseteq D$ if $C^{\mathcal{I}} \subseteq D^{\mathcal{I}}$; $\mathcal{I}$ satisfies a TBox $\mathcal{T}$ if $\mathcal{I}$ satisfies all GCIs in $\mathcal{T}$ - in this case, $\mathcal{I}$ is called a model of $\mathcal{T}$.

An element d with $d^{\mathcal{I}} \in C^{\mathcal{I}}$ is called an instance of C and, if $(d^{\mathcal{I}}, e^{\mathcal{I}}) \in r^{\mathcal{I}}$, the e is called an r-successor of d.

An assertion is of the form $d \in C$ or $(d, e) \in r$. The finite, possibly empty set $\mathcal{A}$ of assertions is called the ABox.

An interpretation $\mathcal{I}$ is a model of the ABox $\mathcal{A}$ if it satisfies all its assertions, i.e., $d^{\mathcal{I}} \in C^{\mathcal{I}}$ holds for all assertions of the form $d \in C$ and $(d^{\mathcal{I}}, e^{\mathcal{I}}) \in r^{\mathcal{I}}$ holds for assertions of the form $(d, e) \in r$.

A knowledge base Σ in a DL is a pair $\Sigma = (\mathcal{T}, \mathcal{A})$, where $\mathcal{T}$ is a TBox and $\mathcal{A}$ is an ABox.

A knowledge base in the DL $\mathcal{ALC}$ is depicted in Figure 3.2. In the following example (in which $C \equiv D$ is the abbreviation for two GCIs $C \sqsubseteq D$ and $D \sqsubseteq C$) we define in the TBox that devices are only linked with configurations and a slot exists for each configuration. In the ABox we assert the instance $device23$ of type $Device$, the instance $conf24$ of type $Configuration$ and the instance $slot25$ of type $Slot$. Furthermore, we assert that $device23$ goes via $hasConfiguration$ to $conf24$, which goes via $hasSlot$ to $slot25$.

TBox:

$$Device \equiv \forall\, hasConfiguration.Configuration$$
$$Configuration \equiv \exists\, hasSlot.Slot$$

ABox:

$$device23 \in Device$$
$$conf24 \in Configuration$$
$$slot25 \in Slot$$
$$(device23, conf24) \in hasConfiguration$$
$$(conf24, slot25) \in hasSlot$$

Figure 3.2. DL knowledge base in $\mathcal{ALC}$.

Transitive Roles

Starting with $\mathcal{ALC}$ we recognize that it does not provide means to express transitive roles. The following concept describes a device, which consists of some configuration that is composed by cards:

$$Device \sqcap \exists\, hasPart.(Configuration \sqcap \exists\, hasPart.Card)$$

This concept is not subsumed by the concept $Device \sqcap \exists\, hasPart.Card$ although it is obviously a specialization of the upper one. Hence, $\mathcal{ALC}$ is extended to $\mathcal{S}$. $\mathcal{S}$ is the description logic, which extends $\mathcal{ALC}$ with transitive roles (cf. Table 3.1).

Role Hierarchies, Inverse and Functional Roles

A role inclusion of the form $hasConfiguration \sqsubseteq hasPart$ is used to define a role $hasConfiguration$ as a subrole of $hasPart$. We are able to express that if two instances are related by the role $hasConfiguration$, they are also related by the role $hasPart$. A finite set of role inclusions builds a role hierarchy. $\mathcal{SH}$ is the extension of $\mathcal{S}$ by role hierarchies (cf. Table 3.1).

It is useful if roles are bidirectional. For example, if we want to express that some $Device$ has as a part (via the role $hasPart$) some $Configuration$, the $Configuration$ belongs to $Device$ (via the role $belongsTo$). To design bidirectional roles, the extension of $\mathcal{SH}$ by $\mathcal{I}$ provides the definition of inverse roles (cf. Table 3.1). In the example $belongsTo$ is the inverse of $hasPart$ ($belongsTo \equiv hasPart^-$, where $R \equiv U$ is the abbreviation for $R \sqsubseteq U$ and $U \sqsubseteq R$).

The description logic $\mathcal{F}$ extends $\mathcal{SHI}$ by the use of functional roles (cf. Table 3.1). Functional roles ensure that for each instance there can be at most one distinct instance via the functional role. For example, the functional role $belongsTo$ ensures that an instance belongs at most to another given instance.

All constructs in Table 3.1 build the description logic $\mathcal{SHIF}$ [Sat03]. $\mathcal{SHIF}$ is equivalent to the ontology language $OWL\text{-}Lite$ [Hor05].

Nominals and Number Restrictions

Nominals are used to define concepts that exactly describe a set of specified instances (cf. Table 3.2). For example, the concept $\exists\, hasPart.\{card256\}$ describes those instances, which are linked via $hasPart$ with the instance $card256$. The description logic $\mathcal{O}$ extends $\mathcal{SHIF}$ by the use of nominals.

The constructs for number restrictions are used to define concepts, which contain those instances that are connected via a role to at least or at most a given number of instances (cf. Table 3.2). The concept $\geq 1\, hasPart$ describes those instances, which are composed by at least one other instance. $\mathcal{N}$ describes the description logic, which provides number restrictions.

Construct	Syntax	Semantics	
atomic concept	A	$A^{\mathcal{I}} \subseteq \Delta^{\mathcal{I}}$	
atomic role	R	$R^{\mathcal{I}} \subseteq \Delta^{\mathcal{I}} \times \Delta^{\mathcal{I}}$	
transitive role	$R \in \mathbf{R}_+$	$\{(x,y),(y,z)\} \subseteq R^{\mathcal{I}} \to (x,z) \in R^{\mathcal{I}}$	
top	$\top$	$\top^{\mathcal{I}} = \Delta^{\mathcal{I}}$	
bottom	$\bot$	$\bot^{\mathcal{I}} = \varnothing$	
conjunction	$C_1 \sqcap C_2$	$(C_1 \sqcap C_2)^{\mathcal{I}} = C_1^{\mathcal{I}} \sqcap C_2^{\mathcal{I}}$	$\mathcal{S}$
disjunction	$C_1 \sqcup C_2$	$(C_1 \sqcup C_2) = C_1^{\mathcal{I}} \sqcup C_2^{\mathcal{I}}$	
negation	$\neg C$	$(\neg C)^{\mathcal{I}} = \Delta^{\mathcal{I}}/C^{\mathcal{I}}$	
universal quantification	$\forall P.C$	$(\forall P.C)^{\mathcal{I}} = \{x \mid \forall y : (x,y) \in R^{\mathcal{I}} \to y \in C^{\mathcal{I}}\}$	
existential quantification	$\exists P.C$	$(\exists P.C)^{\mathcal{I}} = \{x \mid \exists y : (x,y) \in R^{\mathcal{I}} \land y \in C^{\mathcal{I}}\}$	
role hierarchy	$R \sqsubseteq S$	$R^{\mathcal{I}} \subseteq S^{\mathcal{I}}$	$\mathcal{H}$
inverse role	R^-	$\{(x,y) \mid (y,x) \in R\}$	$\mathcal{I}$
functional role	$R \in \mathbf{F}$	$\{(x,y),(x,z)\} \subseteq R^{\mathcal{I}} \to y = z$	$\mathcal{F}$

Table 3.1. DL constructs $\mathcal{SHIF}$.

Extending $\mathcal{SHIF}$ with the constructs in Table 3.2 ($\mathcal{ON}$) builds the description logic $\mathcal{SHOIN}$ [HPS04]. *OWL-DL* ontologies can be transformed into knowledge bases conforming to $\mathcal{SHOIN}$ [HPS04].

Construct	Syntax	Semantics	
nominals	$\{o_1\} \sqcup \ldots \sqcup \{o_n\}$	$(\{o_1\} \sqcup \ldots \sqcup \{o_n\})^{\mathcal{I}} = \{o_1^{\mathcal{I}}, ..., o_n^{\mathcal{I}}\}$	$\mathcal{O}$
at least restriction	$\geq nP$	$(\geq nP)^{\mathcal{I}} = \{x \mid \sharp\{y : (x,y) \in P^{\mathcal{I}}\} \geq n\}$	$\mathcal{N}$
at most restriction	$\leq nP$	$(\leq nP)^{\mathcal{I}} = \{x \mid \sharp\{y : (x,y) \in P^{\mathcal{I}}\} \leq n\}$	

Table 3.2. DL constructs $\mathcal{ON}$.

Generalized Role Inclusion and Qualified Number Restrictions

The description logic $\mathcal{H}$ provides the definition of hierarchies of roles. The description logic $\mathcal{R}$ provides a more general construct for describing hierarchies of roles (cf. Table 3.3). It allows for expressing that if an instance is connected by a sequence of roles with some other instance, then the two instances are also connected to each other by the super role. For example, if an instance is connected via *hasConfiguration* followed by *hasCard* with some other instance, then the two instances are also connected by *hasDeviceCard* if *hasConfiguration* ∘ *hasCard* ⊑ *hasDeviceCard* is defined in the TBox.

In addition, the description logic $\mathcal{R}$ allows for defining concepts that contain all instances, which are connected via a given role to themselves.

While the description logic $\mathcal{N}$ only allows for defining unqualified number restriction, the description logic $\mathcal{Q}$ allows for defining qualified number restrictions. Qualified number restrictions contain those instances that are connected by a role to at least or at most a given number of instances of a specified concept (cf. Table 3.3). While $\geq 1hasPart$ describes those instances, which are composed by at least one other instance (here the type is not specified), $\geq 1hasPart.Configuration$ restricts that the $hasPart$-successors are of type $Configuration$.

Extending $\mathcal{SHOIN}$ with the constructs in Table 3.3 ($\mathcal{RQ}$) builds the description logic $\mathcal{SROIQ}$ [Hor08].

Construct	Syntax	Semantics	
universal role	U	$\Delta^{\mathcal{I}} \times \Delta^{\mathcal{I}}$	
generalized role inclusion axioms	$R_1 \circ R_2 \sqsubseteq R$	$R_1^{\mathcal{I}} \circ R_2^{\mathcal{I}} \sqsubseteq R^{\mathcal{I}}$	$\mathcal{R}$
self concept	$\exists S.SELF$	$(\exists S.SELF)^{\mathcal{I}} = \{x \mid (x,x) \in S^{\mathcal{I}}\}$	
at least restriction	$\geq nS.C$	$(\geq nS.C)^{\mathcal{I}} =$ $\{x \mid \sharp\{y \mid (x,y) \in S^{\mathcal{I}} \wedge y \in C^{\mathcal{I}}\} \geq n\}$	$\mathcal{Q}$
at most restriction	$\leq nS.C$	$(\leq nS.C)^{\mathcal{I}} =$ $\{x \mid \sharp\{y \in \Delta^{\mathcal{I}} \mid (x,y) \in R^{\mathcal{I}} \wedge y \in C^{\mathcal{I}}\} \leq n\}$	

Table 3.3. DL constructs $\mathcal{RQ}$.

Datatypes and Data Values

To complete the presentation of different description logics, Table 3.4 introduces the constructs of $\mathcal{D}$. $\mathcal{D}$ extends every description logic by the support of datatypes and datavalues. In a description logic a datatype theory D is a mapping from a datatype to a set of values. The datatype domain, written $\Delta_D^{\mathcal{I}}$, is the union of the mappings of the datatypes [HPS04]. $\mathcal{D}$ provides constructs to define data type roles and restricting them by quantifications and cardinality restrictions. Its syntax and semantics are presented in Table 3.4.

Construct	Syntax	Semantics	
datatype	D	$D^D \subseteq \Delta_D^{\mathcal{I}}$	
datatype role	U	$U^{\mathcal{I}} \subseteq \Delta^{\mathcal{I}} \times \Delta_D^{\mathcal{I}}$	
data values	v	$v^{\mathcal{I}} = v^D$	
data nominals	$\{v\}$	$\{v\}^{\mathcal{I}} = \{v^{\mathcal{I}}\}$	$\mathcal{D}$
datatype existential quantification	$\exists U.D$	$(\exists U.D)^{\mathcal{I}} = \{x \mid \exists y : (x,y) \in U^{\mathcal{I}} \wedge y \in D^D\}$	
datatype universal quantification	$\forall U.D$	$(\forall U.D)^{\mathcal{I}} =$ $\{x \mid \forall y : (x,y) \in U^{\mathcal{I}} \rightarrow y \in D^D\}$	
data at least restriction	$\geq nU.D$	$(\geq nU.D)^{\mathcal{I}} =$ $\{x \mid \sharp\{y \mid (x,y) \in U^{\mathcal{I}} \wedge y \in D^D\} \geq n\}$	
data at most restriction	$\leq nU.D$	$(\leq nU.D)^{\mathcal{I}} =$ $\{x \mid \sharp\{y \mid (x,y) \in U^{\mathcal{I}} \wedge y \in D^D\} \leq n\}$	

Table 3.4. DL constructs $\mathcal{D}$.

The description logic $\mathcal{SROIQ}(\mathcal{D})$ builds the basis for the ontology language *OWL 2* [Hor08, MPSH09]. OWL 2 is used in the remaining chapters and is discussed in Section 3.3.1.

3.2.2 Relation to First Order Logic and Complexity

The meaning of DL families is usually given in model-theoretic semantics. However, they can be represented by First Order Logic (FOL) terms, where concepts correspond to unary predicates and roles correspond to binary predicates [Bor96]. Table 3.5 summarizes the correspondences.

Construct Name	DL Syntax	FOL Syntax
atomic concept	A	$A(x)$
atomic role	R	$R(x, y)$
transitive role	$R \in \mathbf{R}^+$	$\forall\, x, y, z.(R(x, y) \wedge R(y, z) \rightarrow R(x, z))$
subclass axiom	$A \sqsubseteq B$	$\forall\, x.A(x) \rightarrow B(x)$
disjunction	$C_1 \sqcup \ldots \sqcup C_n$	$C_1(x) \vee \ldots \vee C_n(x)$
conjunction	$C_1 \sqcap \ldots \sqcap C_n$	$C_1(x) \wedge \ldots \wedge C_n(x)$
negation	$\neg C$	$\neg C(x)$
universal quantification	$\forall P.C$	$\forall\, y.(P(x, y) \rightarrow C(y))$
existential quantification	$\exists P.C$	$\exists\, y.(P(x, y) \wedge C(y))$
cardinality restriction	$\leq nS.C$	$\exists\, y_1, \ldots, y_n. \bigwedge_{1 \leq i \leq n}(P(x, y_i) \wedge C(y_i))$
object subproperty	$R \sqsubseteq S$	$\forall\, x, y.R(x, y) \rightarrow S(x, y)$

Table 3.5. Relation between DL and FOL (excerpt).

DL families represent a strict subset of FOL. Although the expressiveness of FOL is higher it does have some significant practical drawbacks. FOL is undecidable in the general case, and often does not allow for sound and complete reasoning [GOS09, GHVD03].

The most widely used reasoning technique for DLs is the tableau-based approach introduced by Schmidt-Schauss and Smolka [MS91]. Given an ABox the tableau-based approach tries to conduct to a model, which is also a model of a corresponding TBox [Baa09]. The tableau-based approach for consistency reasoning in DLs is a decision procedure [Baa09]. A procedure is a decision procedure, if it returns either true or false, and if it is: *sound*, i.e., the positive answers should be correct; *complete*, i.e., the negative answers should be correct; *terminating*, i.e., it should always give an answer in finite time.

In the following, we comment on the complexity of the consistency checking problem. We differ between *data complexity*, *taxonomic complexity*, and *combined complexity*:

Data complexity: the complexity measured with respect to the number of facts in the knowledge base.

Taxonomic complexity: the complexity measured with respect to the size of the axioms in the knowledge base.

Combined complexity: the complexity measured with respect to both, the size of the axioms and the number of facts.

Table 3.6 summarizes the complexity results for OWL 2, OWL DL and OWL Lite for the consistency inference problem (an ABox $\mathcal{A}$ is consistent with regard to the TBox $\mathcal{T}$ if it has a model $\mathcal{I}$, which is also a model of $\mathcal{T}$ [Baa09]).

Language	Taxonomic Complexity	Data Complexity	Combined Complexity
OWL 2	2NP-complete	Open (NP-Hard)	2NP-complete
OWL-DL	NEXPTIME-complete	Open (NP-Hard)	NEXPTIME-complete
OWL-Lite	EXPTIME-complete	NP-complete	EXPTIME-complete

Table 3.6. Complexity of OWL 2 tractable fragments [Gra07].

3.2.3 OWA and CWA

The interpretation of knowledge bases underlies by default the *open world assumption* (OWA). Besides OWA other interpretations like the *closed world assumption* (CWA) may be defined.

The OWA assumes incomplete information by default. That means, if a fact f in a knowledge base is missing, $\neg f$ cannot be inferred. The question if the fact f is *true* or *false* can only be answered with *unknown*. If the fact $\neg f$ is added to the knowledge base, the question if the fact f is true is directly answered with false. The OWA is mainly suitable for systems and application domains, which are assumed to be incomplete and where users do not have full access to all information. Such a prominent system, for example, is the World Wide Web (WWW).

The CWA assumes all relevant facts as part of the knowledge base. If the fact f is not in the knowledge base we can directly infer $\neg f$. A typical example where CWA is used are database systems. Databases only contain information, which is explicitly stored.

Figure 3.3 gives an example of a consistent knowledge base in OWA. The TBox expresses that all devices have at most one configuration and that all configurations are of type *Configuration*. The ABox describes that *device*1 has the two configurations *conf*1 and *slot*1, where *conf*1 is of type *Configuration* and *slot*1 is of type *Slot*. This knowledge base is consistent (since the ABox has a model, which is also a model of the TBox). The fact that the device has two configurations and in addition one configuration is of type *Slot* does not affect the consistency. The reason why the knowledge base is consistent depends on the OWA and the unique name assumption (UNA, cf. Section 3.2.3). A reasoner validating the knowledge base assumes that the type of *slot*1 is *Configuration* (in addition to *Slot*). So far, there is no fact in the knowledge base expressing that *slot*1 is not of type *Configuration*. A contradiction with an inconsistent knowledge base only occurs if the two types are defined as disjoint (*Slot* $\sqsubseteq \neg Configuration$). In addition, a reasoner assumes that the instances *conf*1 and *slot*1 are the same because devices have at most one configuration. If we explicitly define *conf*1 and *slot*1 as different, the knowledge base becomes inconsistent.

TBox:

$$Device \sqsubseteq \forall\, hasConfiguration.Configuration$$
$$\sqcap\, \leq 1\, hasConfiguration.Configuration$$

ABox:

$$Device(device1)$$
$$Configuration(conf1)$$
$$Slot(slot1)$$
$$(device1, conf1) \in hasConfiguration$$
$$(device1, slot1) \in hasConfiguration$$

Figure 3.3. Consistent knowledge base in OWA.

A further characteristic of the OWA is the answering of queries. The following (class-based) query retrieves all instances which are not devices:

$$NotDevice \equiv \neg Device$$

When applying the query on the knowledge base above, the result in OWA is an empty set. We could assume that the instances *conf*1 and *slot*1 possibly have the type *Device*, since it is not specified in the knowledge base that *Configuration* and *Slot* are disjoint with *Device*.

Closing the World

Many approaches were developed for closing knowledge bases and allowing reasoners to validate integrity constraints.

An approach that simulates the local CWA by introducing a new language construct is the one presented in [DLN+96, GM05]. Here a $\mathcal{K}$-operator is introduced, which allows for locally closing concepts and roles. The $\mathcal{K}$-operator only considers instances, which are known by the knowledge base. An extension of OWL by epistemic operators therefore allows for non-monotonic features known from closed world systems, such as default rules, integrity constraints or epistemic querying [GM05].

An implementation of the $\mathcal{K}$-operator is available for the reasoner Pellet [SPG$^+$07], but it is only usable for the description logic $\mathcal{ALC}$.

Ensuring Integrity Constraints

Although the open world assumption has many advantages in software modeling (e.g., reasoning and validation of incomplete models) we have to ensure that the validation of integrity constraints defined in $\mathcal{SROIQ}$ is still possible.

While for a closed world new language constructs (e.g., epistemic operators) are introduces, for a closed domain additional facts using given DL constructs are used.

To establish a closed domain, the $\top$ concept is defined as equivalent with the set of all known instances [MHRS06]. Here, the language construct $\mathcal{O}$ for nominals is considered. Hence, this closing approach, for example, is not available for OWL-Lite [Hor05].

In the following we consider basic integrity constraints and show how to use existing DL constructs to validate them. If the integrity of the data modeled in an ontoware model should be checked, ontoware modeling and validating tools must provide the automatic creation of the additional facts presented in the following.

Simulating Unique Name Assumption

The unique name assumption (UNA) requires that if instances have different names they are understood as being different. In OWA the UNA is not considered since two instances are explicitly not declared as being different. The description logic $\mathcal{O}$ provides a solution for simulating UNA. It provides the nominal concept and thus allows for defining instances as being different from each other. Two instances i_1 and i_2 are different from each other ($i_1 \neq i_2$) if the nominal concept $\{o_1\}$ is disjoint with the nominal concept $\{o_2\}$ ($\{o_1\} \sqsubseteq \neg\{o_2\}$).

Ensuring Types of Instances

To ensure that a given instance *device*1 only has the asserted type *Device*, all other concepts (besides super concepts) must be declared as being disjoint with *Device* (e.g., *Device* $\sqsubseteq \neg(Slot \sqcup Configuration)$). Hence, instances of *Device* cannot be of types *Slot* or *Configuration*.

Ensuring Role Start- and End-Types

The following axiom in the TBox of a knowledge base restricts the instances of *Configuration* to be connected with some instance of type *Slot*.

$$Configuration \sqsubseteq \exists\, hasSlot.Slot$$

In a closed domain we must ensure that the type of instances connected via *hasSlot* to slots is only *Configuration*. We have to add the following axiom to the TBox to close the domain:

$$\exists\, hasSlot.\top \sqsubseteq Configuration$$

Furthermore, all concepts must be declared as disjoint with *Configuration* (*Configuration* $\sqsubseteq \neg(Device \sqcup Slot)$).

To ensure that configuration instances are only connected with slot instances via the *hasSlot* role, we have to introduce the following axiom to close the domain:

$$Configuration \sqsubseteq \forall\, hasSlot.Slot$$

In addition, all concepts in the TBox must be disjoint with the target type *Slot*. For example, *Slot* is declared as disjoint with *Configuration* and *Device* (*Slot* $\sqsubseteq \neg(Device \sqcup Configuration)$).

Ensuring Cardinalities

The following axiom in the TBox of a knowledge base describes the instances of *Configuration* to be connected with exactly two slots.

$$Configuration \sqsubseteq= 2hasSlot.Slot$$

The knowledge base in Figure 3.2 with the cardinality restriction for configurations above and the ABox below, is consistent although the number of slots are either too low (for *conf*1) or too high (for *conf*2).

$$conf1 \in Configuration \qquad\qquad conf2 \in Configuration$$
$$slot1 \in Slot \qquad\qquad slot2, slot3, slot4 \in Slot$$
$$(conf1, slot1) \in hasSlot \qquad\qquad (conf2, slot2) \in hasSlot$$
$$(conf2, slot3) \in hasSlot$$
$$(conf2, slot4) \in hasSlot$$

To validate cardinality constraints in a closed domain, we first of all have to apply the unique name assumption on all instances in the ABox as described above. To avoid the assumption of further instances, which are not explicitly defined in the knowledge base, all concepts are defined as being equivalent to the set of instances they are describing. Thus, for concepts *Configuration* and *Slot* we define:

$$Configuration \equiv \{conf1, conf2\}$$
$$Slot \equiv \{slot1, slot2, slot3, slot4\}$$

Furthermore, *Configuration* and *Slot* are defined as disjoint:

$$Configuration \sqsubseteq \neg Slot$$

To obtain an inconsistency for the numbers of slots for the two configurations (*conf*1 and *conf*2) in the knowledge base given above, we explicitly have to declare which instances of *Slot* are *not* connected with *conf*1 and *conf*2 respectively. Here we use negative role assertions. The description logic $\mathcal{O}$ allows for declaring negative role assertions, e.g., by defining that the instances of the (nominal) concept {*conf*1} have no link via *hasSlot* to the (nominal) concept {*slot*2} ({*conf*1} $\sqsubseteq \neg hasSlot.\{slot2\}$). As an abbreviation we use the $\notin$ symbol:

$$(conf1, slot2) \notin hasSlot$$
$$(conf1, slot3) \notin hasSlot$$
$$(conf1, slot4) \notin hasSlot$$
$$(conf2, slot1) \notin hasSlot$$

In general it is possible to check the validity of integrity constraints. Since modelware models are often processed in a closed world, there are two disadvantages of checking constraints. First, the number of additional axioms in the knowledge base increases and thus reduces the performance of reasoning tools (no scalability). Secondly, if the ABox is modified (e.g., by adding, updating or deleting instances and role assertions) all the additional axioms must be rebuilt (no monotonicity).

3.3 Ontoware Models

An ontoware technological space provides languages to design *ontoware models*. Section 3.2 presented the description logics family and showed how DL knowledge bases are defined. The *Web Ontology Language 2* (OWL 2) is used to design models in an ontoware technological space. Such models are used to model a description logics knowledge base in $\mathcal{SROIQ}(\mathcal{D})$.

3.3.1 Ontoware Models as TGraph

An ontoware model in abstract syntax form is represented by a TGraph. The ontoware model in Figure 3.4 models the knowledge base from Figure 3.2. In the middle of Figure 3.4 an **Ontology** vertex is used to represent the complete knowledge base. The vertex is linked with all axioms. The upper part of Figure 3.4 represents the TBox consisting of vertices for classes and object properties, declarations, and IRIs. In addition, vertices for class axioms (such as the one for equivalent classes) and class expressions (e.g., for universal and

existential quantifications) are declared. In the lower part of Figure 3.4 the
ABox is modeled. Here, vertices for individuals, declarations, and IRIs are
declared and corresponding vertices for assertions are used to represent the
typing and linking of individuals.

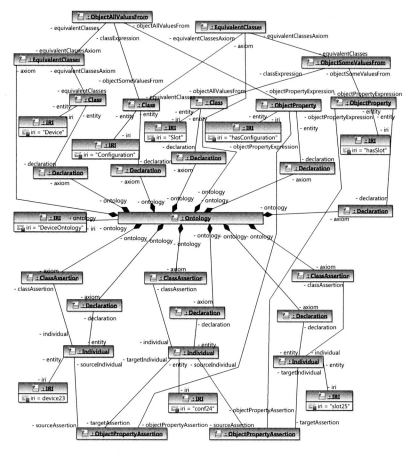

Figure 3.4. Ontoware model as TGraph.

A more user friendly representation of the knowledge base is depicted in
Figure 3.5. The model in Figure 3.5 is a visualization of the TGraph in Figure 3.4 using the textual *OWL 2 Functional-Style syntax*, which is introduced
in the next section.

Since we want to express more ontoware models with the same structure
of axioms, we use the metamodel GS_{OWL}, which is fully presented in Ap-

```
Ontology(DeviceOntology

Declaration(Class(Device))
EquivalentClasses(Device ObjectAllValuesFrom(hasConfiguration Configuration))

Declaration(Class(Configuration))
EquivalentClasses(Configuration ObjectSomeValuesFrom(hasSlot Slot))

Declaration(Class(Slot))

Declaration(ObjectProperty(hasSlot))

Declaration(ObjectProperty(hasConfiguration))

Declaration(Individual(device23))
ClassAssertion(device23 Device)
ObjectPropertyAssertion(hasConfiguration device23 conf24)

Declaration(Individual(conf24))
ClassAssertion(conf24 Configuration)
ObjectPropertyAssertion(hasSlot conf24 slot25)

Declaration(Individual(slot25))
ClassAssertion(slot25 Slot)
)
```

Figure 3.5. Ontoware model representing the knowledge base in Figure 3.2.

pendix A.2. Figure 3.6 just presents a small excerpt of GS_{OWL}, which depicts concepts of the TBox of the ontoware model given in Figure 3.5.

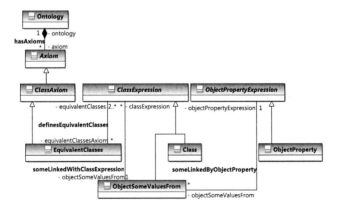

Figure 3.6. OWL 2 metamodel (excerpt).

3.3.2 Concrete Syntaxes

In the following we present two alternative textual concrete syntaxes for ontoware models, namely the *OWL 2 Functional-Style syntax* and the *OWL 2 Manchester syntax*. Both syntaxes are equivalent [HPS09], i.e., an ontoware model designed in Manchester syntax can be translated to a model in Functional-Style syntax, and vice versa.

Axiom-based Syntax

For the visualization of an ontoware model we used in Figure 3.5 the *OWL 2 Functional-Style syntax* [MPSH09]. The syntax allows for designing axiombased ontologies. Figure 3.5 depicts an ontoware model represented in Functional-Style syntax showing an axiom-based ontology. An axiom-based ontology consists of a set of axioms for classes, object properties, data properties, and individuals. Axioms are used in combination with class expressions, object and data property expressions, and individuals.

Frame-based Syntax

Figure 3.7 depicts the ontoware model in Figure 3.5 using the *OWL 2 Manchester syntax* [HPS09]. The syntax is frame-based. Instead of axiom-based ontologies each frame-based ontology consists of a set of frames. Frames are used to define classes, object and data properties, and individuals. Each frame contains axioms restricting the element the frame represents. A frame for classes contains class axioms. A frame for object properties contains object property axioms. A frame for data properties contains data property axioms. A frame for individuals contains individual axioms (assertions).

3.4 Ontoware Reasoning and Querying Services

All services used to reason on ontoware models and to query ontoware models are implemented as static operation and are part of the **Ontoware** API. In Section 3.4.1 we present standard reasoning services to check the consistency of ontoware models, the satisfiability of classes in ontoware models, to classify instances and to validate the subsumption relation between two classes. In Section 3.4.2 we present services used to explain unsatisfiability and inconsistencies in ontoware models. Section 3.4.3 presents a query language for querying ontoware models.

3.4.1 Standard Reasoning Services

In the following we are going to present four standard reasoning services. All services provide means to derive and retrieve implicit knowledge based on the

```
Class: Device
  EquivalentTo:
    hasConfiguration only Configuration

Class: Configuration
  EquivalentTo:
    hasSlot some Slot

Class: Slot

ObjectProperty: hasConfiguration

ObjectProperty: hasSlot

Individual: slot25
  Types:
    Slot

Individual: device23
  Types:
    Device
  Facts:
    hasConfiguration  conf24

Individual: conf24
  Types:
    Configuration
  Facts:
    hasSlot  slot25
```

Figure 3.7. Ontoware Model represented in Manchester-Style Syntax.

logical foundation of ontoware models by DL knowledge bases. In particular we present services for consistency checking, satisfiability checking, classification, and subsumption in Tables 3.7 to 3.10. All services are encapsulations of the correspondent services implemented in Pellet [SPG+07]. In contrast to the services of Pellet they can be directly adopted on ontoware models as defined in Section 3.3.

Name	Consistency Checking
Signature	boolean isConsistent(Ontology o)
Pattern	b=Ontoware.isConsistent(o)
Description	returns true, if the ABox $\mathcal{A}$ of o is consistent with regard to its TBox $\mathcal{T}$. $\mathcal{A}$ is consistent with regard to the TBox $\mathcal{T}$, if it has a model $\mathcal{I}$, which is also a model of $\mathcal{T}$ [Baa09].

Table 3.7. Reasoning service: consistency checking.

3.4.2 Non-Standard Reasoning Services

Reasoning services for inconsistency checking or satisfiability checking allow for detecting problems in ontoware models. Language users create on-

Name	Satisfiability Checking
Signature	boolean isSatisfiable(Ontology o, ClassExpression c)
Pattern	b=Ontoware.isSatisfiable(o, c)
Description	returns true if the class expression c in o is satisfiable. c is satisfiable if $(c)^{\mathcal{I}} \neq \varnothing$ for some model $\mathcal{I}$ of $\mathcal{T}$ [Baa09].

Table 3.8. Reasoning service: satisfiability checking.

Name	Classification
Signature	boolean classify(Ontology o, ClassExpression c, Individual i)
Pattern	b=Ontoware.classify(o, c, i)
Description	returns true if i in o is an instance of the class expression c. i is an instance of c if $(i)^{\mathcal{I}} \in (c)^{\mathcal{I}}$ for all models $\mathcal{I}$ of $\mathcal{T}$ and $\mathcal{A}$ [Baa09].

Table 3.9. Reasoning service: classification.

Name	Subsumption Checking
Signature	boolean subsume(Ontology o, ClassExpression c_{sup}, ClassExpression c_{sub})
Pattern	b=Ontoware.subsume(o, c_{sup}, c_{sub})
Description	returns true if c_{sub} is subsumed by c_{sup}. c_{sub} is subsumed by c_{sup} if $(c_{sub})^{\mathcal{I}} \subseteq (c_{sup})^{\mathcal{I}}$ for all models $\mathcal{I}$ of $\mathcal{T}$ [Baa09].

Table 3.10. Reasoning service: subsumption checking.

toware models and use the consistency checking service or satisfiability service to validate them. If the model has problems, language users require an explanation in order to find out the reason why the problem holds. In [KPSH05, KPHS07, HS05] several techniques are presented for computing justifications (sets of OWL 2 axioms), which entail the problem in the ontology. In Table 3.11 we give the specification of an explanation service, which encapsulates the methods in [KPSH05, KPHS07] for computing justifications and the services implemented in Pellet [SPG+07].

Name	Axiom Explanation
Signature	Set<Set<Axiom>> explainAxiom(Ontology o, Axiom a)
Pattern	S=Ontoware.explainAxiom(o, a)
Description	returns a set S of sets of axioms, where each set $s_i \in$ S of axioms is minimal and entails the axiom a. a is entailed by s_i if all models of s_i also satisfy a.

Table 3.11. Reasoning service: explanation of an axiom.

The explanation service in Table 3.11 can easily be used to compute justifications for an unsatisfiable class C in an ontology o: explainAxiom(o, SubClassOf(C Nothing)).

We present an additional service for inconsistency explanations in Table 3.12. When an inconsistency is detected in the ontoware model, for one inconsistency a single set of axioms causing the problem is extracted [SPG+07].

Name	Inconsistency Explanation
Signature	Set<Set<Axiom>> explainInconsistency(Ontology o)
Pattern	S=Ontoware.explainInconsistency(o)
Description	returns a set S of minimal sets of axioms for each inconsistency. If at least one axiom of each set $s_i \in$ S is removed from o, o becomes consistent.

Table 3.12. Reasoning service: inconsistency explanation.

3.4.3 SPARQL Querying Services

In the following we introduce a query language for RDF graphs, namely *SPARQL*. Since ontoware models may be translated to RDF graphs, the SPARQL query language allows for querying ontologies. An implementation of a SPARQL query engine is provided by Pellet [SPG+07].

RDF Graphs

The *Resource Description Framework* (RDF) is a World Wide Web Consortium (W3C) standard for describing and structuring data in the World Wide Web (WWW). In RDF the data is described and structured by RDF graphs. They describe information about resources and relate them. RDF graphs are built on a vocabulary, which consists of three disjoint sets: A set of unified resource identifiers (URIs) $\mathcal{V}_{uri}$, which refer to resources, a set of blank node (bnode) identifiers $\mathcal{V}_{bnode}$, which refer to nodes in the graph without any meaning, and, a set of literals $\mathcal{V}_{lit}$ used for data values. An RDF graph is a finite set of RDF triples consisting of a subject, a predicate, and an object. RDF triples are of the form $(s, p, o) \in (\mathcal{V}_{uri} \cup \mathcal{V}_{bnode}) \times \mathcal{V}_{uri} \times (\mathcal{V}_{uri} \cup \mathcal{V}_{bnode} \cup \mathcal{V}_{lit})$.

SPARQL Query

The current W3C recommendation for the *SPARQL Protocol and RDF Query Language* (SPARQL is a recursive acronym) corresponds to version 1.1 [HS10]. The main building blocks of a SPARQL query are *Basic Graph Patterns* (BGP). A SPARQL BGP is a set of *triple patterns*. A triple pattern is an RDF triple in which variables might appear. The variables come from the infinite set $\mathcal{V}_{var}$, which is disjoint with the sets $\mathcal{V}_{uri}$, $\mathcal{V}_{bnode}$, and $\mathcal{V}_{lit}$ described above.

The solution of a SPARQL query with regard to an RDF graph G is described by a solution mapping μ from the variables in the query to RDF terms, such that the substitution of variables in the BGP of the query would yield a graph, which is entailed by G (according to the definition of entailments in RDF semantics, e.g., in the *Simple Entailment Regime* [GP10] an RDF graph entails all its subgraphs). In [GP10] different entailment regimes are explained. In this work we consider the *OWL 2 Entailment Regime*, which is presented below.

Based on BGPs, more complex queries can be created by using SPARQL constructs such as projection (**SELECT**), joins (**OPTIONAL**), union (**UNION**), and constraints (**FILTER**) [PS08]. Figure 3.8 depicts a SPARQL query, which asks for all instances of type **Device**.

```
SELECT DISTINCT ?i
WHERE {
      ?i rdf:type Device
}
```

Figure 3.8. Simple SPARQL query.

Translating Ontoware Models to RDF Graphs

In [PSM10] a mapping between ontologies and RDF graphs is presented. This mapping allows for establishing a translation of ontologies described by ontoware models to RDF graphs, and vice versa a translation of RDF graphs satisfying certain restrictions to ontologies [PSM10].

The translation from ontologies to RDF graphs considers all ontoware constructs (axioms, class, object property and data property expressions, and individuals, etc.) and translates them to sets of RDF triples according to the mapping defined in [PSM10].

The translation from RDF graphs to ontologies relies on parsing rules defined by given triple patterns to be matched in the RDF graph. These triple patterns describe which nodes in an RDF graph are representing which constructs of an ontology. Since ontoware models can be translated to RDF graphs they can be queried by SPARQL.

OWL 2 Direct Semantics and Entailment Regime for SPARQL

SPARQL 1.0 has only be defined as a query language over RDF graphs, not taking into account RDF Schema or OWL ontologies [Pol10].

Answering full SPARQL queries on top of OWL has already preliminarily been addressed so far [SP07, KS08] and is proposed to be provided by SPARQL 1.1 [GP10].

The semantics and its entailment is similar to that of description logics (cf. Tables 3.1 to 3.4). It is based on interpretations of basic graph patterns, which are mapped to DL axioms defined in a DL knowledge base.

The solution set $S(Q)$ of a query Q is a set of variable mappings μ : $\mathcal{V}_{var} \to \mathcal{V}_{uri} \cup \mathcal{V}_{lit}$. A variable mapping $\mu(Q)$ is a solution if it is entailed by the knowledge base $\mathcal{K}$ representing the ontoware model. The entailment of $\mu(Q)$ by $\mathcal{K}$ is defined in the OWL 2 entailment regime. In short, it defines that $\mu(Q)$ is entailed by $\mathcal{K}$ if all models for $\mathcal{K}$ are also models for $\mu(Q)$. The OWL 2 entailment regime is explained in [GP10] precisely.

SPARQL Querying Service

Since we are able to transform ontoware models to RDF graphs we can use SPARQL as a query language to query ontoware models. Table 3.13 specifies the available SPARQL querying service.

Name	SPARQL Query Answering
Signature	ResultSet evaluateSparqlQuery(Ontology o, Query q)
Pattern	a=Ontoware.evaluateSparqlQuery(o, q)
Description	evaluates the SPARQL query q on the ontology o and computes the answer a. If there is no answer the service returns null.

Table 3.13. SPARQL querying service.

3.5 Conclusion

In this chapter we presented an ontoware technological space and answered the two research questions RQ3 and RQ4 asking for the concepts and languages, and the tools and services in an ontoware technological space.

The ontoware technological space provides the OWL 2 modeling language to describe ontoware models. Ontoware models are formally represented by TGraphs. The structure of those TGraphs is described by a graph schema, which represents the metamodel of the ontology language OWL 2. Ontoware models have model-theoretic semantics, which are defined by description logics.

The ontoware technological space provides different services for reasoning and querying. Reasoning services allow for checking the consistency of ontoware models and for inferring implicit knowledge. The querying service allows for asking SPARQL queries against ontoware models.

4

Comparison of Modelware and Ontoware

In Chapter 2 we presented the TGraph approach as a modelware technological space, where all models are represented as a TGraph. The space provides services for querying and transforming TGraphs. In Chapter 3 we presented the ontoware OWL 2 technological space. The space allows for designing ontoware models, which conform to the ontology language OWL 2. Additionally it provides a set of reasoning and querying services. Before we combine both spaces in Part III, we are going to describe the commonalities and differences.

To adopt ontology technologies for modelware models we must identify the commonalities of concepts for designing ontoware models and modelware models (Challenge 1). To support the tooling by ontology technologies (Challenge 3) we must identify the advantages of such technologies. Therefore we are going to answer the question:

RQ5: *What are the commonalities and variations of a modelware technological space and an ontoware technological space?*

We are going to show the commonalities and variations of languages and concepts to design data models as well as of services and tools to query and reason on descriptions in data models.

4.1 Chapter Context

In Chapters 2 and 3 we described a modelware technological space and an ontoware technological space. Since we consider the definition given by Kurtev et al. of the term technological space [KBA02], we are interested in a comparison of modeling concepts and tools provided by both technological spaces.

Figure 4.1 depicts an overview of the comparison. In Section 4.2 we are going to compare the grUML language with the ontology language OWL 2. We will establish a mapping between both languages, which represents the common concepts. Additionally, we depict differences of both languages. In Section 4.3 we are going to compare the query languages provided by both technological spaces. We are going to compare GReQL with SPARQL, where the comparison is mainly based on [SE10]. Finally, we are going to consider the reasoning technologies provided exclusively by the ontoware technological space. Since such technologies are not available in the modelware technological space, in Section 4.4 we are going to present the benefits using them in software modeling.

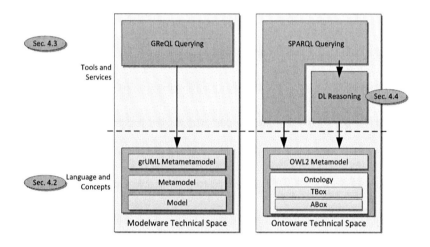

Figure 4.1. Overview of the comparison of modelware and ontoware.

4.2 Comparison of Modeling Languages and Concepts

In this section we are going to compare the modeling languages and concepts the respective spaces provide. As a modelware modeling language we consider grUML, as an ontoware data modeling language we consider OWL 2.

OWL 2 allows for modeling instance layer (ABox) and concept layer (TBox). With respect to the TGraph approach and besides grUML used to model graph schemas, we consider **Vertex**, **Edge**, and **Attribute Assignment** as the concepts to model a TGraph.

We are going to depict a first mapping between concepts of both spaces in Section 4.2.1. In Section 4.2.2 we are going to present its variations. We are going to indicate that the OWL 2 language compared to grUML provides a more expressive set of primitives used to describe data models.

4.2.1 Common Concepts

Comparing Sections 2.2.3 and 3.3, where we have introduced the grUML language and the OWL 2 language, at first glance we intensionally find similar concepts, which are juxtaposed in Table 4.1.

♯	Modelware Concept			Ontoware Concept	
1		VertexClass			Class
2		EdgeClass			ObjectProperty
3		Attribute			DataProperty
4	Graph Schema	Domain	TBox		Datatype
5		Multiplicities			Cardinality class expressions
6		SpecializesVertexClass			SubClassOf
7		SpecializesEdgeClass			SubObjectPropertyOf
8		Vertex			Individual
9	TGraph	Edge	ABox		ObjectPropertyAssertion
10		AttributeAssignment			DataPropertyAssertion

Table 4.1. Mapping between modelware concepts and ontoware concepts.

grUML allows for defining vertex classes in graph schemas, while OWL 2 allows for designing OWL classes in ontoware models. Both concepts are used to classify sets of instances, vertices, and individuals, respectively (1).

Edge classes in graph schemas are used to classify sets of edges between vertices. The counterpart in ontoware is the object property describing a set of relations between two individuals (2).

Attributes in grUML are used to define relations between vertices and edges of a given class (where the attribute is nested) and values of a particular domain. Data properties in OWL are similar to attributes since they define relations between individuals and values (3).

In grUML, domains describe the possible ranges of attributes. In OWL datatypes define the ranges of data properties. Basically, both concepts represent a set of values (4).

The definition of multiplicities of edge classes in graph schemas is achieved by the annotation of the respective incidences. They restrict a vertex to only being connected via edges of a given type with at least and at most a number of vertices typed by a given vertex class. In OWL class expressions for the restriction of cardinalities of individuals may be defined. These class expressions describe those individuals, which are linked via a given object property with at most and at least a given number of instances (5).

grUML allows for defining type hierarchies for vertex classes and edge classes. OWL 2 provides similar concepts. They allow for defining subclass relations between OWL classes and subproperty relations between object properties (6, 7). Specializations defined in grUML require vertices and edges to implement the properties of its type and all supertypes, while subclassing in

OWL declares sets of individuals and sets of relations as subset of other sets of individuals and other sets of relations respectively.

TGraphs are composed of typed vertices, typed edges, and attribute assignments. The counterpart is the ABox of ontoware models, which consists of individuals having a type, object property assertions defining the linking of two individuals via an object property, and, data property assertions defining the assignment of values to a given attribute belonging to some individual (8, 9, 10).

4.2.2 Variations

After we illustrated commonalities of grUML and OWL 2, we continue the comparison by depicting variations. For the ontology language OWL 2, we mention those constructs, which are not replaceable by respective counterparts in grUML-based graph schemas. In the case of the grUML metamodeling language we mention those constructs, which are not directly representable in an ontoware model.

OWL

Besides the description of classes, properties and instances, OWL 2 provides a comprehensive set of class expressions and axioms used to extend the description of modeled data in ontologies.

In OWL 2, class expressions and property expressions are combined to form new class expressions. Class expressions represent sets of individuals by formally describing the properties of individuals. Class expressions in OWL 2, which have no counterpart in grUML, are the ObjectIntersectionOf, ObjectUnionOf, and ObjectComplementOf for the standard set-theoretic operations on class expressions (in logical languages these are usually called conjunction, disjunction, and negation, respectively). Furthermore, constructs for quantified expressions for the description of classes containing those instances being linked with some individual (using the ObjectSomeValuesFrom class expression) or only with individuals (using the ObjectAllValuesFrom class expression) of a given type, are not provided by grUML. OWL 2 provides the description of classes by enumerating individuals. A counterpart of the ObjectOneOf class expression is not available in grUML.

The following class expression, which is defined as equivalent to the class Device describes those individuals, which are linked via the property hasConfiguration with at least one individual of type ComplexConfiguration or with one of the individuals config7603 or config7604.

EquivalentClasses(Device ObjectSomeValuesFrom(hasConfiguration ObjectUnionOf(ComplexConfiguration
    ObjectOneOf(config7603 config7604))))

OWL 2 provides an extensive set of axioms used to state what is true in the domain [MPSH09]. In particular OWL 2 provides the use of class axioms and property axioms.

Class axioms are used to express relationships between two or more class expressions. The EquivalentClasses axiom states that two class expressions describe the same set of individuals, while the DisjointClasses axiom states that the sets of individuals described by both class expressions are disjoint. In the listing above the EquivalentClasses axiom states the equivalence of the set of individuals described by Device and the set described by the ObjectSomeValuesFrom class expression. grUML allows for relating classes by specialization relationships. Additional relations between the sets of instances described by classes are not possible.

Object property axioms are used to characterize and establish relationships between object property expressions. An OWL 2 object property transitivity axiom describes that an object property expression is transitive. Furthermore, OWL 2 allows for stating that two object properties are equivalent or disjoint. If two object properties are equivalent or disjoint, the sets of relations between individuals they describe are equivalent or disjoint. grUML does not provide constructs to relate the sets of edges described by an edge class.

OWL 2 allows for composing two or more object properties to one object property chain being the specialization of another object property. The object property hasDeviceCard in the following is defined as the composition of hasCard and hasDeviceCard. In grUML the composition of edge classes is not possible.

```
SubObjectPropertyOf(SubObjectPropertyChain(hasConfiguration hasCard) hasDeviceCard)
```

grUML

The main distinction of the grUML metamodeling language compared to OWL 2 is the definition of attributes for edge classes. Hence, edges in TGraphs may be attributed. OWL 2 does not allow for defining attributes (or data properties) assigned to object properties. In OWL 2 only classes can be defined as a domain of a data property.

Edges in TGraphs may be traversed in both forward and backward direction.

In addition grUML allows for (sub-)packaging vertex classes and edge classes. The hierarchical (sub-)packaging concepts are not available for ontoware models.

Concluding Section 4.2 we state that OWL 2, compared to usual metamodeling languages like grUML, provides a rich set of primitives for the description of data models.

4.3 Comparison of Query Technologies

In this section we compare the query language GReQL from the modelware technological space with SPARQL from the ontoware technological space. This comparison is mainly based on the work by Schwarz and Ebert. For technical details of the comparison we refer to [SE10].

4.3.1 Query Language Concepts

As shown in [SE10], SPARQL and GReQL provide various features, which partially are not shared by both language. For example, the construction of RDF graphs by SPARQL CONSTRUCT queries and the usage of stand-alone GReQL regular path expressions. Hence, SPARQL and GReQL are not mutually substitutable, i.e., it is not always possible to replace a SPARQL query by an equivalent GReQL query and vice versa.

Anyway, there is an intersection of constructs, which are mapped in Table 4.2 (which is taken from [SE10]). The central concepts to be compared are SELECT and ASK queries in SPARQL and FWR expressions in GReQL.

4.3.2 Semantics and Entailment

The translations and mappings mentioned in Table 4.2 are syntactic translations of query languages where constructs may have similar semantics.

SPARQL with *Simple Entailment* [HS10] behaves similarly to GReQL: it only retrieves information explicitly defined in an RDF graph. In this case the different semantics of RDF and TGraphs do not bear any relevance to the mapping and translation of the query languages.

SPARQL with *OWL 2 Direct Semantics Entailment Regime* allows for querying RDF graphs (which can be mapped to OWL 2 ontologies) plus the entailed facts. The semantics and their entailment is similar to that of description logics (cf. Tables 3.1 to 3.4).

In Section 4.4 we comment in more detail on the querying of inferred facts.

4.3.3 Constraint Validation

In [ST09], Sirin et al. show that constraint validation can be reduced to SPARQL query answering. They consider three kinds of constraints:

Typing constraints require that individuals that participate in a relation should be instances of certain types.

Participation constraints require that instances of the constrained class should be involved in an object property assertions (existence).

Uniqueness constraints require that an individual cannot participate in multiple object property assertions with the same property (functional properties).

The following SPARQL query gives an example for a participation constraint check. As mentioned in Table 4.2, ASK queries are used to ensure existential quantifications. The query given below checks whether one device without configuration exists. Here the well-known method for representing

SPARQL query part		GReQL concept	Comment
prologue		—	no correspondence for base URI or prefixes in GReQL
query form	SELECT	report part of (a union of) FWR expression(s)	if UNION or OPTIONAL are used, it maps to the union of multiple FWR expressions instead of a single one. In SPARQL, pattern alternatives are syntactically specified with the UNION keyword. Optional parts of the graph pattern may be specified syntactically with the OPTIONAL construct. If DISTINCT or REDUCED are specified, reportSet is used. The DISTINCT keyword ensures that solutions in the sequence are unique. The REDUCED keyword permits the elimination of some non-unique solutions.
	CONSTRUCT	—	no support in GReQL for building graphs. In SPARQL, the CONSTRUCT query form returns a single RDF graph specified by a graph template.
	ASK	existentially quantified expression	ASK queries in SPARQL are used to test whether or not a query pattern has a solution.
	DESCRIBE	—	no support for returning descriptions specified in graphs in GReQL. The DESCRIBE form returns a single result RDF graph containing RDF data about resources.
dataset		—	no support for querying multiple graphs in GReQL.
where clause	with SELECT query form	from and with parts of (a union of) FWR expression(s)	Variables in the where clause are mapped to declarations in the from part(s). Triple patterns and FILTERs are mapped to the with part(s). FILTER in SPARQL restricts the solutions of a graph pattern match according to a given expression.
	with ASK query form	declaration part and boolean expression in existentially quantified expression	Variables in the where clause are mapped to declarations in the declaration part of the quantified expression. Triple patterns and FILTERs are mapped to the boolean expression.
solution modifier		—	no support in GReQL for sorting or controlling the number of solutions.
—		*all other expressions, e.g., regular path expressions*	no support in SPARQL for other GReQL concepts.

Table 4.2. Mapping between SPARQL and GReQL concepts [SE10].

negation as failure (NAF)[1] is based on a pattern of OPTIONAL / FILTER / !BOUND operators.

```
ASK WHERE { ?x rdf:type Device .
        OPTIONAL {
                ?x hasConfiguration ?y .
                ?y rdf:type Configuration .
                }
        FILTER(!BOUND(?y))}
```

Experience shows that path expressions are a powerful means for prescribing properties of user models in practical applications [EWD⁺96].

In the W3C working draft SPARQL 1.1 is extended by the definition of *property paths*[2]. A property path is a possible path through an RDF graph between two nodes. Property paths may be composed of constructs for alternative and sequenced paths or paths of arbitrary length. Unlike regular path expressions in GReQL, variables (nodes) cannot be used as part of the path itself, only at the begining and the end.

Since SPARQL 1.1 is still a working draft, we were not able to test these additional constructs with Pellet[3] in version 2.1.1 and the Jena API[4] in version 2.6.3.

We may conclude the comparison of GReQL and SPARQL with the message that the use of a respective query language depends of the kind of application.

GReQL seems to be more applicable for constraint definition. GReQL provides support for regular path expressions. SPARQL 1.1 will support path expressions. Furthermore, in most cases the GReQL syntax seems to be more concise. This especially applies to the fact that all constraints evaluated by a SPARQL query must be formulated as a set of RDF triples. Consequently, complex GReQL constraints should be more easily graspable than their SPARQL counterparts.

On the other hand SPARQL provides the querying of entailed facts, or the construction of new RDF graphs for the results of a query.

4.4 Reasoning Technologies

Modelware technologies as presented in Section 2.3 mainly do not provide reasoning facilities. Reasoning on modelware models is principally enabled after a translation to a logic-based representation, e.g to Alloy [ABGR07], Description Logics [BCG05], OWL 2 [WSR10], or Object-Z [Eva98, EWD⁺96]. When using such formal representations, one could reason on modelware models

---

[1] http://www.w3.org/TR/rdf-sparql-query/

[2] http://www.w3.org/TR/sparql11-query/

[3] http://clarkparsia.com/pellet/

[4] http://jena.sourceforge.net/

and formally prove properties through inference and make implicit knowledge of interest explicit [BCG05]. Description Logics reasoners (such as Pellet [SPG+07], or Racer [HM01]) allow for joint as well as for separate sound and complete reasoning at both, the schema and the instance layers.

4.4.1 Schema Reasoning

Schema reasoning considers all concept descriptions in ontoware models independent of their instances. Based on the descriptions in the schema, schema reasoning allows for inferring new facts, which might be queried, e.g., using SPARQL, or detected by reasoning services.

Language designers creating graph schemas may possibly be interested in computing the vertex classes and edge classes, which are not satisfiable, i.e., classes, which cannot be instantiated without the graph becoming inconsistent. The following GReQL constraint is not satisfiable because it simultaneously forbids and requires that **Configuration** vertices have a successor.

```
forall c:V{Configuration} @ exists s:V{Slot} @ not(c −−>{hasSlot} s) and (c −−>{hasSlot} s)
```

The tools available in the modelware technological space presented in Chapter 2 do not allow for detecting the unsatisfiability of elements in graph schemas. If we encode the GReQL constraint as an axiom of an ontoware model, we will be able to reason and infer new facts. The listing below represents the GReQL constraint above as class description being part of an OWL 2 ontology.

```
SubClassOf(Configuration ObjectIntersectionOf(ObjectComplementOf(ObjectSomeValuesFrom(hasSlot
    Vertex)) ObjectSomeValuesFrom(hasSlot Vertex)))
```

Facts for unsatisfiability of class expressions may be derived by queries or the given reasoning service presented in Table 3.8. The SPARQL query below queries for the fact of unsatisfiability. It uses the ontology with all additional facts inferred by a DL reasoner as data model:

```
SELECT DISTINCT ?t
WHERE {
    ?t rdfs:subClassOf owl:nothing
}
```

The satisfiability checking service presented in Table 3.8 considers an ontoware model and may infer the unsatisfiability based on all descriptions. The result of this check is that the OWL class **Configuration** described above is not satisfiable.

4.4.2 Schema+Instance Reasoning

Description logics reasoners allow for joint reasoning on both schema and instance layer. Given an ontoware model describing TBox concepts and ABox instances, reasoners allow for classifying individuals to find their possible types described in the schema.

The following excerpt of an ontoware model depicts a TBox axiom stating that every device is linked via **hasConfiguration** with some configuration. The corresponding ABox consists of two individuals **d** and **c**. **d** is linked with **c**, which is of type **Configuration**.

```
// TBox axiom
EquivalentClasses(Device ObjectSomeValuesFrom(hasConfiguration Configuration))

// ABox axioms
Declaration(Individual(d))
ObjectPropertyAssertion(hasConfiguration d c)
Declaration(Individual(c))
ClassAssertion(c Configuration)
```

Based on a common description of schema and instance layer within one ontoware model, reasoners may infer new facts. Based on the descriptions in TBox and ABox, the SPARQL query below asks for all named types, that an individual **i** has. In the case of the individual **d** it returns the type **Device**.

```
SELECT DISTINCT ?t
WHERE {
        i rdf:type ?t
}
```

Using the reasoning service specified in Table 3.9, we are able to classify the individual **d** to find its possible type. The result is the class **Device**, since **d** fulfills all descriptions defined by the class expression.

4.4.3 Open World Reasoning

The *Open World Assumption* (OWA) assumes incomplete information as default and allows for reasoning on incomplete models, while the *Closed World Assumption* (CWA) assumes all positive to be facts as part of the knowledge base (cf. Section 3.2.3).

For quantified expressions a reasoner assumes that a given individual is linked with other individuals. Although an individual is not linked with a given number (cardinality) of other individuals, a reasoner would assume by default that cardinality restrictions are fulfilled by assumed individuals in the domain.

The ontoware model below describes an incomplete knowledge base. In the TBox we define that each device must have a configuration and that each configuration must have a slot. In the ABox we declare the individuals **d** and **c**. **d** is linked with **c**, which is of type configuration.

```
// TBox axiom
EquivalentClasses(Device ObjectSomeValuesFrom(hasConfiguration Configuration))
EquivalentClasses(Configuration ObjectSomeValuesFrom(hasSlot Slot))

// ABox axioms
Declaration(Individual(d))
ObjectPropertyAssertion(hasConfiguration d c)
```

Declaration(Individual(c))
ClassAssertion(c Configuration)

Although the knowledge base is incomplete (c is not linked with a slot), reasoners are able to infer facts based on all descriptions in TBox and ABox. In the example above a reasoner infers that the individual d is of type device, because it is linked with some configuration although the configuration c is not complete (i.e., it is not linked with a slot).

4.5 Conclusion

In this chapter we have answered RQ5 asking for the commonalities and variations of the TGraph modelware technological space and the ontoware technological space.

We compared the data modeling languages grUML and OWL 2. We detected many common concepts having similar semantics. In addition to the common concepts, OWL 2 provides a comprehensive set of class expressions and axioms used to extend the description of modeled data in ontologies. grUML is more powerful in the definition of attributes since it allows for attributing edge classes.

In the second part of this chapter we compared the query technologies of both technological spaces. SPARQL and GReQL provide various features, which are not shared by the respective other language. In the case of querying and constraining modelware models, GReQL with its regular path expressions is more applicable. Advantages of SPARQL are detected if we add DL reasoning capabilities. Based on the descriptions in data models, reasoning allows for inferring new facts, which might be queried.

Part III

Combinations

5

Bridging Technologies

Model-driven engineering (MDE) makes use of concrete modeling languages for the description of models. Often a variety of different modeling languages is used simultaneously to describe a software system from several viewpoints. In the context of MDE, several models in different standardized languages may be combined to form a complete and consistent overall model of the system under development.

In the context of this thesis we consider the combination of modelware technological spaces with ontoware technological spaces. Appropriate techniques are required to combine technological spaces (Challenge 1). We constitute these techniques as *bridges*. A modeling environment provides the *establishment of a bridge* and the *use of a bridge*. We need to answer the question:

RQ6:   *What are the techniques to bridge technological spaces?*

In this chapter we develop four kinds of bridges, namely a *transformation bridge*, an *integration bridge*, a *mapping bridge*, and an *API bridge*. All bridges represent generic ways for combining two modeling languages. In the context of this work, they are used to combine a modelware modeling language with the ontology language OWL 2.

5.1 Chapter Context

In this section we present a domain-specific modeling language, which is an example for bridging it with the ontology language OWL 2. Finally we present this chapter's road map where we classify all kinds of bridges to be presented.

5.1.1 Example Modeling Language

In this chapter we consider BEDSL, the *Business Entity Domain-Specific Language* [KMS09], to be integrated with the ontology language OWL 2. We consciously choose a simple modeling language, which is worthwhile for being integrated with a more expressive language such as OWL 2.

BEDSL is a structural modeling language for describing several entities, attributing them and relating them by specialization relationships and references between two entities.

Figure 5.1 depicts an example model in textual concrete syntax of BEDSL. The model consists of one data type definition and three entity definitions. The entity **Device** consists of a **name** attribute, whose datatype is **String** and of a reference **hasCard**, which defines a connection from entity **Device** to the entity **Card**. The opposite reference of **hasCard** is **belongsToDevice**, which is defined in the entity **Card**. Entity **Router** is a specialization of **Device**, while entity **Card** contains the reference **belongsToDevice**.

```
model DeviceModel {
  datatype String;

  entity Device {
    attribute name : String;
    reference hasCard : Card oppositeOf belongsToDevice;
  }

  entity Router specializes Device {
  }

  entity Card {
    reference belongsToDevice : Device;
  }
}
```

Figure 5.1. BEDSL model.

Figure 5.2 depicts the metamodel of BEDSL, which conforms to the grUML metaschema. The language is used to describe business entity models, which consist of sets of entities and data types. Each entity can have an optional super type, a set of references and attributes. Each reference (and its reverse reference) is used to point from one entity to some other entity, while each attribute is used to store data values conforming to some data type. A special kind of a data type is an enumeration, which consists of a number of entries.

5.1.2 Bridge Classification and Chapter's Road Map

All bridges are defined at the level of graph schemas by language designers. Here graph schemas represent metamodels as well as metametamodels. After the bridge has been designed its adoption by language users takes place at the model layer. Figure 5.3 depicts this chapter's road map and illustrates the description of the following bridges:

Transformation: The first class of bridges provides *transformations* to create for an input model a respective output model according to a transformation definition. The transformation definition established by a language

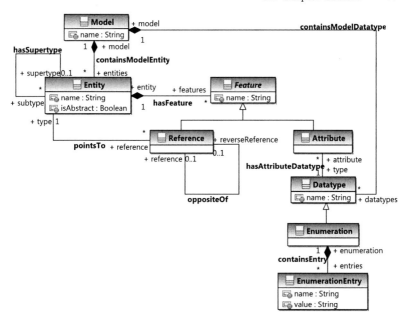

Figure 5.2. Metamodel of BEDSL.

designer describes which types of elements in the input model are considered to build an element in the target model. The transformation bridge is presented in Section 5.2.

Integration: The second class of bridges we discuss are the integration bridges. The result of the bridge establishment is an *integrated metamodel*, which is the merge of the abstract syntax definitions of two modeling languages. An integrated metamodel allows language users to create *hybrid models*. Hybrid models are build by constructs conforming to an integrated modeling languages. Language users use projection services to build models conforming to one of the metamodels to be combined for a given hybrid model. The *projection* of a hybrid model is a model, which consists only of the elements that conform to concepts of one given metamodel to be integrated, or, of merged concepts of the integrated metamodel. The integration bridge is presented in Section 5.3.

Mapping: The third class of bridges supports the *mapping* of models, which may be developed separately. Based on a mapping definition describing which constructs in metamodels can be mapped, users are able to declare mappings between elements of two different modeling languages. Language users consider derive services to trace mappings. The *derivation* of a mapped model consists of those elements of the opposite model, which are incident with mappings. The mapping bridge is presented in Section 5.4.

Implementation: The fourth class of bridges is the API bridge (a bridge between *Application Programming Interfaces*). API bridges are established by the *implementation* of services using the operations and services of given APIs used to traverse models and those services of another API to build new models. The API bridge is presented in Section 5.5.

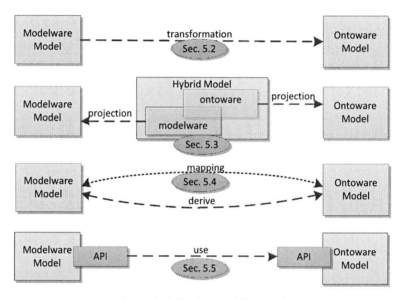

Figure 5.3. Road map of Chapter 5.

In addition, we compare all bridges and discuss advantages and disadvantages of the bridges respectively. Section 5.6 concludes this chapter by presenting related work in the field of bridging modeling languages.

5.2 Transformation Bridge

The transformation bridge is considered to switch automatically from a given modelware model (as the input) to an ontoware model (as the output). The bridge is established as a transformation service developed by the language designer and used by the language user.

5.2.1 Transformation Definition

The establishment of the transformation bridge consists of the definition how modelware models conforming to a modeling language are transformed to ontoware models.

A transformation service that transforms a modelware model conforming to a metamodel GS to an ontoware model conforming to the metamodel GS_{OWL} is specified as follows (cf. Table 5.1). All transformation services are implemented as a static method being part of the class TransformationBridge.

Name	Transformation Service
Signature	GS_{OWL} transform(GS m)
Pattern	m_{owl}=TransformationBridge.transform(m)
Description	transforms a model m to an ontoware model m_{owl} according to a *transformation definition*.

Table 5.1. Transformation service: transform.

The first step in the establishment of a transformation service is the *mapping of concepts* provided by the metamodel GS of the modelware modeling language (e.g., GS_{BEDSL}) and the metamodel GS_{OWL} of the ontology language OWL 2. In the case of a transformation bridge the mapping is needed to denote which elements from a modelware model are transformed to which elements in a newly created ontoware model. The relation is mainly based on intensional knowledge of both languages and is defined by the language designer.

With regard to our example modeling language BEDSL from the modelware and the ontology language OWL 2 from the ontoware, we can identify the following vertex classes and edge classes, which are presented in Table 5.2.

Relation Nr.	BEDSL	OWL 2
1.	Model	Ontology
2.	Entity	Class
3.	Datatype	Datatype
4.	Reference	ObjectProperty
5.	Attribute	DataProperty
6.	Enumeration, EnumerationEntry	DataOneOf, Literal
7.	hasSupertype	SubClassOf
8.	hasOpposite	InverseObjectProperty

Table 5.2. Mapping of concepts of BEDSL metamodel and OWL 2 metamodel.

In general all model elements of BEDSL models are transformed to OWL 2 elements such as Class, ObjectProperty, DataProperty, etc. (Relation 2-8, cf.

Table 5.2). The creation of an **Ontology** element is necessary to define an element that contains all other ontology elements and the axioms predicating them (Relation 1, cf. Table 5.2).

We mentioned that the output of the transformation service returns an ontoware model, which is created according to transformation rules. To describe these transformation rules we use the three GReTL transformation operations that allow for creating vertices, edges, and defining attribute values. In Section 2.3.2, GReTL and the three operations are introduced.

In Appendix A.3.1 we exemplify the implementation of the transformation. Here, GReTL is used to transform models conforming to the BEDSL metamodel to ontoware models written in OWL 2.

5.2.2 Transformation Use

As specified in Table 5.1 the transformation service requires a modelware model m and delivers a corresponding ontoware model m_{owl}. Thus, when using the transformation bridge, one must first create a modelware model, which conforms to the source metamodel GS of the given modeling language.

Example

Figure 5.1 depicts a modelware model m, which conforms to the BEDSL metamodel GS_{BEDSL}. Using the transformation service **transform** the ontoware model m_{owl} is created:

```
m_owl=TransformationBridge.transform(m);
```

Figure 5.4 depicts the target ontoware model m_{owl}. Here we have a pure OWL 2 ontology document that is processable by ontoware reasoning tools.

5.2.3 Discussion

A transformation generates a new model conforming to the target language from a given model, which in turn conforms to the source language. This kind of bridging usually implies some loss of information, since both languages have different properties not all of which are transformable into the other languages [EW10].

Based on the mapping of the modeling language to be transformed and the ontology language the transformation bridge is established. It is realized by a transformation service, which is used for automatically producing ontoware models from given modelware models.

Having a transformation service, language users are able to build modelware models with the modeling language and concrete syntaxes they are familiar with. But the users are restricted to the expressiveness (e.g., different syntactic constructs) of the modeling language they are working with.

```
Ontology(DeviceModel

Declaration(Class(Device))

Declaration(Class(Router))
SubClassOf(Router Device)

Declaration(Class(Card))

Declaration(ObjectProperty(belongsToDevice))
ObjectPropertyDomain(belongsToDevice Card)
ObjectPropertyRange(belongsToDevice Device)

Declaration(ObjectProperty(hasCard))
ObjectPropertyDomain(hasCard Device)
ObjectPropertyRange(hasCard Card)

InverseObjectProperties(hasCard belongsToDevice)

Declaration(DataProperty(name))
DataPropertyDomain(name Device)
DataPropertyRange(name xsd:string)
)
```

Figure 5.4. Visualized ontoware model.

5.3 Integration Bridge

Due to the needs of multiple modeling languages and their simultaneous use, we present an integration bridge for the combination of two modeling languages to one integrated language. The integration bridge we are going to present supports language designers in the construction of an integrated metamodel, a combined representation of the abstract syntax definition of two modeling languages. The integrated metamodel allows for designing one integrated overall view representing a hybrid merge of different views of the system to be modeled. Since the integration bridge provides a loss-free merge of modeling languages, the overall model can still be projected to its parts representing just one view.

Figure 5.5 depicts a hybrid model, which is visualized by a textual concrete syntax. It is built by constructs of BEDSL and OWL 2, which are integrated seamlessly. Besides the typical BEDSL elements the hybrid model contains an object property with name **belongsToDevice** and two axioms for domain and range. Here, the integrated modeling language provides the definition of both, references and object properties. In addition, a **DisjointClasses** axiom is defined, which is directly adopted on **Device** and **Card**, since they provide the properties of both, BEDSL **Entity** and OWL **Class**.

For the need of interoperability between a modeling environment and reasoning tools, a projection service is realized. It translates hybrid models to ontoware models, which are the input for reasoning tools.

```
model DeviceModel {

  entityClass Device disjointWith Card{
    reference hasCard : Card;
  }

  entityClass Router subClassOf Device{
  }

  entityClass MobileDevice subClassOf Device{
  }

  entityClass Card {
  }

  objectProperty belongsToDevice{
    domain: Card;
    range: Device;
  }
}
```

Figure 5.5. Hybrid model in concrete syntax.

5.3.1 Integration Definition

The establishment of the integration bridge consists of the definition how the metamodels of a modeling language and the ontology language are integrated. The integration is supported by a set of integration services. These services are provided by the modeling environment and used by the language designer. The integration of two modeling languages consists of three steps.

In the first step, the *mapping* as introduced in Section 5.2.1 is necessary where language designers relate the different constructs provided by the modeling languages to be integrated.

The second step creates a *disjoint union* of the two metamodels. The sets for vertex classes, edge classes, and attributes are united.

In the third step, different *integration services* are applied on the united graph schema to either merge two vertex classes, edge classes or attributes to one single vertex class, edge class or attribute, respectively, to relate two vertex classes by an edge class, or to create hierarchies of types for vertex classes or edge classes, respectively.

The result is the integrated metamodel, which represents the abstract syntax definition of an integrated modeling language.

The integration bridge itself is encapsulated in one object of type IntegrationBridge, which is initialized by the respective constructor specified in Table 5.3.

1. Mapping and Adaptations

Before an integration bridge is established, a mapping is performed, equal to that in Section 5.2.1. In the mapping step different constructs of the two modeling languages are compared and related.

Name	Integration Bridge Constructor
Signature	IntegrationBridge IntegrationBridge(Schema GS_1, Schema GS_2)
Pattern	b = new IntegrationBridge(GS_1, GS_2)
Description	initializes the integration bridge object b with the schemas GS_1 and GS_2.

Table 5.3. Integration bridge constructor.

Sometimes, related constructs in the metamodels to be integrated are realized by different constructs. For example, in BEDSL an association is used to define the specialization relationship between two entities, while in OWL 2 a separate class is used to define an OWL class expression being a subclass of another class expression. To relate an association with a class an adaptation of the metamodels is performed.

For all adaptations of metamodel GS to a metamodel GS^a, language designers have to implement a service, which gets as input a model conforming to GS and returns a model conforming to GS^a. Models must also be adapted since the adapted metamodels are integrated. Adaptation services are required by language users to automatically change the structure of models in such a way that they are useable for the integration bridge. In Table 5.4 we specify a respective static adaptation service, which is provided by the Convert class. The service may be implemented as a transformation with source metamodel GS and target metamodel GS^a.

Name	Adaptation Service
Signature	GS^a adaptation(GS m)
Pattern	m_a=Convert.adaptation(m)
Description	adapts a model m by refactoring its structure according to the adaptation of GS to GS^a.

Table 5.4. adaptation service.

2. Disjoint Union of Metamodels

For the initial union of two metamodels we specify a **metamodelUnion** service. It considers the two graph schemas GS_1 and GS_2 representing the metamodels to be unified and initializes the metamodel GS_{Int}. The **metamodelUnion** service is specified in Table 5.5, which may be invoked directly in the integration bridge constructor.

3. Applying Integration Services

All integration services directly consider elements of the metamodel GS_{Int} and either merge them, or relate them by a specialization relationship or an

Name	Metamodel Union Service
Signature	void metamodelUnion( )
Pattern	b.metamodelUnion( )
Description	constructs the graph schema GS_{Int}, which is the disjoint union of the two graph schemas GS_1 and GS_2. GS_1 and GS_2 are taken from the integration bridge object. After the union the object provides a reference to GS_{Int} . All incidences of edge classes and specialization relationships between classes, all multiplicities annotating edge classes, and all attributes nested in vertex classes or edge classes in GS_{Int} are kept as defined in the two graph schemas GS_1 and GS_2. b is the integration bridge object.

Table 5.5. metamodelUnion service.

association. The result of applying a set of integration services is an integrated metamodel that is represented by GS_{Int}, which consists of parts of GS_1 and GS_2, which are connected seamlessly.

After the definition of the integration services and an example, in this section we are going to show how to store the information within which elements of the two metamodels are integrated. This information is considered in Section 5.3.2 where we introduce projection services.

Merge Vertex Classes Service

The *mergeVertexClasses* service, specified in Table 5.6, is used if the meaning of two vertex classes is the same. The two vertex classes are replaced by a new single vertex class. All properties of the two vertex classes to be merged (e.g., incidences with edge classes or specialization relationships and attributes) are moved to the new vertex class.

Name	Merge Vertex Class Service
Signature	VertexClass mergeVertexClasses(VertexClass t_1, VertexClass t_2, String qualifiedName)
Pattern	t_m=b.mergeVertexClasses(t_1, t_2, s)
Description	merges the two vertex classes t_1 and t_2 by replacing them with a new vertex class t_m with name s in GS_{Int}. t_m is newly created in GS_{Int}. All incidences with edge classes and specialization relations, which are incident with t_1 or t_2, and all attributes nested in t_1 or t_2 are moved to the new vertex class t_m. b is the integration bridge object.

Table 5.6. Integration service: mergeVertexClasses.

Specialization Service

The *specializeClasses* service, specified in Table 5.7, is used if two vertex classes or two edge classes in a graph schema are related where one of them specializes the other. Subsequently the two vertex or edge classes are related by a specialization relation.

Name	Specialization Service
Signature	void specializeClasses(GraphElementClass t_{sub}, GraphElementClass t_{sup})
Pattern	b.specializeClasses(t_{sub}, t_{sup})
Description	creates a specialization relationship between two given vertex classes or edge classes t_{sub} and t_{sup} in GS_{Int}. b is the integration bridge object.

Table 5.7. Integration service: specializeClasses.

Associate Classes Service

The *associateClasses* service, specified in Table 5.8, is used if two vertex classes in a graph schema should be associated by an edge class. Two incidences are required to define precisely the edge class between the two vertex classes.

Name	Association Service
Signature	EdgeClass associateClasses(VertexClass t_s, IncidenceClass i_s, VertexClass t_t, IncidenceClass i_t, String name)
Pattern	t_{ec}=b.associateClasses(t_s, i_s, t_t, i_t, n)
Description	associates two vertex classes t_s and t_t by a newly created edge class t_{ec} with name n in GS_{Int}. t_{ec} has the two incidences i_s (for vertex class t_s) and i_t (for vertex class t_t). b is the integration bridge object.

Table 5.8. Integration service: associateClasses.

Merge Edge Classes Service

The *mergeEdgeClasses* service, specified in Table 5.9, is used if two edge classes are identified to represent the same relations between two vertex classes. Furthermore, the multiplicities must match for both incidences. Incident vertex classes at one edge class end must be the same or specializations for the other edge class.

Merge Attribute Service

The *mergeAttributes* service, specified in Table 5.10, is taken into account if one vertex class or edge class contains two attributes that are identified to be merged. Both attributes to be merged must have the same domain.

The set of integration services presented in this section is easily extendable. But it depends on the technological space where the integration services are

Name	Merge Edge Classes Service
Signature	EdgeClass mergeEdgeClasses(EdgeClass t_1, EdgeClass t_2, String qualified-Name)
Pattern	t_m =b.mergeEdgeClasses(t_1, t_2, s)
Description	merges two edge classes t_1 and t_2 by replacing them with a new edge class t_m with name s in GS_{Int}. All specialization relations and all nested attributes are moved to the new edge class. b is the integration bridge object. Before the merge, the service ensures that the multiplicities at the incidences of t_2 are the same or more specific than the multiplicities at the incidences of t_1, and that the vertex classes at the incidences of t_2 are the same or specializations of vertex classes at the incidences of t_1.

Table 5.9. Integration service: mergeEdgeClasses.

Name	Merge Attributes Service
Signature	Attribute mergeAttributes(Attribute a_1, Attribute a_2, String name)
Pattern	a_m=mergeAttributes(a_1, a_2, s)
Description	merges two attributes by replacing them with a new attribute with name s. The service ensures that the domains of a_1 and a_2 are the same or that of a_2 describes a subset of the domain of a_2. Furthermore, attributes must be in the same vertex class or edge class, or a_2 is in a specialization of that of a_1. b is the integration bridge object.

Table 5.10. Integration Service: mergeAttributes.

being implemented. E.g., in the EMOF technological space [OMG06] a special-ize-service for references is not implementable because EMOF does not allow for specializing references, while in the CMOF technological space [OMG06] an associateClasses and specializeClasses service to create an association or specialization relationship between two associations may be used.

Example

In the following we are going to present the creation of the integration bridge for BEDSL and OWL 2. The metamodels of both languages are described the by graph schemas GS_{BEDSL} and GS_{OWL}.

1. Mapping and Adaptation. Before applying any integration services a *mapping* (comparable to that in Section 5.2.1) is necessary. This step is needed to denote which constructs can be integrated and how they must be integrated. The mapping is mainly based on intensional knowledge on GS_{BEDSL} and GS_{OWL}.

To integrate the two languages based on the mapping, an adaptation of the BEDSL metamodel is necessary. Figure 5.6 depicts the metamodel GS^a_{BEDSL}, which is the adapted version of GS_{BEDSL}. We adapt four parts of GS_{BEDSL}.

The hasSupertype association is materialized by a new class because it should be integrated with the SubClassOf class from the OWL 2 metamodel

(1). The hasFeature association in BEDSL relates entities with features. Because subsequent to an integration the relation should model domain axioms for object properties and data properties, we have to materialize the hasFeature association by two new classes HasReference and HasAttribute (2). The pointsTo association is materialized by a new class because it should be integrated with the object property range class from the OWL 2 metamodel (3). The hasAttributeDatatype association is materialized by a new class because it should be integrated with the data property range class from the OWL 2 metamodel (4).

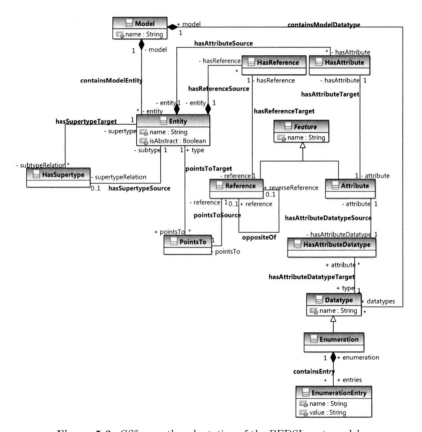

Figure 5.6. GS^a_{BEDSL}, the adaptation of the BEDSL metamodel.

With all metamodels in its adapted version being ready to be integrated, the integration bridge object is instantiated.

b = **new** IntegrationBridge(GS^a_{BEDSL}, GS_{OWL});

2. Metamodel Union. The second part of the integration consists of a simple metamodel union, which constructs the initial integrated metamodel GS_{Int}. It contains all elements (vertex classes, edge classes, and attributes) of the two source metamodels.

```
b.metamodelUnion();
```

3. Integration Services. In the third part of the integration, several integration services are applied on the initial GS_{Int} where the integration services to be executed are intensionally based on the mapping defined in step 1. Subsequent to applying the integration services on related constructs we get a new integrated metamodel represented by GS_{Int}. The listings below may represent scripts designed by a domain-specific language used to declaratively describe the integration. These integration scripts may be executed and its result is the integrated metamodel.

Since the integrated metamodel is complex we present excerpts in Figures 5.7, 5.8, and 5.9 and illustrate the respective use of integration services. Figure 5.7 depicts the integration of the BEDSL constructs Model, Entity, and HasSupertype with the respective OWL constructs. Model becomes a specialization of Ontology since all constructs provided by OWL should be part of a BEDSL model (1). Entity and Class are merged to a new vertex class called EntityClass (2). It allows on the one hand for defining references and attributes, on the other for several OWL class axioms. Expressions can also be applied on it. In steps (3) to (5) the concerns of HasSupertype in BEDSL and SubClassOf in OWL are merged. The new vertex class SubClassOf allows for defining several subclass relations between several class expressions, for instance EntityClass.

```
b.specializeClasses(Model, Ontology); // (1)
EntityClass=b.mergeVertexClasses(Entity, Class, "EntityClass"); // (2)
SubClassOf=b.mergeVertexClasses(HasSupertype, SubClassOf, "SubClassOf"); // (3)
hasSuperClass=b.mergeEdgeClasses(definesSuperClass, hasSupertype, "definesSuperClass"); // (4)
definesSubClass=b.mergeEdgeClasses(definesSubClass, hasSubtype, "definesSubClass"); // (5)
```

Figure 5.8 depicts the integration of the BEDSL construct Reference with the respective OWL constructs. Reference becomes a specialization of ObjectProperty (6). Thus, references can be involved in object property axioms and expressions. References are connected via the classes HasReference and PointsTo with EntityClass. These relations in OWL 2 are designed by ObjectPropertyDomain and ObjectPropertyRange constructs. Hence, in steps (7) to (12), the concerns of links between entity classes and references are becoming specializations of the respective constructs in OWL.

```
b.specializeClasses(Reference, ObjectProperty); // (6)
b.specializeClasses(HasReference, ObjectPropertyDomain); // (7)
b.specializeClasses(hasReferenceSource, definesDomainClassExpression); // (8)
b.specializeClasses(hasReferenceTarget, definesDomainObjectProperty); // (9)
b.specializeClasses(PointsTo, ObjectPropertyRange); // (10)
b.specializeClasses(pointsToSource, definesRangeClassExpression); // (11)
b.specializeClasses(pointsToTarget, definesRangeObjectProperty); // (12)
```

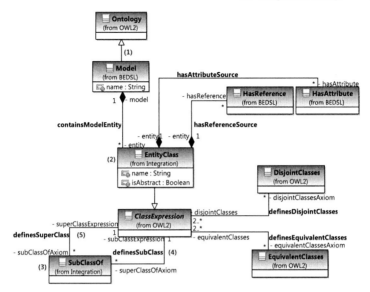

Figure 5.7. Integration of BEDSL Model, Entity, and HasSupertype with OWL constructs.

Figure 5.9 depicts the integration of the BEDSL construct **Attribute** and **Datatype** with the respective OWL constructs. **Attribute** becomes a specialization of **DataProperty** (13). Thus, attributes can be involved in data property axioms and expressions. Attributes are connected via the classes **HasAttribute** and **HasAttributeDatatype** to the **EntityClass**. These relations in OWL 2 are designed by **DataPropertyDomain** and **DataPropertyRange** constructs. Hence, in steps (14) to (19) the concerns of links between entity classes and references become specializations of the respective constructs in OWL. The vertex classes for data types are merged to one single class (20). Thus, data types can be used by attributes and data properties. In steps (21) to (24) the concerns of **Enumeration** and **DataOneOf** are merged. The new vertex class **DataEnumeration** allows for modeling a set of literal entries, while the vertex class **LiteralEntry** is the result of the merge of **Entry** and **Literal**. To provide only one relation between the new vertex classes **DataEnumeration** and **LiteralEntry**, the edge classes **containsEntry** and **containsLiteral** are merged. Furthermore, the attributes **value** and **lexicalForm** are merged to have only one attribute for defining the literal value.

```
b.specializeClasses(Attribute, DataProperty); // (13)
b.specializeClasses(HasAttribute, DataPropertyDomain); // (14)
b.specializeClasses(hasAttributeSource, definesDataPropertyDomainClassExpression); // (15)
b.specializeClasses(hasAttributeTarget, definesDomainDataProperty); // (16)
b.specializeClasses(HasAttributeDatatype, DataPropertyRange); // (17)
b.specializeClasses(hasAttributeDatatypeSource, definesRangeDataProperty); // (18)
b.specializeClasses(hasAttributeDatatypeTarget, definesRangeDataRange); // (19)
```

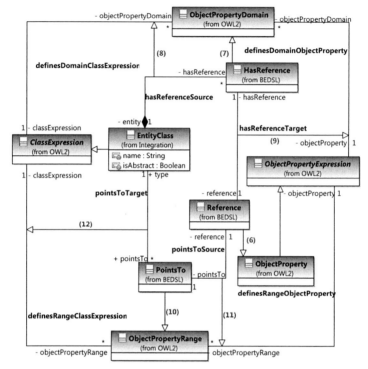

Figure 5.8. Integration of BEDSL Reference with OWL constructs.

Datatype=b.mergeVertexClasses(Datatype, Datatype, "Datatype"); // (20)
DataEnumeration=b.mergeVertexClasses(Enumeration, DataOneOf, "DataEnumeration"); // (21)
LiteralEntry=b.mergeVertexClasses(EnumerationEntry, Literal, "LiteralEntry"); // (22)
containsLiteralEntry=b.mergeEdgeClasses(containsEntry, containsLiteral, "containsLiteralEntry"); // (23)
lexicalValue=b.mergeAttributes(value, lexicalForm, "lexicalValue"); // (24)

Integration Tracing

In the following we are going to describe how to keep the information which metamodel elements of an integrated metamodel, especially the elements built by integration services, originate from which metamodel elements of the languages being integrated. This information is considered in Section 5.3.2 where we introduce projection services. A projection service for a given language is used to extract those parts of a model conforming to the integrated metamodel, which are built by constructs of the given language to be integrated. For example, a projection service for the ontology language OWL gets as input a model conforming to the integrated metamodel and returns a pure ontoware

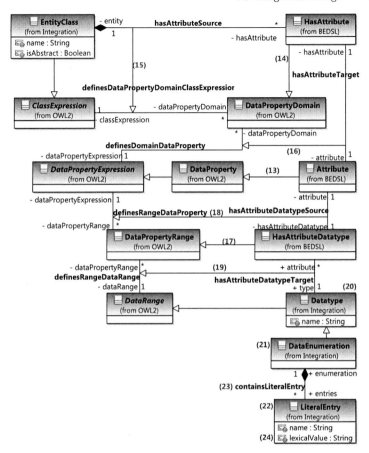

Figure 5.9. Integration of BEDSL Attribute and Datatype with OWL constructs.

model. The projection service for BEDSL gets the same model as an input but returns only those parts, which are built by using BEDSL constructs.

To keep the information of the mapping step (cf. Section 5.2.1) we use traceability techniques as introduced in [SEW10].

Defining Traceability Links

In order to trace metamodel elements we extend the grUML metaschema (cf. Section 2.2.3) by the traceability reference schema as it is suggested in [SEW10]. Since we want to define traceability relations expressing the merge of two vertex classes, edge classes, and attributes to a new respective one and specializations of classes we identify vertex classes, edge classes and attributes as traceable entities. We create a specialization relation between the grUML classes GraphElement (representing vertex and edge classes), Attribute and TraceableEntity.

In addition we want to express how the metamodel elements are related to each other by means of the integration services used to integrate them. For each integration service we define specializations of TraceabilityRelationship, which is the association in the traceability reference schema used to define traceability links between entities. We define the edge classes MergeVertex-Classes, MergeEdgeClasses, MergeAttributes, SpecializeClasses, and Associate-Classes.

Two vertex classes are linked via two MergeVertexClasses edges with the vertex class representing the merge of both. Two edge classes are linked via two MergeEdgeClasses edges with the edge class representing the merge of both. Two attributes are linked via two MergeAttributes edges with the attribute representing the merge of both. Two vertex classes or edge classes are linked via two SpecializeClasses edges with the two vertex classes and edge classes, respectively, being linked via a specialization relationship. Two vertex classes are linked via two AssociateClasses edges with the edge class connecting them.

Figure 5.10 depicts the extension of the grUML metaschema by the new classes for modeling traceability links between metamodel elements.

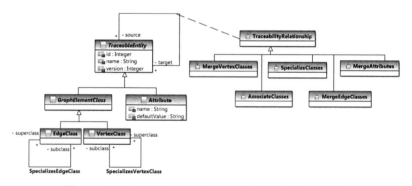

Figure 5.10. grUML metaschema extended for Traceability.

Recording Traceability Links

The recording of the integration steps is achieved in a separate schema graph named GS_{Int}^t, which conforms to the extended grUML metaschema (cf. Figure 5.10). GS_{Int}^t is initialized during the use of the metamodelUnion service adopted on the schema graphs of GS_1 and GS_2 (cf. Table 5.5). Firstly, GS_1 and GS_2 are two disjoint parts of GS_{Int}^t.

For each integration service executed, new corresponding traceability relationships between the two elements considered by the service are created in GS_{Int}^t. These traceability relationships are linked with the element, which is the result of an integration service (a merged vertex class, edge class or attribute, or a new edge class). In the case of the specialization service, the two vertex classes or edge classes being specialized are linked via two SpecializeClasses edges with two new classes, which represent the two classes that are connected by a specialization edge.

Example

Above we illustrated 24 integration services applied on GS_{Int}. As mentioned above for each integration service a new traceability relationship edge must be created in GS_{Int}^t.

Figure 5.11 presents an excerpt of the (isolated) schema graph GS_{Int}^t where 8 traceability relationships are created to describe the 4 steps 1, 2, 8 and 9 of the integration of GS_{BEDSL} and GS_{OWL}.

In Figure 5.11, the vertex classes bedsl.Model and owl2.Ontology are linked via SpecializeClasses edges with two vertex classes representing the counterparts in the integrated metamodel; they are also linked with a specialization edge. The vertex classes bedsl.Entity and owl2.Class are both linked via a MergeVertexClasses edge with the vertex class representing the merged integration.EntityClass. The edge classes bedsl.containsEntry and owl2.containsLiteral are linked via a MergeEdgeClasses edge with the edge class representing the merge of both. The attributes value and lexicalForm are linked via a MergeAttributes edge with the attribute representing the merge of both.

5.3.2 Integration Use

The use of the integration bridge allows for combined modeling and is separated in the creation of hybrid models, models that conform to the metamodel of an integrated modeling language, and its projection to ontoware models.

Creating Hybrid Models

When using an integration bridge, the first step is to create hybrid models. Hybrid models are models, which conform to the metamodel of an integrated modeling language. An example of a hybrid model is depicted in Figure 5.5.

Since we are bridging modeling languages with ontology languages, the graph schema GS_{Int} results from the integration of the graph schema of a modeling language (e.g., GS_{BEDSL}) and that of the ontology language (e.g., GS_{OWL}).

Load Models

Existing models are taken into consideration as an alternative to the creation of hybrid models. The reuse of existing models to be extended by additional

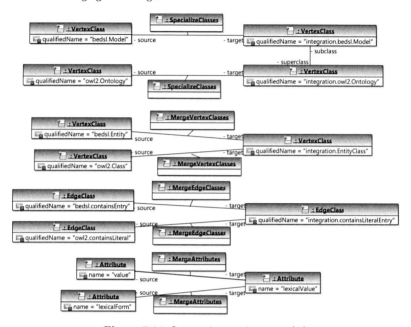

Figure 5.11. Integration services recorded.

OWL constructs is based on a load service, which may be implemented by a transformation. In the case of the BEDSL language the service transforms models conforming to the BEDSL metamodel into models conforming to the integrated metamodel. In general, the integration bridge object provides two services to load models conforming to GS_1 and GS_2, respectively. The load service for GS_i (with $i \in \{1,2\}$) is specified in Table 5.11.

Name	Load BEDSL Service
Signature	GS_{Int} load(GS_i m)
Pattern	m$_h$=b.load(m)
Description	transforms model m to a hybrid model m$_h$. b is the integration bridge object providing the service. For all elements of a model m conforming to GS_i, corresponding elements in the hybrid model are created where the type of the element in the hybrid model is the same as the element to be transformed has in the GS_i model. If the type is not available in GS_{Int} (e.g., because it is merged) the type of the element to be created in the hybrid model is the final integrated type.

Table 5.11. Load service.

Name	*Projection Service*
Signature	GS_i project$_{GS_i}(GS_{Int}\ m_h)$
Pattern	m=b.project$_{GS_i}$(m$_h$)
Description	returns a model m, which conforms to GS_i. m consists of those vertices and edges in m_h, which conform to vertex classes or edge classes in GS_i or conform to merged or specialized elements in GS_{Int} which can be traced back to constructs of GS_i. All attribute assignments in m conform to attributes nested in vertex classes or edge classes in GS_i or conform to merged attributes, which can be traced back to attributes in GS_i.

Table 5.12. Projection service.

Projection to Ontoware Models

An important service on a hybrid model is its projection to a TGraph conforming purely to one of the respective original metamodels (e.g., to GS_{OWL} or GS_{BEDSL}). Language users require projection services because they need interoperability with tools they used before the integration; for example, ontology reasoners only allow ontology models (TGraphs conforming to GS_{OWL}) as input, while BEDSL tools only work with BEDSL models.

The projection of integrated models depends on the integration. A projection service creates a TGraph conforming to a metamodel, which has been integrated. The projected TGraph contains elements, which are projections of elements in the integrated metamodel. The projection service selects only those elements in the integrated model, which conform to integrated constructs (e.g., merged classes and classes integrated by specialization) or, which conform to pure language constructs.

The IntegrationBridge object provides such projection services, one for each metamodel GS_1 or GS_2 to be integrated. Table 5.12 depicts the specification of the projection service for GS_i (where $i \in \{1, 2\}$) getting as input an integrated model and returning a model conforming to GS_i.

For each element in a hybrid model the projection service project$_{GS_i}$ must check where the type of the element originates from. To identify the type of an element, the type function as specified in Definition 1 is used.

If the type is a vertex class or edge class in GS_i, the service creates a new element in the projected model having the same type.

If the service cannot find the type in GS_1 or GS_2 the service must consider the traceability information stored in GS_{Int}^t. The service iterates through all vertex classes and edge classes and checks if the type name is stored in some qualifiedName attribute. If the element having the right qualifiedName attribute is the target of a MergeVertexClasses or MergeEdgeClasses edge, a new element in m is created having as type the one being defined in GS_i, which is the start of a sequence of traceability edges leading to the merged type. Additionally, the projection service has to analyze traceability relationships of type SpecializeClasses. If the type originates from the graph schema GS_i and if it is linked via a SpecializeClasses edge with a vertex class or edge

class being part of the integrated metamodel, and, if it is defined as superclass, then for all instances of the corresponding subclass, elements in m are
created, which have the type of the superclass.

Besides the creation of a new model m for a hybrid model m_h the projection service establishes a *projection function* p_{m_h} with

$$p_{m_h} : Vertex \cup Edge \nrightarrow Vertex \cup Edge,$$

and $p_{m_h}(x) = x'$ where x is some vertex or edge in m_h and x' is the projection
of x created in m_o. This function is encapsulated by the integration bridge
object for each hybrid model that is projected and keeps the relation between
elements in m and m_h.

Besides vertices and edges, attribute assignments are also projected. For
each attribute assignments $(value(x))(a)$ (where $x \in V \cup E$ is in m_h and
$a \in AttrId$) the service checks if a originates from GS_i. If a originates
from GS_i, the service defines an attribute assignment $(value(p_{m_h}(x)))(a) =
(value(x))(a)$. If a does not originate from GS_i, the service checks if a is a
merged attribute in GS_{Int} by analyzing all traceability relationships of the
type MergeAttributes. If it is a merged attribute the service defines an attribute assignment $(value(p_{m_h}(x)))(a) = (value(x))(a')$ where a' is the start
of a sequence of MergeAttributes edges to a in the schema graph GS_{Int}^t.

Example

In the following we present an example where the projection service for GS_{OWL}
($=GS_2$) is used. The service is provided by the integration bridge object b
encapsulating the integration of GS_{BEDSL} and GS_{OWL}.

Figure 5.5 depicts a hybrid model, which is visualized by a textual concrete
syntax. It conforms to the integrated metamodel, which (partially) is depicted
in Figures 5.7, 5.8, and 5.9.

The projection service is applied on the integrated model m_h in Figure 5.5
and returns the ontoware model m_o in Figure 5.12.

```
mₒ = b.project_GS_OWL(mₕ);
```

The instances of SubClassOf, DisjointClasses, or ObjectProperty (with domain and range axioms) are elements that come from GS_{OWL}. They are projected directly to correspondent elements in the ontoware model m_o.

The type EntityClass is neither defined in GS_{BEDSL} nor in GS_{OWL}. But
in GS_{Int}^t a MergeVertexClass traceability relationship edge exists, which is
incident with a vertex class with a qualified name attribute set to "integra-
tion.EntityClass". The edge starts at the vertex class with a qualified name
attribute set to owl2.Class. Thus, for all EntityClass vertices a correspondent
OWL class is created in m_o.

Reference and Attribute are integrated with ObjectProperty and DataProperty via a specialization relationship (cf. GS_{Int}^t). Thus, for all instances of
Reference and Attribute an object property or data property is created in m_o.

Figure 5.12 depicts the final ontoware model represented in OWL 2 Functional style syntax, which is the projection of the hybrid model in Figure 5.5.

```
Ontology(DeviceModel

Declaration(Class(Device))
DisjointClasses(Device Card)

Declaration(Class(Card))
DisjointClasses(Card Device)

Declaration(Class(Router))

Declaration(Class(MobileDevice))
SubClassOf(MobileDevice Device)

Declaration(ObjectProperty(belongsToDevice))
ObjectPropertyDomain(belongsToDevice Card)
ObjectPropertyRange(belongsToDevice Device)

Declaration(ObjectProperty(hasCard))
ObjectPropertyDomain(hasCard Device)
ObjectPropertyRange(hasCard Card)
)
```

Figure 5.12. Visualized ontoware model.

5.3.3 Discussion

The integration of two languages results in one all-embracing new modeling language. To achieve the integration the mapping of concepts (which defines an intersection of both languages) has to be used to define a new modeling language, which corresponds to the union of the source languages [EW10].

From the perspective of language designers, the integration bridge provides a set of services for building integrated modeling languages. From the perspective of language users, the integration bridge provides a common view on modelware models and ontoware models by using hybrid models.

The modeling of hybrid models requires an understanding of both integrated languages. A language designer starts with the mapping of constructs of the metamodels to be integrated. Depending on how different constructs relate to each other, specific integration services are applied. A language user has to be familiar with different concrete syntaxes (at least one for each modeling language) and how they are used in combination.

To provide interoperability between different tools, projection services are given by the integration bridge. Projection services extract all relevant information from hybrid models and translate them to models understandable by given tools.

Integration Bridge vs. Transformation Bridge

To compare both bridges we consider any existing BEDSL model m, which conforms to GS_{BEDSL}. We assume the transformation service specified in Section 5.2.1, which transforms BEDSL models to ontoware models, and, the integration bridge combining GS_{BEDSL} and GS_{OWL} as established in Section 5.3.1.

To get an ontoware model m_o^t for the BEDSL model m we use the transformation service as follows:

```
m_o^t=TransformationBridge.transform(m);
```

If b is the integration bridge object encapsulating the integration of BEDSL and OWL, we are able to adapt, load, and project the BEDSL model m as follows:

```
m_a=Convert.adaptation(m);
m_h=b.load(m_a);
m_o^i=b.project_GS_OWL(m_h);
```

Without any change of m_h using the integrated modeling language, we can state that the two bridges return equal ontoware models:

$$m_o^i =_o^t$$

In the next listing the same BEDSL model m is adapted and loaded but using the new integrated modeling language some ontology construct is added:

```
m_a'=Convert.adaptation(m);
m_h'=b.load(m_a);
m_h'.createVertex("owl2.DisjointClasses");
...
m_o''=b.project_GS_OWL(m_h);
```

Having the change in m_h' the projected model is different from the transformed model, because projection services also consider additional OWL constructs:

$$m_o^{i'} \neq m_o^t$$

The main difference between the two bridges is the use of the new integrated language provided by the integration bridge. It allows the use of additional constructs exclusively provided by the ontology language OWL 2. These constructs are projected to a pure ontoware model. The transformation service only considers pure BEDSL constructs for the creation of ontoware models. The parallel use of both modeling languages is not possible.

5.4 Mapping Bridge

While the integration bridge allows for hybrid modeling, the mapping bridge allows for the separate design and use of different modeling languages. Both languages can be developed independently by a language designer. They are bridged by integrating them with a given mapping metamodel. Language users can use the mapped modeling languages separately. In addition, mappings can be defined to declare relations between model elements.

5.4.1 Mapping Definition

In the following we present the establishment of a mapping bridge, which is used in Section 5.4.2.

Mapping Metamodel

The establishment of a mapping bridge is mainly based on a generic mapping metamodel, which defines how mappings are organized. Figure 5.13 depicts the mapping metamodel, which describes mapping models. Here, a mapping model connects a modelware model and an ontoware model and consists of a set of mapping assertions. These mapping assertions (represented by the class Mapping in the metamodel) are first-class elements that exist independently of the modelware models and ontoware models. The mapping metamodel is represented by the graph schema GS_{map}

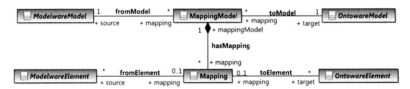

Figure 5.13. Mapping metamodel.

In the context of bridging modeling languages with ontology languages, the mapping metamodel allows for defining mappings between ontoware model elements and modelware model elements. Hence, the metamodel provides classes for both kinds of elements. We define that several modelware elements may be mapped to an arbitrary number of ontoware elements. Each modelware element may have a counterpart in the ontoware model where the counterpart may consist of complex constructs (e.g., properties with domain and range axioms). Vice versa, ontoware elements may have counterparts in modelware models via mappings.

Integration

To use the mapping metamodel with concrete modeling languages and ontology languages, and, to define concrete mappings between modelware and ontoware elements, the mapping metamodel must be integrated with the corresponding languages.

Figure 5.14 depicts the integrated mapping metamodel where the metamodels of BEDSL and OWL 2 are combined with the mapping metamodel.

To map modelware elements with ontoware elements its types are defined as a specialization of ModelwareElement. We define that BEDSL models can be mapped with OWL 2 ontologies. Each entity and feature from BEDSL can be mapped with ontoware elements. Furthermore, we define that each OWL 2 class, individual, object property, data property, and in addition each OWL 2 axiom can be mapped with modelware elements. Thus we define the corresponding classes coming from the OWL 2 metamodel as specialization of OntowareElement.

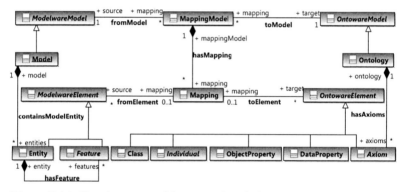

Figure 5.14. Mapping metamodel integrated with the BEDSL and OWL 2 metamodel.

Constraints

Since the pure mapping metamodel allows for example to map BEDSL entities with OWL properties or BEDSL references with OWL classes, there is a need for constraining the metamodel. Constraints (e.g., defined in GReQL, cf. Section 2.3.1) restrict the definitions of mappings, such that attributes are only mapped with OWL data properties, or entities are only mapped with OWL classes or individuals.

forall e:V{Entity} **@ forall** v:V **@** e <−−{fromElement}−−>{toElement} & {Class, Individual} v
forall e:V{Attribute} **@ forall** v:V **@** e <−−{fromElement}−−>{toElement} & {DataProperty} v

5.4.2 Mapping Use

The mapping bridge is taken into consideration if the modelware model and the ontoware model are developed separately. Instead of the integration bridge both models stay separate from each other.

The mapping bridge is encapsulated by an object **b** of type **Mapping-Bridge**. It contains the integrated mapping metamodel GS_{Int} (accessible via o.getMappingMetamodel()) defining which constructs of the two languages can be mapped. In addition, it provides the services for loading existing models, for defining mappings between models and for deriving counterparts of a model.

Load Models

Before mappings between modelware model and ontoware model can be defined, the models must be loaded into the mapping bridge.

The mapping bridge provides two services to load a modelware model and an ontoware model respectively. The services are defined in Tables 5.13 and 5.14.

Name	Load Modelware Model Service
Signature	void load(ModelwareModel m_m)
Pattern	b.load(m_m)
Description	creates a modelware model m_m, which conforms to the integrated mapping metamodel. The modelware model b.m_m is referenced by the mapping bridge object.

Table 5.13. Load modelware model service.

Name	Load Ontoware Model Service
Signature	void load(OntowareModel m_o)
Pattern	b.load(m_o)
Description	creates an ontoware model m_o, which conforms to the integrated mapping metamodel. The ontoware model b.m_o is referenced by the mapping bridge object.

Table 5.14. Load ontoware model service.

Mapping Models

As mentioned in the definition of the mapping bridge, modelware elements can be mapped with ontoware elements. In Table 5.15 we specify a mapping service, which describes how two elements v_m and v_o a mapped.

Name	Mapping Service
Signature	void mapping(ModelwareElement v_m, OntowareElement v_o)
Pattern	b.mapping(v_m, v_o)
Description	maps the modelware element v_m with the ontoware element v_o via a Mapping vertex. v_m and v_o are part of b.m_m and b.m_o, respectively. The mapping is encapsulated by the mapping bridge object b.

Table 5.15. Mapping service.

The mapping service is used to model the relation between a modelware element and an ontoware element. In Figure 5.15 we present an example model consisting of a BEDSL part, an OWL 2 part and a part where the mappings between the two models are modeled.

Derive Models

Having a mapping established between a modelware model and ontoware model, the mapping bridge provides a **derive** service for deriving a concrete ontoware model for a given modelware model.

The **derive** service checks if a mapping in the mapping model exists for elements of a given modelware model. If such mapping exists, the counterpart in the ontoware model is put into a new ontoware model representing the *derivation* of the given modelware model. The derivation of a mapped model consists of those vertices of the opposite model, which in turn are incident with mappings, plus all edges, which are connecting mapped elements.

The **derive** service is represented in Table 5.16.

Name	Derive Service
Signature	OntowareModel derive(ModelwareModel m_b)
Pattern	m_o=b.derive(m_b)
Description	checks if for the elements in m_b a mapping in m_m exists. If a mapping exists, the counterpart in the ontoware model is put into a new ontoware model m_o. All edges between derived vertices in m_o are created in m_o with respect to GS_{OWL}.

Table 5.16. Derive Service.

Analogously we can implement a derive service, which gets as input an ontoware model and returns a modelware model. In the following we present an example model consisting of a BEDSL part, an OWL 2 part and a part where the mappings between the two models are modeled.

Example

Figure 5.15 depicts an example model, which consists of a modelware model, an ontoware model, and a mapping model.

In the upper part a modelware model is designed by creating entities and connecting them by references. In particular, modelware.Device and modelware.Card are declared. Furthermore, modelware.deviceInstance and modelware.cardInstance are defined and connected by references modelware.instanceOfDevice and modelware.instanceOfCard with modelware.Device and modelware.Card.

To semantically define that modelware.deviceInstance and modelware.cardInstance are instances of modelware.Device and modelware.Card, the modelware model is mapped to an ontoware model expressing these facts. Hence, in the second part of Figure 5.15 the two correspondent OWL classes ontoware.Device and ontoware.Card and the OWL individuals ontoware. deviceInstance and ontoware. cardInstance are declared.

In the third part of Figure 5.15 they are mapped with the correspondent modelware elements. Since axioms are not named elements they are directly listed in the mapping, but originally they belong to the ontoware model part. For example, the two class assertion axioms are directly mapped to the references modelware.instanceOfDevice and modelware.instanceOfCard.

Mappings are defined by using the mapping keyword. They are declared using the mapping service defined in Table 5.15, where both parameters within the round brackets are the elements to be mapped. The mapping model itself is not directly given as parameter because it is encapsulated by the mapping bridge object.

Having the modelware model m_m depicted below, which is just a part of that displayed in Figure 5.15, we can use the derive service to get those parts of m_o in Figure 5.15, which are mapped with the device model below.

```
model DeviceModel {
  entity modelware.Device{
  }
  entity modelware.Card {
  }
}
```

Using the derive service, we get the ontoware model m_o.

```
m_o=b.derive(m_m);
```

The ontoware model m_o depicted below consists of the two classes ontoware.Device and ontoware.Card since they are linked via mappings with the entities modelware.Device and modelware.Card.

```
Ontology(DeviceOntology
  Declaration(Class(ontoware.Device))
  Declaration(Class(ontoware.Card))
)
```

5.4.3 Discussion

The mapping bridge allows for designing and using different modeling languages separately. From the perspective of a language designer, the modeling

```
model DeviceModel {
  entity modelware.Device{
  }
  entity modelware.Card {
  }
  entity modelware.deviceInstance{
      reference modelware.instanceOfDevice : modelware.Device;
      reference modelware.hasCardInstance : modelware.cardInstance;
  }
  entity modelware.cardInstance{
      reference modelware.instanceOfCard : Card;
  }
}
**************************************************
Ontology(DeviceOntology
  Declaration(Class(ontoware.Device))
  Declaration(Class(ontoware.Card))

  Declaration(Individual(ontoware.deviceInstance))
  Declaration(Individual(ontoware.cardInstance))
)
**************************************************
MappingModel{
  mapping(modelware.Device, ontoware.Device)
  mapping(modelware.Card, ontoware.Card)

  mapping(modelware.deviceInstance, ontoware.deviceInstance)
  mapping(modelware.cardInstance, ontoware.cardInstance)

  mapping(modelware.instanceOfDevice, ClassAssertion(ontoware.deviceInstance ontoware.Device))
  mapping(modelware.hasCardInstance, ClassAssertion(ontoware.cardInstance ontoware.Card))
}
```

Figure 5.15. Mapping of modelware model and ontoware model (concrete syntax).

language and the ontology language are bridged by integrating them with a mapping metamodel defining which modelware model and ontoware model elements can be mapped. From the perspective of language users, all languages are used separately. The user must be familiar with syntax and semantics of both languages. In addition a mapping language is provided to define mappings. Having mappings established between a modelware model and an ontoware model, the counterparts of modelware elements can be derived.

Because different languages and their models can be designed and used independently, modeling environments and reasoning tools can be used separately.

Mapping Bridge vs. Integration Bridge

To compare both bridges we consider any existing BEDSL model m_m and any existing OWL 2 model m_o. We assume that the mapping bridge combining BEDSL and OWL is encapsulated by the object b_m, and that the integration bridge combining BEDSL and OWL is encapsulated by the object b_i.

To define any mappings between m_m and m_o using the mapping bridge we must load the two models. After the load, different mappings may be defined between two elements e_1 and c_2, where e_1 belongs to m_m and c_2 belongs to m_o. We are able to derive those parts of m_o, which are mapped with elements in m_m. The Result is the ontoware model m_o'.

```
bₘ.load(mₘ);
bₘ.load(mₒ);
bₘ.mapping(e₁, c₂);
...
m'ₒ=bₘ.derive(mₘ)
```

To load the model m_m into the integration bridge we may have to adapt it first. After loading, we are able to project the hybrid model m_h to the ontoware model m_o''.

```
m'ᵧ=Convert.adaptation(mₘ);
m'ₕ=bᵢ.load(mₐ);
m''ₒ=bᵢ.project_{GS_{OWL}}(mₕ);
```

When comparing m_o' and m_o'', generally both ontoware models are not equal ($m_o' \neq m_o''$). The reason is that the integration of constructs and the respective projection service, both encapsulated by b_i, is established by language designers before using the bridge. Using the integration bridge the language user has no choice to affect the counterpart in ontoware models, as it is possible with the **mapping** service using the mapping bridge. For example, using the integration bridge, all BEDSL entities are projected to OWL classes. The mapping bridge allows a less restrictive combination of modelware and ontoware model elements at the level of language users (e.g., BEDSL entities may be mapped to OWL classes or individuals.), but therefore requires a better understanding of ontology languages.

Mapping Bridge vs. Transformation Bridge

To compare both bridges we once again consider any existing BEDSL model m_m and any existing OWL 2 model m_o. We assume that the mapping bridge combining BEDSL and OWL is encapsulated by the object b_m.

To define any mappings between m_m and m_o using the mapping bridge, we must load the two models. After loading different mappings may be defined between two elements e_1 and c_2, where e_1 belongs to m_m and c_2 belongs to m_o. We are able to derive those parts of m_o, which are mapped with elements in m_m. The result is the ontoware model m_o'.

```
bₘ.load(mₘ);
bₘ.load(mₒ);
bₘ.mapping(e₁, c₂);
...
m'ₒ=bₘ.derive(mₘ)
```

The transformation bridge provides a **transform** service, which directly gets the BEDSL model m_m and returns the ontoware model m_o''. When comparing m_o' and m_o'', generally both ontoware models are not equal ($m_o' \neq m_o''$). A transformation service prescribes which types of elements are produced in an ontoware model according to a transformation definition. A language user has no option to define the possible type of target elements, since the transformation is predefined by the language designer. Compared to the transformation bridge, the mapping bridge allows for defining a less restrictive relation of modelware model elements with ontoware model elements, but therefore requires an understanding of ontology languages.

5.5 API Bridge

In this section we are going to present the API bridge. In Section 5.5.1 we show how to design an API bridge. The example we present allows for translating BEDSL graphs to ontoware models. In Section 5.5.2 we show how to use the API bridge.

API bridges are established by the *implementation* of services using the operations and services of given APIs used to traverse models and those services of another API to build new models. The API bridge is designed by the language designer and used by the language user.

In the following we are going to exemplify the use of the *OWL API* in version 3.0.0[1]. It is developed primarily at the University of Manchester [HB09]. Before we go into detail how to use the OWL API we comment on its architecture depicted in Figure 5.16. Here, the OWLOntologyManager provides a central point for creating, loading, changing, and saving many ontologies. Ontologies are represented by the interface OWLOntology. An ontology is created or loaded by an ontology manager and each ontology is unique to a particular manager by its IRI. Each ontology consists of a set of OWL axioms and a set of OWL annotations (which are not discussed in this thesis).

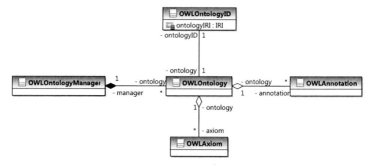

Figure 5.16. Architecture showing the management of ontologies of the OWL API [HB09].

---

[1] http://owlapi.sourceforge.net/

In the next subsections (and in the Appendix A.3.2) we present Java methods. These methods show how to use the services provided by the OWL API to create a new ontology based on the result of services used to traverse BEDSL models.

5.5.1 API Bridge Implementation

The API bridge to translate BEDSL graphs to ontoware models is established by a language designer. He implements the Java class **APIBridge**, which is partially depicted in Figure 5.17 and later provided to the language user. The bridge uses the JGraLab library[2] to read BEDSL graphs and it uses the OWL API [HB09] to build ontologies.

Before the bridge for the separate constructs of BEDSL is implemented, the relation between constructs of BEDSL and corresponding OWL entities and axioms relies on a *mapping*. We use the mapping presented in Table 5.2. This mapping is defined by the language designer and it is based on intensional knowledge.

The API bridge keeps a reference to the **OWLOntologyManager**, which provides the central point for creating, loading, changing, and saving different ontologies. All changes to an ontology are applied via the manager. An **OWLDataFactory** is obtained from the manager. It is used to create entities and different axioms.

A map in the **APIBridge** class manages the relation between vertices in a BEDSL graph and OWL entities in an ontology. The method **bridgeBEDSL-Graph** gets as input a BEDSL graph and iterates through all models in the graph. Each model is translated by the method **bridgeModel** to a separate ontology.

An implementation of the **bridgeModel** method is shown in the Appendix A.3.2.

5.5.2 API Bridge Use

In the following we comment on the use of the API bridge.

Translation of Models

Figure 5.18 illustrates the use of the API bridge. Here, for a given BEDSL graph (e.g., loaded from the file **networkDeviceModel.tg**) a new APIBridge object is created, which provides the public method **bridgeBEDSLGraph**. For each model in the BEDSL graph, this method directly creates a new ontology and saves them in separate files.

---

[2] http://jgralab.uni-koblenz.de

```
public class APIBridge {

  OWLOntologyManager manager;
  OWLDataFactory factory;

  HashMap<Vertex, OWLEntity> owlEntityMap = new HashMap<Vertex, OWLEntity>();

  public APIBridge() {
    manager = OWLManager.createOWLOntologyManager();
    factory = manager.getOWLDataFactory();
  }

  public void bridgeBEDSLGraph(BEDSL g) {
    Iterator<Model> iteratorModel = g.getModelVertices().iterator();

    while(iteratorModel.hasNext()){
      bridgeModel(iteratorModel.next());
    }
  }
  ...
}
```

Figure 5.17. API bridge class.

```
public static void main(String[] args) {
  Graph graph = null;
  try{
    graph = GraphIO.loadGraphFromFile("networkDeviceModel.tg", BEDSLSchema.instance(), new
        ProgressFunctionImpl());
  }catch(Exception e){
    e.printStackTrace();
  }
    new APIBridge().bridgeBEDSLGraph((BEDSL)graph);
}
```

Figure 5.18. Using the API bridge.

Reasoning Services

Reasoners, which should process ontologies managed by the ontology manager of the OWL API are declared by a separate reasoner interface. It gets as parameter the manager and provides methods for all common reasoning services. Figure 5.19 shows how to adopt the consistency checking service on the device ontology and how to check if the class Device is satisfiable.

```
Reasoner reasoner = new Reasoner(manager);
reasoner.loadOntology(deviceOntology);
boolean consistent = reasoner.isConsistent();
boolean satisfiable = reasoner.isSatisfiable(device);
```

Figure 5.19. Using reasoning services.

5.5.3 Discussion

The API bridge allows for building ontologies. It is defined via a programming interface provided by an existing API. The bridge itself encapsulates the modeling of ontology constructs by services and methods. On the one hand, this ensures a higher consistency of ontologies with regard to the OWL 2 language definition, since the methods have well-defined pre- and post-conditions (for example, only instances of ClassExpression can be connected with class axioms). On the other hand, the API is restricted by the set of methods and services it provides (for example, only those elements can be created for which a get-method in the OWL-API data factory exists).

To access and use the API, other tools must provide an implementation interface as well. Metamodels and models to be translated to ontologies must be accessible via services provided by a respective API. The JGraLab library provides such an interface for accessing graph schemas and graphs.

Comparison with other Bridges

The transformation bridge allows for producing ontoware models by a given modelware model according to some transformation definition. The API bridge, if the modelware model is accessible via an implementation interface, provides services and methods to produce an ontology. Both bridges provide a service/method, which gets a modelware model as input and returns an ontoware model. Nevertheless, the API bridge establishment relies on the existing methods a respective API provides. A transformation service may be implemented with access to all model elements.

In contrast to the integration bridge, the API bridge does not allow for modeling hybrid models. The API bridge gets a modelware model as input and allows for producing a correspondent ontoware model using a set of predefined methods.

The mapping bridge allows for modeling modelware and ontoware models separately, which is not possible with the API bridge. In addition it allows for defining mapping relations between different modelware and ontoware elements.

5.6 Related Work

The related work for this chapter is separated into related work for each of the four bridges. Before dealing with related approaches concerning a concrete bridge, we refer to a paper also dealing with different kinds of bridges.

In [KBJK03] three metamodel integration patterns are presented, which are equal to our set of metamodel bridges. The *reference pattern* in [KBJK03] allows for integrating two complementary metamodels. Similar to our mapping bridge it supports loose coupling and navigation between complementary parts via reference links. The *transformation pattern* in [KBJK03] allows for describing transformations between a source metamodel and a target metamodel. A transformation allows for generating models conforming to a target metamodel from models conforming to a source metamodel. The *merge pattern* in [KBJK03] is used if two metamodels are used concurrently and are tightly coupled. Each merge pattern consists of a set of merge rules used to merge parts of source and target metamodel.

The *transformation bridge* is the most commonly used bridge. The main differences are the transformation language (e.g., ATL [JABK08], QVT [Kur08]) and the modeling languages involved in the transformation. In the example in Section 5.2 we used GReTL as a transformation language, which transforms BEDSL models to ontoware models. Our transformation bridge is similar to the transformation pattern given in [JABK08, Kur08]. Our transformation service, implementing the transformation, gets a source model conforming to the source metamodel as input and transforms it to a target model conforming to a target metamodel (in our case the OWL 2 metamodel). In contrast, our transformation service itself is not a model conforming to the transformation language metamodel. It is implemented in Java using the GReTL library. A further transformation bridge is described in [SE10]. Here a schema-aware translation from schema-like RDF graphs to grUML schemas and TGraphs is presented. The mutual transformation of the respective query languages SPARQL and GReQL is also described in this work. The transformation is also implemented in GReTL.

In [NE93] a reference model for frameworks of software engineering environments is presented. Here, the reference model addresses interoperability and integration of different software engineering environment. One issue of a software engineering environment is the functionality for integration. As proposed in [NE93], our integration bridge provides from the perspective of a language user a common view into a hybrid model consisting of modelware and ontoware constructs. Via the projection services it allows different tools (e.g., reasoning tools) to process hybrid models. As required in [NE93], from the perspective of a language designer, the *integration bridge* provides a consistent interface for integrating languages.

In [Süt01] the *syntactic integration* of visual modeling languages is considered. In particular, [Süt01] mentions three ways of integrating the abstract syntax: integration of types by merging two concepts, connecting two concepts by a specialization relationship, and integrating two concepts by an associations. In general, our integration approach extends the three ways of integration by allowing the merge of associations and attributes. In addition, our approach provides the projection of hybrid models (integrated models) to models conforming to one of the modeling languages to be integrated.

In [LBM+01, LNK+01] a framework for *metamodel composition* is presented. It consists of operators (equivalence and inheritance operators) for combining metamodels. In addition, the framework provides operations for translating models. [LNK+01] describes translation operations, which allow for translating models conforming to some metamodel to be combined into models conforming to the integrated metamodel. Furthermore, [LBM+01] presents translation operations to map integrated models to executable modeling languages. Compared to our integration approach, we provide a set of integration services, which are similar to the composition operators relating concepts of the metamodels to be integrated and combining them. Instead of translations to executable languages we provide a projection service. However, the idea of projection is similar to the translation in [LBM+01], since we must project our hybrid models to ontoware models to have a consistent input for reasoning tools executing the ontoware models. A translation from a model conforming to a modeling language to be integrated to a model conforming to the integrated language can be realized by implementing a transformation service, which uses the integrated metamodel as a target metamodel and the metamodel to be integrated as source metamodel.

Kolovos et al. describe in [KPP06] the Epsilon Merging Language (EML) used to merge two source models being instances of two given source metamodels to a target model being instance of a given target metamodels. In a comparison phase equivalent elements of the source models are identified by match-rules. Each match-rule can compare pairs of instances of two specific metaclasses and decides if they match and conform to each other. In the merging phase, two activities produce elements in the target model. The elements that have been identified as matching are merged into a sequence of model elements in the target model and the elements for which a match has not been found in the opposite model are transformed into elements of the target model. In contrast to our integration bridge, we are first building a new integrated metamodel for the two given source metamodels. This integrated metamodel is either directly used for hybrid modeling, or models conforming to source metamodels are transformed (loaded) to hybrid models. While our integration bridge supports the design of new integrated metamodels and provides projection of hybrid models, the Epsilon Merging Language targets the merge of instance models.

In [Hei09], Heidenreich et al. present a *mapping bridge*. It allows for mapping feature models with any arbitrary Ecore-based metamodel. Compared to our approach, mappings are declaratively defined and a mapping metamodel is used to express the relation between the Ecore language and the feature description language. In contrast to our approach the two languages to be mapped are fixed and instead of features, elements of ontoware models can be mapped. We allow for integrating our mapping metamodel with any language metamodel to map its instances to ontoware elements.

Kappel et al. present in [KWRS11] a mapping bridge for model-based tool integration. Given a mapping language, different operators are used to relate classes, attributes, and references (CAR - the name of the mapping language) of two metamodels. Given a mapping model and source and target metamodels, transformations may be generated. They are used to apply the mappings on models from both languages. In contrast to our mapping bridge, the CAR language is restricted to class based modeling languages (only classes, references and attributes can be mapped), while our mapping metamodel has the capability of being integrated with several DSLs. Therefore, CAR mapping models may be translated to transformations. This however is not provided by our approach.

Whenever metamodels or models are accessible via an implementation interface, an *API bridge* can be realized. Object-oriented and ontological representations are integrated in the paper of Puleston et al. [PPCR08]. In particular a framework is described that combines Java programs with OWL ontologies to support hybrid modeling, where parts of the model are developed directly in Java and other parts of the model are developed directly in OWL. The connections between both representations are established by APIs, which allow for accessing knowledge resources (RDF-based repositories) or object-oriented models (written in Java). In [SEL+10] an API bridge between the JGraLab library and its query language GReQL and the ADOxx platform[3] is mentioned to facilitate efficient querying as well as constraint specifications by GReQL and their automated checking for ADOxx models.

5.7 Conclusion

In this chapter we presented four different bridging approaches. All bridges provide methods for combining different modeling languages. We answered RQ6 by developing the bridging technologies for the combination of modelware modeling languages and the ontology language OWL 2.

The transformation bridge is used to translate modelware models into ontoware models according to some transformation definition.

The integration bridge supports language designers to combine different modeling languages. Language users are able to use both languages simultaneously and to create hybrid models. The use of the integration bridge is proposed if language users want to design models with the language they are familiar with, but in addition want to simply annotate model elements with ontology constructs.

The mapping bridge allows for using modeling languages separately and combining models by just declaring mappings between model elements. The use of the mapping bridge is suggested if ontoware models already exist or the languages to be combined are complementary.

---

[3] ADOxx® is the extensible, multi-lingual, multi-os, repository-based platform for the development of modeling tools of the BOC Group. ADOxx® is a registered trademark of the BOC Group, `http://www.boc-group.com`.

The API bridge provides services to create, modify, and save ontologies. In addition, it provides services for different reasoning tasks. The API bridge is used if modelware models and metamodels to be translated to an ontoware model are only accessible via an implementation interface, which might be also given by an API.

6

Language Engineering and Use with Ontology Technologies

Language engineering is concerned with linguistic metamodeling, where the abstract syntax of a modeling language is designed by a metamodel to prescribe the structure of user models. Language designers are responsible for the correctness of instance models built by language users (Challenge 2). A modeling environment should provide a metamodeling language with formal semantics to language designers that enables the combined definition of metamodels and constraints. Since ontology languages provide formal semantics, we need to answer the question:

RQ7:   *How may ontology languages be used to define semantics and constraints of modeling languages?*

Since language designers rely on the metamodeling languages they are familiar with, the ontology language used to write constraints must be bridged with the languages they use (Challenge 1).

Language users are using a modeling language by creating user models. They require services for checking the consistency of a model with regard to its metamodel. If the model is not consistent they require services to detect the inconsistency in the model and to get suggestions on how to repair the model (Challenge 3). Based on a bridge combining the design of metamodels and conforming models with ontologies, ontology technologies can help to ensure model correctness. We answer the following question:

RQ8:   *How do ontology technologies support model correctness?*

Modeling environments should provide ontology technologies encapsulated as user services to languages users. Hence, language users do not need any experience for using ontoware tools.

6.1 Chapter Context

In this section we present the context of this chapter. We start with the technological space used in this chapter and present examples used in the following sections. In Section 6.1.2 we consider the notion of linguistic metamodeling. Section 6.1.3 presents a road map for the remaining sections of this chapter.

6.1.1 Technological Space

Models and metamodels are defined in the TGraph technological space. Hence, models are represented by a TGraph conforming to a metamodel represented by a grUML diagram (cf. Section 2.2).

An example grUML diagram is given in Figure 6.1. It describes the Ecore metametamodel, which represents the abstract syntax of a language to specify metamodels. Here, metamodels are composed of packages, which contain model elements. Model elements are characterized by its name. Model elements as well as packages are located elements. Classes are model elements that can be specialized and contain several structural features. Structural features are either references or attributes and have a type. In the case of references the type is a class. In the case of an attribute the type is a datatype or an enumeration consisting of literals. Several attributes of structural features allow for defining multiplicities of features and whether their instances are ordered or unique. In addition, references can be defined as a container of the elements they point to. A reference can also have an opposite reference.

The Ecore language is supported by KM3 [JB06, ATL05] (where KM3 is the abbreviation for *Kernel MetaMetaModel*). KM3 provides a textual concrete syntax that eases the implementation of Ecore-based metamodels. Its syntax is simple and has some similarities with the Java notation [ATL05]. TGraphs conforming to the grUML diagram representing the Ecore metametamodel are visualized by this textual concrete syntax. Figure 6.2 depicts such a visualized TGraph representing the metamodel of an activity diagram language (similar to that in [OMG07b]).

Activity diagrams consist of activity nodes and activity edges. Action nodes are activity nodes, which model concrete actions within an activity. Object nodes can be used in a variety of ways, depending on where values or objects are flowing from and to. Control nodes (e.g., initial and final nodes, decision and merge nodes, and fork and join nodes) are used to initialize, coordinate, and finalize the flows between other activity or object nodes.

Activity diagrams contain two types of edges, where edges have exactly one source and one target node. One edge is used for object flows and another edge for control flows. An object flow edge models the flow of values to or from object nodes. A control flow is an edge that starts an action or control node subsequent to the previous one finishing.

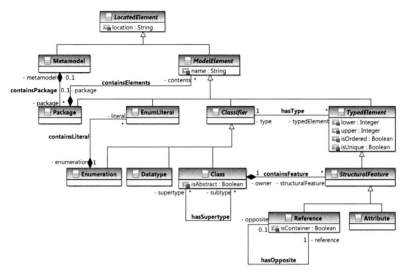

Figure 6.1. Ecore metametamodel as grUML diagram.

```
package ActivityLanguage {
  abstract class ActivityNode {
    reference incoming [0−∗] : ActivityEdge oppositeOf target;
    reference outgoing [0−∗] : ActivityEdge oppositeOf source;
    attribute name : String;
  }
  class ObjectNode extends ActivityNode {
  }
  class Action extends ActivityNode {
  }

  abstract class ControlNode extends ActivityNode { }
  class Initial extends ControlNode { }
  class Final extends ControlNode { }
  class Decision extends ControlNode { }
  class Merge extends ControlNode { }
  class Fork extends ControlNode { }
  class Join extends ControlNode { }

  abstract class ActivityEdge {
    reference source [1−1] : ActivityNode;
    reference target [1−1] : ActivityNode;
    attribute condition : String;
  }
  class ObjectFlow extends ActivityEdge { }
  class ControlFlow extends ActivityEdge { }
}
```

Figure 6.2. Visualized TGraph representing the metamodel of an activity language.

6.1.2 Linguistic Metamodeling

Environments for model-driven engineering (MDE) provide the facility for defining and using modeling languages.

One part of the language definition is the definition of the abstract syntax by designing metamodels. The abstract syntax definition is used to prescribe the structure of models conforming to the metamodel. The metamodel layer is known as the language definition layer, since it defines the abstract syntax of a modeling language.

A metamodel is instantiated to define models at the model layer. For example, the model in Figure 6.2 (representing the metamodel of an activity language) is built by instantiating the Ecore metametamodel in Figure 6.1. Here the Ecore metametamodel representing the abstract syntax of a metamodeling language prescribes the structure of metamodels (represented as TGraphs and used to design Ecore conformant metamodels).

The relation between language definition layers and the model layer consisting of its instances is known as *linguistic instanceOf relationship*. The elements at the model layer are known as *linguistic instances* [AK03]. *Linguistic metamodeling* means the definition of metamodels, which represent the abstract syntax of a modeling language and prescribe the structure of models [AK03].

6.1.3 Chapter Road Map

Figure 6.3 depicts this chapter's road map. In Section 6.2.1 we start with the establishment of an integration bridge between Ecore and OWL 2. The result is an integrated metamodel, which conforms to the grUML metaschema (cf. Section 2.2.3). The bridge is used to define hybrid metamodels. Since the hybrid metamodels are instantiable, we show how they are represented in set notation. They are projected together with corresponding linguistic instances to ontoware models as shown in Section 6.2.2. In Section 6.3.1, we show how to define constraints in hybrid models that prescribe the structure of corresponding linguistic user models. In Section 6.3.2, the inconsistency management for user models is presented.

We conclude this chapter by presenting related approaches in Section 6.4.

6.2 Integration Bridge for Linguistic Instantiable Models

Language designers creating metamodels are responsible for the correctness of instance models built by language users. Language designers require a metamodeling language, which enables the combined definition of metamodels and constraints. Below we depict the design of the class ObjectNode, this being part of the metamodel for the activity diagram language. Here, a language designer has seamlessly annotated the class definition by an OWL 2 SubClassOf axiom, which states that object nodes are only incident with object flows.

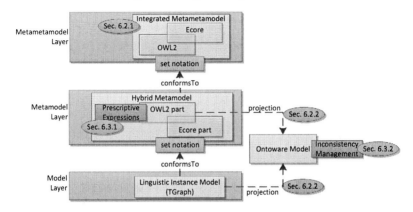

Figure 6.3. Road map of Chapter 6.

...
class ObjectNode **subClassOf** (outgoing **only** ObjectFlow) **and** (incoming **only** ObjectFlow)
...

In Section 6.2.1 we present the establishment of the bridge where the integration services presented in Section 5.3.1 are used. This bridge supports language designers in defining Ecore-based metamodels together with integrated OWL 2-based annotations.

Since language users are creating linguistic instances of metamodels, we present a method to project both the metamodel and model to one common ontoware model in Section 6.2.2. Given such ontoware model building the description of metamodel and model reasoning technologies from Chapter 3 may be used to validate the correctness of instance models with respect to their metamodel.

6.2.1 Integration Definition

The integration bridge between Ecore and OWL is established as suggested in Section 5.3.1.

1. Mapping and Adaptation

In the first step a mapping is established, which is based on the intensional knowledge of the two languages to be integrated. In [KKK+06], Kappel et al. present a mapping between Ecore concepts and concepts in the OMG *Ontology Definition Metamodel* [OMG07a]. We adapted this mapping by juxtaposing Ecore concepts with OWL 2 concepts in Table 6.1.

♯	Ecore	OWL 2
1.	Metamodel	Ontology
2.	Class	Class
3.	Datatype	Datatype
4.	Reference	ObjectProperty
5.	Attribute	DataProperty
6.	Enumeration	DataOneOf
7.	Literal	Literal
8.	hasSuperType	SubClassOf

Table 6.1. Mapping of Ecore and OWL 2.

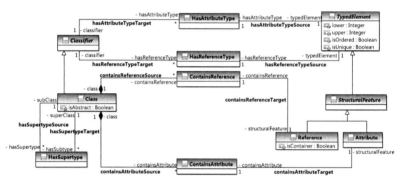

Figure 6.4. Adapted Ecore metametamodel GS^a_{Ecore} (excerpt).

In addition, the Ecore metametamodel GS_{Ecore} is adapted to make it capable of being integrated with the metamodel of OWL 2. An excerpt of the adapted Ecore metametamodel is depicted in Figure 6.4.

We adapt three parts of GS_{BEDSL}. The hasSupertype association is materialized by a new class, since it should be integrated with the SubClassOf class from the OWL 2 metamodel (1). The containsFeature association in Ecore relates entities with features. Since subsequent to an integration the relation should model domain axioms for object properties and data properties, respectively, we have to materialize the containsFeature association by two new classes ContainsReference and ContainsAttribute (2). The hasType association is materialized by two new classes, since it should be integrated with the classes for object property and data property range from the OWL 2 metamodel (3). The new classes representing the range of an Ecore feature are HasReferenceType and HasAttributeType.

With all metamodels in their adapted versions being capable of being integrated, the integration bridge object b is instantiated.

b = **new** IntegrationBridge(GS^a_{Ecore}, GS_{OWL});

2. Metamodel Union

The second part of the integration consists of a simple metamodel union, which constructs the initial integrated metamodel GS_{Int}. It contains all elements (vertex classes, edge classes, and attributes) of the two source metamodels.

```
b.metamodelUnion();
```

3. Integration Services

In the third part of the integration, several integration services are applied on the initial GS_{Int} where the integration services to be executed are intensionally based on the mapping defined in step 1. After applying the integration services on related constructs, we get a new integrated metamodel represented by GS_{Int}.

Since the integrated metamodel is complex, we present excerpts in Figures 6.5, 6.6, and 6.7 and illustrate the respective use of integration services.

Figure 6.5 depicts the integration of the Ecore constructs Metamodel, Class, and HasSupertype with the respective OWL constructs. Metamodel becomes a specialization of Ontology, since all OWL 2 constructs should be available for the design of Ecore metametamodels (1). Ecore Class and OWL Class are merged to a new vertex class called Class (2). The new class allows on the one hand for defining references and attributes, on the other hand several OWL class axioms and expressions can be applied to it. In steps (3) to (5) the concerns of HasSupertype in Ecore and SubClassOf in OWL 2 are merged. The new vertex class SubClassOf allows for defining several subclass relations between several class expressions.

```
b.specializeClasses(Metamodel, Ontology); // (1)
EntityClass=b.mergeVertexClasses(Class, Class, "Class"); // (2)
SubClassOf=b.mergeVertexClasses(HasSupertype, SubClassOf, "SubClassOf"); // (3)
hasSuperClass=b.mergeEdgeClasses(definesSuperClass, hasSupertypeTarget, "definesSuperClass"); // (4)
definesSubClass=b.mergeEdgeClasses(definesSubClass, hasSupertypeSource, "definesSubClass"); // (5)
```

Figure 6.6 depicts the integration of the Ecore construct Reference with the respective OWL constructs. Reference becomes a specialization of ObjectProperty (6). Thus, references can be involved in object property axioms and expressions. References are connected via the classes ContainsReference and HasReferenceType with Class. These relations in OWL 2 are designed by ObjectPropertyDomain and ObjectPropertyRange constructs. Hence, in steps (7) to (12), the concerns of relations between classes and references are becoming specializations of the respective constructs in OWL.

```
b.specializeClasses(Reference, ObjectProperty); // (6)
b.specializeClasses(ContainsReference, ObjectPropertyDomain); // (7)
b.specializeClasses(containsReferenceSource, definesDomainClassExpression); // (8)
b.specializeClasses(containsReferenceTarget, definesDomainObjectProperty); // (9)
b.specializeClasses(HasReferenceType, ObjectPropertyRange); // (10)
b.specializeClasses(hasReferenceTypeSource, definesRangeObjectProperty); // (11)
b.specializeClasses(hasReferenceTypeTarget, definesRangeClassExpression); // (12)
```

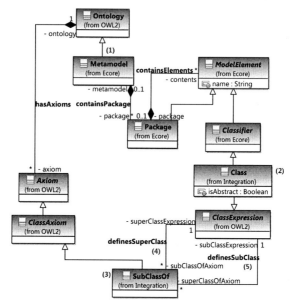

Figure 6.5. Integration of Ecore Metamodel, Class, and HasSupertype with OWL 2 constructs.

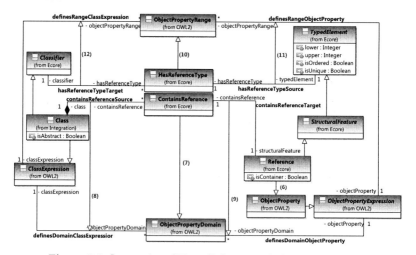

Figure 6.6. Integration of Ecore Reference with OWL 2 constructs.

Figure 6.7 depicts the integration of the Ecore constructs **Attribute** and **Datatype** with the respective OWL constructs. **Attribute** becomes a specialization of **DataProperty** (13). Thus, attributes can be involved in data property axioms and expressions. Attributes are connected via the classes **ContainsAttribute** and **HasAttributeType** with **Class**. These relations in OWL 2 are designed by **DataPropertyDomain** and **DataPropertyRange** constructs. Hence, in steps (14) to (19), the concerns of links between entity classes and references become specializations of the respective constructs in OWL. The vertex classes for data types are merged to one single class (20). Thus, data types can be used by attributes and data properties. In steps (21) to (23) the concerns of **Enumeration** and **DataOneOf** are merged. The new vertex class **DataEnumeration** allows for modeling a set of literal entries, while the vertex class **Literal** is the result of the merge of **EnumLiteral** and **Literal**. To provide only one relation between the new vertex classes **DataEnumeration** and **Literal**, the edge classes **containsLiteral** in Ecore and **containsLiteral** in OWL 2 are merged.

```
b.specializeClasses(Attribute, DataProperty); // (13)
b.specializeClasses(ContainsAttribute, DataPropertyDomain); // (14)
b.specializeClasses(containsAttributeSource, definesDataPropertyDomainClassExpression); // (15)
b.specializeClasses(containsAttributeTarget, definesDomainDataProperty); // (16)
b.specializeClasses(HasAttributeType, DataPropertyRange); // (17)
b.specializeClasses(hasAttributeTypeSource, definesRangeDataProperty); // (18)
b.specializeClasses(hasAttributeTypeTarget, definesRangeDataRange); // (19)

Datatype=b.mergeVertexClasses(Datatype, Datatype, "Datatype"); // (20)
DataEnumeration=b.mergeVertexClasses(Enumeration, DataOneOf, "DataEnumeration"); // (21)
LiteralEntry=b.mergeVertexClasses(EnumLiteral, Literal, "Literal"); // (22)
containsLiteralEntry=b.mergeEdgeClasses(containsLiteral, containsLiteral, "containsLiteral"); // (23)
```

6.2.2 Integration Use

Having an integration bridge established as described above, a language designer can create hybrid models. Hybrid models in the context of this chapter represent language metamodels with integrated OWL 2 constructs. For example, in Figure 6.8 a language designer enriches the activity diagram language metamodel from Figure 6.2 by extending the class **ActivityNode** by an additional reference called **edge**. With the pure Ecore language it is not possible to define references as transitive or as a chain of many references. Using an integrated language, a language designer declares the reference **edge** as transitive (using the keyword **transitive**) and defines that the reference **edge** is composed by a chain of the references **outgoing** and **target** (using the keyword **subPropertyChain**).

Besides OWL object property axioms and OWL object property expressions, which are adopted by Ecore references, a language designer is also able to create OWL class axioms and OWL class expressions. In Figure 6.8 he defines that the class **ActivityNode** is equivalent to a class expression, which requires, via the reference **edge**, to be connected to some **Final** node. A language designer restricts the class representing initial nodes in such a way so

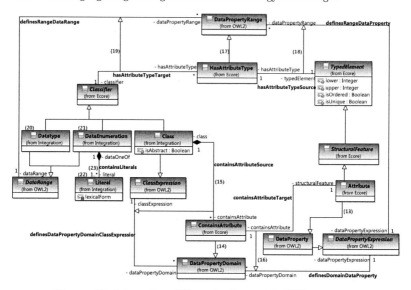

Figure 6.7. Integration of Ecore **Attribute** with OWL constructs.

that each node, which directly appears after an initial node, must have the type **Action** or **ControlNode**. Thus, no object nodes are allowed directly after the initial node. In addition, all object nodes only have incoming and outgoing object flows and control flows do not have object nodes as target or source.

As mentioned in Section 6.1.2 metamodels such as the one in Figure 6.8 allow for creating linguistic instances. All linguistic instances build a model whose elements are structured according to the prescriptive metamodel.

Since we are in a graph-based technological space, all models, especially instance models in abstract syntax, are represented as a TGraph. The structure of TGraphs is defined by its schema. We state that if a model is linguistically instantiable, it can be represented in *set notation* defined for schemas in Section 2.2.2. In set notation it describes which elements are instantiated to vertices in the model, which elements are instantiated to edges linking vertices in the model, and how vertices and edges are attributed.

The definition how a model is represented in set notation must be established separately for each metametamodel, a metamodel whose instance models in turn are instantiable. In Table 6.2 we precisely describe a service named **toSchema**, which as an input gets a hybrid model conforming to $GS_{EcoreOWL}$ and returns a graph schema defined by its set notation that allows for creating linguistic instances. The service must be established by the Ecore language designer and is implemented into the modeling environment. The language designer might rely on a mapping between concepts in the Ecore metametamodel [SBPM08] and the grUML metaschema. This mapping is presented

```
class ActivityNode subClassOf edge some Final{
    reference incoming [0−∗] : ActivityEdge oppositeOf target;
    reference outgoing [0−∗] : ActivityEdge oppositeOf source;
    attribute name : String;
    transitive reference edge [0−∗] : ActivityNode subPropertyChain outgoing o target;
}

...

class Initial subClassOf outgoing only ControlFlow { }

...

class ObjectNode subClassOf (outgoing only ObjectFlow) and (incoming only ObjectFlow) { }

...

abstract class ActivityEdge {
    reference source [1−1] : ActivityNode;
    reference target [1−1] : ActivityNode;
}

class ObjectFlow subClassOf ActivityEdge { }
class ControlFlow subClassOf ActivityEdge and (target only (not ObjectNode)) and (source only (not
    ObjectNode)) { }
```

Figure 6.8. Hybrid model representing a metamodel with integrated OWL 2-based annotations.

in [Hec10]. The toSchema service is implemented as a static method being part of the Convert class.

Name	Convert Service
Signature	Schema toSchema($GS_{EcoreOWL}$ G)
Pattern	GS=Convert.toSchema(G)
Description	converts a hybrid metamodel G (represented by a TGraph) to a graph schema GS. All classes in the hybrid metamodel G become vertex classes. All references define an edge class. The set of attributes is composed by all attributes in a hybrid metamodel G, where all possible domains provided by a graph schema are defined by datatype definitions in G.

Table 6.2. toSchema Service.

To convert a TGraph representing an Ecore-based metamodel to a new graph schema, we have to set up the graph schema by its set notation as introduced in Definitions 2 and 4.

Hence, the service sets up the following sets and archetype functions for a TGraph G and the schema GS which is returned:

- $V_{GS} = \{v \mid v \in repr_m^G(Class)\}$ defines the set of vertex classes. The function $c_{GS} : V_{GS} \to Class$ describes the archetype of the vertex classes in GS.

- $E_{GS} = \{e \mid e \in repr_m^G(Reference)\}$ defines the set of edge classes. The function $c_{GS} : E_{GS} \to Reference$ describes the archetype of the edge class in GS.
- $Attr_{GS} = \{a \mid a \in repr_m^G(Attribute)\}$ defines the set of attributes. The function $c_{GS} : Attr_{GS} \to Attribute$ describes the archetype of the attributes in GS.
- $Domain = \{d \mid d \in repr_m^G(Datatype)\}$ defines the set of all possible domains for attributes. The function $c_{GS} : Domain \to Datatype$ describes the archetype of the datatypes in GS.

$repr_m^G$ is the function which returns all instances for a given schema element and a given instance graph (cf. Appendix A.1.3). For each class in a hybrid model a vertex class to be instantiated is defined in V_{GS}. All references in the hybrid model define an edge class in E_{GS}. The set of attributes is composed by all attributes in a hybrid model, where all possible domains provided by a graph schema are defined by datatypes in the schema.

In addition to the four sets above, the service sets up the following functions and relations:

- $typeDefinition_{GS} : V_{GS} \cup E_{GS} \to (Attr_{GS} \twoheadrightarrow Domain)$
  with $(typeDefinition_{GS}(v))(a) = d$ if
  $c_{GS}(v) \to \{\mathsf{containsAttributeSource}\} \to \{\mathsf{containsAttributeTarget}\} c_{GS}(a)$
  $\to \{\mathsf{hasAttributeTypeSource}\} \to \{\mathsf{hasAttributeTypeTarget}\} c_{GS}(d)$
- $isA_{GS} : V_{GS} \cup E_{GS} \leftrightarrow V_{GS} \cup E_{GS}$ with $isA_{GS} = \{(v, w) \mid c_{GS}(v) \to \{\mathsf{hasSupertypeSource}\} \to \{\mathsf{hasSupertypeTarget} c_{GS}(w)\}\}$
- $relates_{GS} : E_{GS} \to V_{GS} \times V_{GS}$ with $relates(e) = (v, w)$ if
  $c_{GS}(v) \to \{\mathsf{containsReferenceSource}\} \to \{\mathsf{containsReferenceTarget}\}$
  $\to \{\mathsf{hasReferenceTypeSource}\} \to \{\mathsf{hasReferenceTypeTarget}\} c_{GS}(w)$.
- $multiplicity_{GS} : E_{GS} \to Multiplicity \times Multiplicity$ with $multiplicity_{GS}(e) = ((0, *), (min, max))$ and
  $min = (value(c_{GS}(e)))(\mathsf{lower})$ and $max = (value(c_{GS}(e)))(\mathsf{upper})$

The *typeDefinition* function assigns those attributes to classes, which are linked via a ContainsFeature class with the respective Class instance in the hybrid model. The domain of an attribute is defined via the sequence of hasAttributeTypeSource and hasAttributeTypeTarget edges. Specialization relations in hybrid models conforming to the metamodel $GS_{EcoreOWL}$ are only defined between two classes. All pairs connected via the HasSupertype class are related by isA. Two vertex classes are related by an edge class if they are linked via a Reference instance in the hybrid model. The multiplicities for an edge class are defined by the lower and upper attributes defined for reference vertices in the hybrid model. Because references only have multiplicities for the target end, the multiplicities for the source are set to 0 to any (0,*).

Having defined when a model is linguistically instantiable, we define a specific projection service, which projects an Ecore-based metamodel with

OWL 2 annotations and a conforming model to one ontoware model. The service is provided by the IntegrationBridge class and requires an IntegrationBridge object representing the combination of Ecore and OWL 2 as established in Section 6.2.1. The service is invoked each time, when a language user requires reasoning facilities for the current model under developmentt. The service is specified in Table 6.3.

Name	Multi-layer Projection Service
Signature	GS_{OWL} project$_{GS_{OWL}}$($GS_{EcoreOWL}$ m_h, Graph g, IntegrationBridge b)
Pattern	m_o=IntegrationBridge.project$_{GS_{OWL}}$(m_h, g, b)
Description	projects a linguistic instantiable metamodel m_h and an instance graph g to an ontoware model m_o. b is the IntegrationBridge object encapsulating the integration of GS_{Ecore}^a and GS_{OWL} and providing the projection of m_h to the TBox part of m_o. For each vertex in g, m_o is extended by an individual. For each edge e in g an object property assertion is created in m_o. For each attribute assignment a data property assertion is created in m_o.

Table 6.3. Multi-layer projection service.

Having an integration bridge object b for the integration of Ecore and OWL 2 and the projection function p_{m_h} as defined in Section 5.3.2 for each projection of a hybrid model, we are able to precisely describe the steps of building the ABox in the ontoware model m_o.

m_o is initially created by the projection service provided by b: $m_o =$ b.project$_{GS_{OWL}}$(m_h). Furthermore, a new projection function p_g : $Vertex \cup Edge \rightarrow Vertex \cup Edge$ is declared (besides p_{m_h}) for each instance model projected.

1. For each vertex v in g, m_o is extended by an individual i, which is asserted by $p_{m_h}(c_{GS}(type(v)))$ the projection of the type of v in m_h. In addition, p_g defines $v \mapsto_{p_g} i$
2. For each edge e in g an object property assertion v_{opa} is created in m_o connecting $p_g(\alpha(e))$ and $p_g(\omega(e))$, the projections of source and target vertex. The object property assertion instantiates the object property $p_{m_h}(c_{GS}(type(e)))$, the projection of the type of e in m_h. In addition, p_g is extended by $e \mapsto_{p_g} v_{opa}$
3. For each attribute assignment $(value(x))(a)$ ($x \in V \cup E$ of g, $a \in AttrId$) a data property assertion v_{dpa} is created in m_o connecting $p_g(x)$, the projection of x with the value $(value(x))(a)$. The data property assertion instantiates the data property $p_{m_h}(c_{GS}(a))$, the projection of a.

Example

Based on the metamodel depicted in Figure 6.8, we present an example of the extended projections service.

In Figure 6.9(a) a TGraph is depicted. The model it represents is visualized in Figure 6.9(b) using the concrete syntax of UML activity diagrams [OMG07b]. The TGraph is a linguistic instance of the schema converted from the metamodel in Figure 6.8. For instance, its vertices have the types Initial, Action, ControlFlow, Decision, Merge or Final. Edges in the TGraph are linguistic instances of edge classes, which in turn are converted from references. In the TGraph one edge represents the instances of two opposite references.

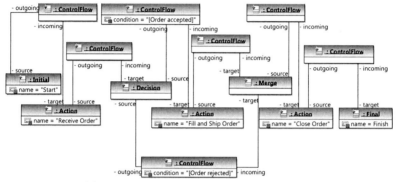

(a) Inconsistent process model in concrete syntax

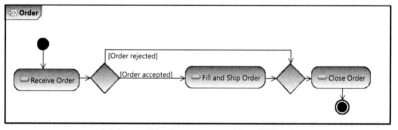

(b) Inconsistent process model as TGraph

Figure 6.9. Process models.

The projection service specified in Table 6.3 is able to project the TGraph in Figure 6.9(a) together with the hybrid metamodel in Figure 6.8 to one ontoware model. An excerpt of the ontoware model is depicted in Figure 6.10. It depicts the two axioms for restricting activity nodes and initial nodes, the declarations for object properties and also the definition of the transitive edge object property building a chain of outgoing and target. In the lower part, three individuals are created for defining the initial action, the Receive Order action, and the final action. In addition, a control flow individual connects the initial individual with that of the Receive Order action.

```
Ontology(OrderDiagram

EquivalentClasses(ActivityNode ObjectSomeValuesFrom(edge Final))

SubClassOf(Initial ObjectSomeValuesFrom(outgoing ObjectSomeValuesFrom(target ObjectUnionOf(
    ControlNode Action))))

...

Declaration(ObjectProperty(target))
Declaration(ObjectProperty(outgoing))
Declaration(ObjectProperty(source))
Declaration(ObjectProperty(incoming))

Declaration(ObjectProperty(edge))
TransitiveObjectProperty(edge)
SubObjectPropertyOf(SubObjectPropertyChain(outgoing target) edge)

Declaration(Individual(f1))
ClassAssertion(f1 Final)
DataPropertyAssertion(name f1 "Finish")

Declaration(Individual(i1))
ClassAssertion(i1 Initial)
DataPropertyAssertion(name i1 "Start")

Declaration(Individual(a1))
ClassAssertion(a1 Action)
DataPropertyAssertion(name a1 "Receive Order")

Declaration(Individual(c1))
ClassAssertion(c1 ControlFlow)
ObjectPropertyAssertion(target c1 a1)
ObjectPropertyAssertion(source c1 i1)

...
)
```

Figure 6.10. Ontoware model representing the hybrid model and the linguistic user model (excerpt).

6.3 Defining and Validating Constraints

In this section we are going to show which OWL 2-based expressions language designers are able to formulate within metamodels. All expressions are defined by an integrated ontology language and restrict the structure of user models.

User models are created by language users. They want to ensure the consistency of their models. Many works deal with inconsistency management using description logics [Van05] and the debugging of ontoware models [Kal06]. In this section we are going to present basic services for inconsistency management and guidance of user models represented as a TGraph.

6.3.1 Defining Constraints

In the following we present a set of expressions used to constrain the structure of user models. All expressions are defined by language designers in metamodels using an integrated metamodeling language. The grammar for the textual design of Ecore-based metamodels with integrated OWL 2-based annotations is given in the Appendix A.4.

Class Expressions

Classes are used to define types for instances and to prescribe instances, e.g., to be connected to other instances of a given type. For more complex types, class expressions are defined and bound to classes by using class axioms.

A class is combined with a class expression by an equivalent classes axiom, if the set of instances described by the class expression should be equal to the set of instances typed by the class. In the following example we declare the class ObjectNode as being equivalent to a class expression describing those instances, which are either of type DataStore or DataBuffer. Thus, instances are of type ObjectNode, if, and only if they are instance of DataStore or DataBuffer.

class ObjectNode **equivalentTo** DataStore **or** DataBuffer { }

In the following example, the subclass of axiom is used to state that the set of instances having the type Initial is a subset of instances having an outgoing edge. The class expression prescribes initial nodes to have at least one outgoing edge.

class Initial **subClassOf** outgoing some (ObjectFlow **or** ControlFlow) { }

Class expressions are also used to prescribe the use of attributes in instances, which can only be assigned by a given value or values of a specific datatype. In the following example, we prescribe instances of ActivityNode to have a name, which is not the empty string. The data range representing the empty string is described by a DataOneOf construct (defined by { }) and is negated by the DataComplementOf construct (defined by the not-operator). It is bound to name using the DataAllValuesFrom construct (using the only keyword).

class ActivityNode **subClassOf** name only (not {"" })

To prescribe instances of ActivityNode to have at least one name, we use the DataAllValuesFrom construct. In the following example, we define a superclass of ActivityNode representing those instances, which have a name attribute set to some string value.

class ActivityNode **subClassOf** name some String

Path- and Multiplicity Expressions

Experience shows that path expressions are a powerful means for prescribing properties of user models in practical applications [EWD+96]. In the following paragraphs, we present all basic path and multiplicity expressions, which are used to prescribe the relation between two instances in a model. All expressions are defined in a hybrid model designed by using the integrated Ecore+OWL metamodel. They can be composed to more complex path expressions.

Start- and Target-Restriction

To prescribe the type of an instance where edges of a given type start, we define a subclass of the start type. This subclass describes all instances where an edge of the given type starts. The subclass is restricted by a superclass, which describes the start type. The following example prescribes all instances where an **outgoing** edge to an object flow vertex starts to be an object node or an action. Here, the subclass axiom is used to relate two (anonymous) classes.

(outgoing **some** ObjectFlow) **subClassOf** (ObjectNode **or** Action)

To prescribe the type of an instance where an edge of a given type should end, we define a superclass, which describes those instances, which are connected via the edge only to instances of the given type. In the following example for each **target** edge, which starts at some object node, we prescribe that its target is only an object node or an action.

class ObjectFlow **subClassOf** (target **only** (ObjectNode **or** Action)) { }

Sequential Edges

To prescribe instances of a given type to be connected with a sequence of edges, the sequence is described as a superclass consisting of nested class expressions. Each class expression prescribes instances to be connected with a sequence of an **outgoing** and a **target** edge. The following example prescribes initial nodes to be connected with some activity node via a sequence of two edges.

class Initial **subClassOf** (outgoing **some** (target **some** ActivityNode)) { }

Alternative Edges

To allow instances to be connected with two alternative paths, the class expressions representing the paths are combined by the **or** operator. The example in the following allows all instances of **ObjectFlow** to be connected with some object node or alternatively with some action.

class ObjectFlow **subClassOf** ((target **some** ObjectNode) **or** (target **some** Action)) { }

Optional Edges

To prescribe instances of a given type to be connected with optional paths, a superclass is created describing the default path and the optional path using the **or** operator. In the superclass the optional edge is separated by the **or** operator. In the following example, all object nodes must have some edge to an action node, or optionally a second edge, which ends at an action node.

```
class ObjectNode subClassOf (edge some (Action or (edge some Action))) {}
```

Iterated Edges

Iterated edges are realized by object property expressions that are declared as transitive. To prescribe instances of a given type to be connected with some other instance of a specific type via a sequence of edges, a superclass is created. The superclass describes those instances, which are connected via a transitive edge with the instances of the given type. In the example, we prescribe the initial nodes to be connected via an arbitrary length of a sequence of edges with some final node, i.e., each final node must be reachable from all nodes in the diagram.

```
class Initial subClassOf edge some Final{}
```

Multiplicities

Cardinality restrictions are used to prescribe instances to be connected with a number of other instances. They are defined as class expressions, which describe those instances connected with at least (using the **min**-keyword), at most (using the **max**-keyword), or exactly (using the **exact**-keyword) a given number of instances of a given type via edges of a given type. In the following example, we define a superclass of **Final**, which restricts its instances to be connected with at least one incoming control flow.

```
class Final subClassOf incoming min 1 ControlFlow {}
```

Property Axioms

The use of references and attributes may be restricted by additional OWL 2 object and data property axioms. In the following we give two examples for references and attributes. The full list of axioms is presented in the Appendix A.4.

Axioms for References

References in metamodels may be annotated by OWL 2 axioms for object properties. The reference **edge** specified in the class **ActivityNode** is defined as transitive.

In addition, as a subproperty it has the chain of **outgoing** and **incoming** where both are also references.

```
class ActivityNode {
  ...
  transitive reference edge [0−∗] : ActivityNode subPropertyChain outgoing o target;
}
```

Axioms for Attributes

Such as the additional axioms for references, attributes specified in classes can be annotated. In the example below the attribute id is defined as functional.

```
class ActivityNode {
  ...
  functional attribute id : Integer;
}
```

6.3.2 Validating Constraints

Modeling environments should check whether models fulfill the prescription of the metamodel or not. If the models do not conform to the metamodel, language user need suggestions to where and how to repair the model. In the following we are going to present services, which allow for inconsistency management and for suggesting model elements to be used. All services are based on ontoware models, which are projections of the metamodel (with additional constraints) and a user model.

Validation in Open World and Closed Domain

The services presented in the following may be adopted on ontoware models which may be assumed in an open or closed world. In Table 6.4 we illustrate the decision when to use OWA and when to use CWA or a closed domain, respectively.

World Assumption	OWA	CWA/Closed Domain
Model State	under development	ready for deployment

Table 6.4. Use of OWA and CWA for model validation.

We differ between the states a model has in the development. If a model is under development, then all (reasoning) services applied consider an open world. Hence, facts that are missing may be assumed by default by reasoners. If a model is in a final state, i.e., it is ready for deployment, then all services are applied under closed world assumption. Hence, the model must be complete and missing facts are not assumed.

Inconsistency Detection

Syntactic consistency ensures that a specification conforms to the metamodel of the modeling language specified by the language designers. This guarantees that the model is well-formed [Van05].

Inconsistency Management

In [FST96] inconsistency management is defined as the process by which inconsistencies in software models are handled to support the goals of the stakeholders concerned. The process of inconsistency management consists of activities for *detecting*, *diagnosing*, and *handling* inconsistency [NER00].

Detecting: The detection of inconsistencies is the activity of checking for inconsistencies in user models with regard to a metamodel. Different approaches for the detection of inconsistencies are possible [SZ01]. In this work we consider a logic based approach with detecting logical inconsistency [HS05], where models together with metamodels are projected to ontoware models, and, which are consistent if an interpretation exists. Otherwise they are inconsistent.

Diagnosing: The diagnosis of inconsistencies is concerned with the identification of the elements causing an inconsistency [SZ01]. The diagnosis is a basic for inconsistency handling. Several methods are available for debugging ontoware models and identifying inconsistent parts [Kal06]. Since models specified by language users are graphs, we are going to develop a service delivering the vertices of the graph causing the inconsistency.

Handling: Inconsistency handling is concerned with identifying possible actions for dealing with an inconsistency [SZ01]. For ontoware models several repair strategies are developed [Kal06]. In the following we develop a service suggesting valid types for instances involved in an inconsistency.

All services are subsumed by an API for inconsistency management. The API consists of services for inconsistency detection, diagnosis and handling. The services are implemented as static methods in the class InconsistencyManagement.

Services for Inconsistency Management

Figure 6.11 depicts an incomplete process model (in abstract and concrete syntax). It consists of an initial node, an action node, and an object node. All nodes are connected by control flow edges. With respect to the metamodel in Figure 6.8, the model is incomplete because a final node is missing. Furthermore the model obviously contains one inconsistency in an open world, which is detected, diagnosed, and handled in the following.

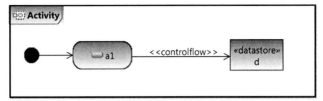

(a) Inconsistent process model in concrete syntax

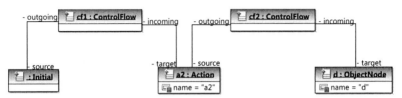

(b) Inconsistent process model as TGraph

Figure 6.11. Inconsistent process model.

Name	Inconsistency Detection Service
Signature	boolean isConsistent(Metamodel mm, TGraph g, IntegrationBridge b)
Pattern	r=InconsistencyManagement.isConsistent(mm, g, b)
Description	returns r=true if the instance model represented as a TGraph g is consistent with regard to the metamodel mm. b is the integration bridge object, which encapsulates the integration of Ecore and OWL and provides the projection service.

Table 6.5. Inconsistency detection service.

Detection. A language user who wants to detect if his model is consistent uses the consistency checking service specified in Table 6.5 provided by the inconsistency management API.

This service uses the inconsistency service specified in Table 3.7, which gets an ontoware models as input. This ontoware model is built by the projection of the hybrid metamodel and an instance model using the multi-layer projection service.

For the model in Figure 6.11 and the metamodel in Figure 6.8 the service isConsistent returns false.

Diagnosis. Having an inconsistent model such as the activity diagram in Figure 6.11(b), language users want to diagnose the inconsistency. To identify which elements of the model are involved in the inconsistency, the language users require a service, which returns a set of vertices. The service, specified in Table 6.6, reuses the explanation service for inconsistent ontoware models in Table 3.12. We assume that the metamodel is consistent and that all classes are satisfiable.

Name	Inconsistent Elements Service
Signature	Set<Set<Vertex>> getInconsistentElements(Metamodel mm, TGraph g, IntegrationBridge b)
Pattern	S=InconsistencyManagement.inconsistentVertices(mm, g, b)
Description	returns a set of sets S of vertices in the instance model g, which are involved in the inconsistency of g with respect to the metamodel mm. b is the integration bridge object, which encapsulates the integration of Ecore and OWL and provides the projection service.

Table 6.6. Inconsistent elements service.

Since an instance model can have multiple inconsistencies, the service may return multiple sets of vertices being involved in the respective inconsistency.

To compute sets of vertices leading to inconsistencies, the service in Table 6.6 uses the projection m_o of a hybrid metamodel mm and a respective instance model g achieved by the multi-layer projection service. The service uses an explanation set E for the inconsistent ontoware model m_o using the inconsistency explanation service specified in Table 3.12. For each set in E the service puts those vertices into one result set S, which occur in some construct for the given set in E.

Since the model in Figure 6.11 has just one inconsistency, the ontoware explainInconsistency service returns the following set of axioms:

```
1)
SubClassOf(ControlFlow ObjectIntersectionOf(ObjectAllValuesFrom(target ObjectComplementOf(
    ObjectNode)) ObjectAllValuesFrom(source ObjectComplementOf(ObjectNode))))

ObjectPropertyAssertion(target cf d)
ClassAssertion(cf ControlFlow)
ClassAssertion(d ObjectNode)
```

For the explanation given above, the getInconsistentElements service returns the set {cf,d}. Modeling environments may highlight these vertices in the editors to illustrate where the language users may look for problems in their models.

Handling. Several strategies for ontology debugging and repairing have been developed. A simple strategy is to analyze the sets of vertices separately. A solution for handling inconsistencies and to repair models, is to provide a set of valid types for one vertex leading to an inconsistency. Replacing the type of the given vertex by exactly one valid type leads to a consistent model. This is realized by a type suggestion service specified in Table 6.7.

To suggest valid types, the service uses the projection m_o of a hybrid metamodel mm and a respective instance model g achieved by the multi-layer projection service. For a vertex v causing an inconsistency, the service returns a named type t for v if the inconsistency in which v is involved is solved and no other inconsistencies in m_o occur.

Name	Type Suggestion Service
Signature	Set<Class> suggestType(Metamodel mm, TGraph g, Vertex v, IntegrationBridge b)
Pattern	s=InconsistencyManagement.suggestType(mm, m, v, b)
Description	returns a set s of classes from mm, which are valid types for the vertex v in g, i.e., replacing the type of v by a valid type corrects the inconsistency caused by the wrong type. b is the integration bridge object, which encapsulates the integration of Ecore and OWL and provides the projection service.

Table 6.7. Type suggestion services.

The type suggestion service applied on cf returns the valid type ObjectFlow. Applying the type suggestion service on vertex d in Figure 6.11(b) returns Action and all possible control nodes.

Further complex strategies analyze all explanation sets and for instance base on axiom rating as shown in [Kal06]. A simple strategy is to compute the frequency of an axiom. Here the number of times the axiom appears in each set of the various inconsistencies is counted. If an axiom appears in all sets for n different inconsistencies, removing or changing the axiom from the ontology ensures that n inconsistencies are repaired. Thus, the higher the frequency, the lower (better) the rank assigned to the axiom.

6.4 Related Work

In the following we are going to present related work concerning the approaches presented in Chapter 6. We separate the related approaches in two parts. The first part deals with related work in the field of prescribing the structure of user models. In the second part we consider related work concerned with services for inconsistency management and user guidance.

Among approaches with constraints to prescribe the structure of user models, one can use languages such as OCL, F-Logic or Alloy to formally describe models.

In [ABGR07] a transformation of UML class diagrams with OCL constraints [WK03] to Alloy is proposed to exploit analysis capabilities of the Alloy Analyzer [Jac06]. Compared to our work, [ABGR07] considers only one model layer in which the UML models (e.g., class diagrams) are designed. In contrast, we consider two layers (metamodel layer and instance layer) to be transformed into a logic representation. Hence, the capabilities of our approach are more language user oriented, in the sense that we provide services for problems (e.g., inconsistencies) language users have in the design of user models.

F-Logic is a further prominent rule language that combines logical formulas with object oriented and frame-based description features. Different works (e.g., [GLR+02]) have explored the usage of F-Logic to describe and validate well-formedness constraints and expressions for MOF conformant metamodels. F-Logic rules can be interpreted at both the model and instance levels. In contrast to our work, the integration cited above is achieved by transforming MOF models into a knowledge representation language. Thus, the expressiveness available for language designers is limited to MOF. Our approach extends these approaches by enabling language designers to use an integrated ontology language, to specify classes with additional integrated constraints increasing the expressiveness of the language.

Many papers are dealing with inconsistency management and assisting modeling and debugging models.

In [Van05] the detection and resolution of inconsistencies in UML models with description logics (DL) is presented. Here, UML models are translated to DL knowledge bases, which allow for querying and reasoning. Similar to our approach of linguistic metamodeling, [Van05] presents an approach for checking structural inconsistencies of UML models with regard to its metamodel. Here, the DL knowledge base ABox represents the user model where the TBox encodes the UML metamodel. In contrast to our approach, the bridge between UML and DL is established by a transformation, which precisely defines, which UML metamodel elements are translated to DL constructs. The bridge is adequate since [Van05] is dealing with the UML language only. Generally, for linguistic metamodeling and consistency checks of user models, we propose an integration bridge. The bridge allows language designers to define their own constraints embedded within an arbitrary language metamodel.

There are quite a few works in the field of assisting modeling and debugging models. For example, [CK05, CP06] deals with tool support for creating feature models. Here the prescription of valid feature configuration is based on OCL constraints [WK03]. They provide the propagation of configuration choices, auto-completion of configurations, and the debugging of incorrect configurations. [WSN+08] deals with model intelligence where existing constraint specifications in OCL [WK03] are used to query for valid endpoints of relationships in models. Such queries guide users towards correct solutions.

[MM09, MMM08] present a modeling editor for process models with syntax-based assistance. The editor provides the completion and preservation of model correctness. The syntax of the process modeling language is formally defined by graph grammars. Compared to our approach of validating and guiding user modeling, all approaches mentioned above base on a formal representation of the abstract syntax of a modeling language (either by constraint languages like OCL, graph grammars, or by description logics). But in contrast to our approaches, no integrated modeling of constraints is possible.

6.5 Conclusion

In this chapter we used the integration bridge presented in Section 5.3 and extended its projection service. We answered RQ7, asking for design of modeling languages with OWL, by presenting an integration bridge, which allows the definition of language metamodels with integrated ontology-based constraints to restrict the structure of user models. In addition to the integration bridge, metamodels as well as conforming models are projected to one ontoware model. Thus, the language specifications as well as the user models are formally and simultaneously represented by one ontoware model. Based on this formalization, different services for language users are automatically provided. As an answer for RQ8, asking for the use of ontology technologies in software modeling, we showed how language users benefit from services for inconsistency detection to localize problems in models, inconsistency diagnosis to explain problems in models, and inconsistency handling to repair models.

7

Conceptual Domain Engineering with Ontological Instantiation

Besides language engineering and use, modeling environments may support the tasks of domain engineering with ontology languages and technologies. One task of domain engineering is the design of *conceptual domain models*, which describe an application domain. Conceptual domain models are built by *domain modelers* and consist of domain instances representing objects in the real world and types classifying these instances (Challenge 4). We are going to show how to design modeling languages for the creation of conceptual domain models. We need to answer the question:

RQ9: *What are the structures of modeling languages for conceptual domain models?*

To adopt ontology technologies for conceptual domain models, we integrate the domain engineering languages with ontology languages. Based on the integrated ontology language, domain modelers are able to define ontology based expressions to describe types as well as instances in domain models. The projection of domain models delivers an ontoware model. This ontoware model is the input for several domain engineering services provided by a modeling environment to domain modelers (Challenge 3). We need to answer the question:

RQ10: *How do ontology technologies support conceptual domain modeling?*

7.1 Chapter Context

A *domain* is described by an area of knowledge or activity characterized by a set of concepts and terms understood by practitioners in that area. Such areas, for example, are network devices or order processing systems.

7.1.1 Domain Engineering

In [Cza98] the term *domain engineering* is defined as follows:

Domain Engineering is the activity of collecting, organizing, and storing past experience in building systems or parts of systems in a particular domain in the form of reusable assets (i.e., reusable work products), as well as providing an adequate means for reusing these assets (i.e., retrieval, qualification, dissemination, adaptation, assembly, etc.) when building new systems.

Domain Engineering is composed of three main processes: *Domain Analysis, Domain Design*, and *Domain Implementation*. Figure 7.1 illustrates all parts. We comment on each of the processes but in this chapter we mainly concentrate on domain analysis and the design of conceptual domain models.

Figure 7.1. Domain engineering according to [Cza98].

The objective of *domain analysis* is to select and define the domain of focus and to collect relevant domain information and to integrate this information into a coherent domain model [Cza98]. One result of the domain analysis is a *conceptual domain model*. It describes the concepts in a domain expressed in some appropriate modeling formalism (e.g., using ontology languages [Gui05] or domain-specific languages [WPSE10]).

The task of *domain design* is to develop an architecture for the systems in the domain. *Domain implementation* follows after domain design. During domain implementation several appropriate technologies to implement components are applied.

7.1.2 Ontological Metamodeling

In this chapter we consider special kinds of models, namely *conceptual domain models*, which describe the concepts of an existing or new application domain. The conceptual domain model consists of both domain instances and domain types, which classify the instances.

In contrast to linguistic instances (cf. Section 6.1.2) domain instances in conceptual domain models are so-called *ontological instances* of domain types. The hasType relation between domain instances and domain types is the *ontological instantiation relation*, which in contrast to the linguistic instanceOf relation lies in one model. Within one conceptual domain model, domain types and domain instances are subsumed in layers, respectively. These layers are called *ontological layers*.

Conceptual domain models are used in the domain analysis to describe the problem domain a software system should support. Hence, conceptual domain models are of descriptive nature. A schematic conceptual domain model is depicted in the left column of Figure 7.2. It consists of domain instances, which describe the system instances in the real world. All domain instances and their relations build the ontological O1 layer, which is part of the conceptual domain model. To classify domain instances, domain modelers define domain types lying in the ontological O2 layer.

A conceptualization of the domain is represented by the O2 layer. The design of a domain specific language inevitably requires conceptual domain modeling. The derivation of a metamodel for a new modeling language is a way to interpret the type layer in a domain model into a suitable form that possesses pragmatic values [AZW06].

While the problem space is used to analyze a domain, the solution space is responsible for the design of new system models representing systems from the domain. The main differences to conceptual models are that they are prescriptive, i.e., they prescribe the design of a system. Metamodels prescribe the structure of models representing a system (cf. Section 6.1.2).

In software product line engineering, domain modelers identify the domain types for given domain instances, language designers formalize them for a new modeling language and application engineers (language users) use modeling language to create models describing products within the domain [WL99].

In general a new language metamodel prescribes the structure of further models describing system instances within the same domain.

For conceptual domain modeling, ontology languages are often considered since they support the distinction between type and instance layer within one model. Since domain modelers may not be experienced in the use of ontology languages, they require domain-specific languages to describe conceptual domain models with concepts and notations they are familiar with.

Figure 7.3 depicts an extended BEDSL model (a model of the business entity domain-specific language (BEDSL) which consists of a type and an instance layer. The new language BEDSL+DE provides the capability for domain analysis. In the type layer of the model in Figure 7.3 the entities Cisco, CiscoConfiguration, CiscoSlot, CiscoCard, HotSwappableOSM, and Supervisor are defined. In the instance layer the domain instances cisco7603, ciscoConfiguration7603, cisco7604, slot1, supervisor720, and supervisor360 are defined.

Since a conceptual domain model consists of both domain instances and domain types, instances can be classified by domain types via an explicit *hasType* relation. In Figure 7.3, ciscoConfiguration7603 and slot1 are connected via the hasType relation with the respective entities classifying them. In addition instances are linked with each other using references.

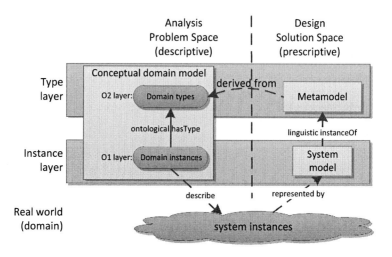

Figure 7.2. Relation between conceptual domain models and metamodels.

In [AK03], Atkinson and Kühne describe the capability of infrastructures for model-driven engineering. One capability is to dynamically extend the set of domain types available for describing the domain instances in the conceptual domain model (for instance by introducing a new domain type, e.g., **Netgear**). This requires the capability to define new types of instances. Atkinson and Kühne refer to this as *ontological metamodeling* because it is concerned with the description of concepts that exist in a certain domain and have different properties.

7.1.3 Chapter Road Map

Figure 7.4 represents the road map belonging to this chapter. In Section 7.2 we show how modeling languages must be extended to provide ontological metamodeling. We present a generic extension for metamodels, which allows for describing ontological instances and which must be integrated with that of a (domain-specific) modeling language. In Section 7.3 we describe how to integrate the OWL 2 ontology language with modeling languages providing ontological metamodeling. The integrated ontology language allows for the creation of hybrid models with descriptive expressions enriching a conceptual domain model. Based on the underlying model-theoretic semantics of conceptual domain models, different services are provided. The expressions are presented in Section 7.4.1 and the services are presented in Section 7.4.2.

Section 7.5 concludes this chapter by presenting related work in the field of conceptual domain modeling.

```
model DeviceModel {
  // ontological domain type layer
  entity Cisco {
    reference hasConfiguration : CiscoConfiguration;
  }

  entity CiscoConfiguration {
      reference hasSlot : CiscoSlot;
  }

  entity CiscoSlot {
    reference hasCard : CiscoCard;
  }

  entity CiscoCard { }

  entity HotSwappableOSM specializes CiscoCard { }

  entity Supervisor { }


  // ontological domain instance layer
  instance cicso7603{
    hasConfiguration ciscoConfiguration7603;
  }

  instance cisco7604 { }

  instance ciscoConfiguration7603 hasType CiscoConfiguration{
      hasSlot slot1;
  }

  instance slot1 hasType CiscoSlot {
    hasCard supervisor360;
  }

  instance supervisor720 { }

  instance supervisor360 { }
}
```

Figure 7.3. Device conceptual domain model.

7.2 Extending Modeling Languages for Ontological Metamodeling

In this section we are going to show how to extend modeling languages with the capability for designing conceptual domain models.

In particular we show how to extend the modeling language BEDSL (the business entity domain-specific language presented in Section 5.1) to allow the description of domain types and instances in conceptual domain models such as the one shown in Figure 7.3.

To extend modeling languages with the capability for designing conceptual domain models, the metamodel of a modeling language is integrated with a generic metamodel for modeling ontological instances.

Figure 7.5 depicts the generic metamodel extension, which is represented by the graph schema GS_{DE}. Since we are in a graph-based technological space

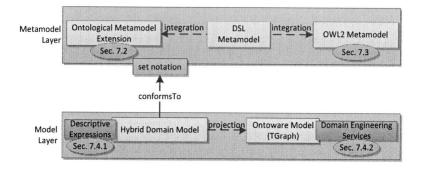

Figure 7.4. Road map of Chapter 7.

ontological instances are structured as a directed graph. The metamodel allows for describing ontological instances. They are connected by links and have attributes assigned by a given value.

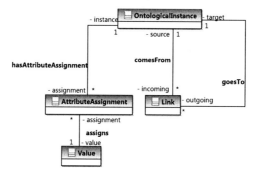

Figure 7.5. Metamodel extension GS_{DE} for languages with ontological instantiation.

To extend BEDSL with the capability for describing BEDSL models consisting of entities and ontological instances, the BEDSL metamodel GS_{BEDSL} is integrated with the metamodel GS_{DE} using the integration bridge.

In particular, the **associateClasses** service (cf. Table 5.8) is used by the language designer to create three designated associations:

hasInstanceType: The association **hasInstanceType** allows for defining the *has-Type* relation between a domain instance and an entity in a BEDSL+DE model. Each instance has optionally one to many entities as domain types.

hasLinkType: The association **hasLinkType** allows for defining the *hasType* relation between a link and a reference in a BEDSL+DE model. Each link has exactly one reference as type.

hasAttributeType: The association **hasAttributeType** allows for defining the *hasType* relation between an attribute assignment and an attribute in a BEDSL+DE model. Each attribute assignment has exactly one attribute as type.

Figure 7.6 depicts an excerpt of the metamodel for the new BEDSL+DE language represented by the graph schema $GS_{BEDSL+DE}$. It allows for modeling explicit ontological instantiation relationships between instances and entities, links and references, and attribute assignments and attributes, respectively.

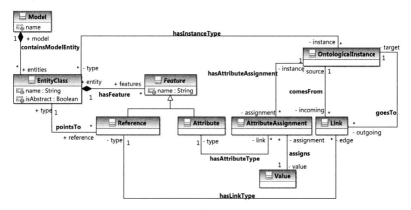

Figure 7.6. BEDSL+DE metamodel.

7.3 Integrating Ontological Metamodeling with Ontology Languages

In this section we are going to show how to bridge ontology languages with modeling languages allowing the design of conceptual domain models with two ontological layer. We are going to show how to integrate a modeling language for ontological metamodeling with the OWL 2 metamodel. We exemplify the integration by bridging the new BEDSL+DE language with OWL 2.

7.3.1 Integration Definition

The integration of BEDSL+DE with OWL 2 is an extension of the one presented in Section 5.3.1. We present the integration in three steps as introduced in Section 5.3.

1. Mapping and Adaptation

The first step in the establishment of an integration bridge is a *mapping* where language designers intensionally relate corresponding constructs of the two languages to be integrated.

As mentioned the integration of BEDSL+DE and OWL 2 depends on the one already shown in Section 5.3.1. Table 7.1 is an extension of Table 5.2 (which relates BEDSL with OWL 2).

♯	BEDSL+DE	OWL 2
1.	OntologicalInstance	Individual
2.	Link	ObjectPropertyAssertion
3.	AttributeAssignment	DataPropertyAssertion
4.	Value	Literal

Table 7.1. Mapping of BEDSL+DE and OWL 2 (extension for Table 5.2).

As shown in Section 5.3.1 we use the adaptation of GS_{BEDSL} to be capable of being integrated with GS_{OWL}. In addition to the adaptations in Section 5.3.1, the relation hasInstanceType in $GS_{BEDSL+DE}$ is materialized by a separate class, because the type relation in OWL 2 is represented as an own class (ClassAssertion) as well.

The adapted metamodel of the new variant of BEDSL is represented by the graph schema $GS^a_{BEDSL+DE}$. Together with GS_{OWL} it is put into the integration bridge constructor specified in Table 5.3.

b = **new** IntegrationBridge($GS^a_{BEDSL+DE}$, GS_{OWL});

b is the new integration bridge object, which encapsulates all metamodels to be integrated and provides the respective services.

2. Metamodel Union

The second part of the integration consists of a simple metamodel union, which constructs the initial integrated metamodel GS_{Int}. It contains all elements (vertex classes, edge classes, attributes) of the two source metamodels $GS^a_{BEDSL+DE}$ and GS_{OWL}.

b.metamodelUnion();

3. Integration Services

Since in Section 5.3.1 all integrations of BEDSL constructs with OWL 2 constructs are given, we are going to show how to integrate the additional BEDSL+DE constructs for instance modeling with the constructs of the ontology language OWL 2. To do this we use the integration bridge object **b**, which already encapsulates the integration of the BEDSL language constructs with OWL 2 constructs as described in Section 5.3.1.

In the following we describe the integration of the BEDSL constructs for defining instantiations of entities with the corresponding constructs OWL 2 provides. OntologicalInstance becomes a specialization of Individual. Both classes are used to represent instances in BEDSL models and ontoware models, respectively. HasInstanceType and ClassAssertion are combined using a specialization relationship, since both classes are used to define the instantiation of an Entity to an instance and a ClassExpression to an individual, respectively. In Step 27 and 28 the associations linking the above mentioned concepts are integrated.

```
b.specializeClasses(OntologicalInstance, Individual) // (25)
b.specializeClasses(HasInstanceType, ClassAssertion) // (26)
b.specializeClasses(instantiatesEntity, instantiates); // (27)
b.specializeClasses(types, asserts); // (28)
```

Figure 7.7 illustrates the integration steps presented in the listing above by showing the correspondent excerpt of GS_{Int}.

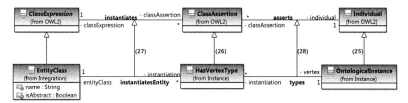

Figure 7.7. Part of GS_{Int} relevant for the instantiation of EntityClasses.

The next use of integration services builds the integration of the BEDSL+DE constructs for defining instantiations of references with corresponding OWL 2 constructs. In particular, BEDSL+DE Link becomes a specialization of OWL 2 ObjectPropertyAssertion. Both describe the relation between two instances with respect to some object property or reference, respectively. In steps 30 to 32 the concerns of the associations connecting Link and ObjectPropertyAssertion with OntologicalInstance and Individual, and Reference and ObjectPropertyExpression, respectively, are integrated.

```
b.specializeClasses(Link, ObjectPropertyAssertion); // (29)
b.specializeClasses(comesFrom, definesSource); // (30)
b.specializeClasses(goesTo, definesTarget); // (31)
b.specializeClasses(hasLinkType, hasProperty); // (32)
```

Figure 7.8 illustrates the integration steps presented in the listing above by showing the correspondent part of GS_{Int}.

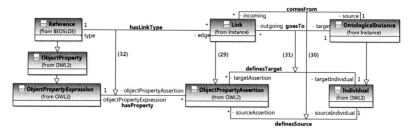

Figure 7.8. Part of GS_{Int} relevant for the instantiation of **References**.

The next listing describes the integration of the BEDSL+DE constructs for defining instantiations of attributes with corresponding OWL 2 constructs for defining data property assertions. In particular, BEDSL+DE Value becomes a specialization of OWL 2 Literal. Both describe an atomic value. The attributes describing the value are merged in step 34. BEDSL+DE Attribute-Assignment becomes a specialization of OWL 2 DataPropertyAssertion. Both describe the relation between one instance and a literal value with respect to some data property or attribute, respectively. In steps 36 to 38 the concerns of the associations connecting AttributeAssignment and DataPropertyAssertion with OntologicalInstance and Individual, and Attribute and DataPropertyExpression, respectively, are integrated.

```
b.specializeClasses(Value, LiteralEntry); // (33)
b.mergeAttributes(value, lexicalForm, "lexicalValue"); // (34)
b.specializeClasses(AttributeAssignment, DataPropertyAssertion); // (35)
b.specializeClasses(hasAttributeAssignment, definesSourceIndividual); // (36)
b.specializeClasses(assigns, definesTargetLiteral); // (37)
b.specializeClasses(hasAttributeType, hasDataProperty) // (38)
```

Figure 7.9 illustrates the integration steps in the listing above by presenting the corresponding part of GS_{Int}.

7.3.2 Integration Use

The integrated metamodel (partially depicted in Figures 5.7, 5.8, 5.9, 7.7, 7.8, and 7.9) allows for describing models such as the one shown in Figure 7.3. In addition, after the integration with GS_{OWL}, it allows for defining OWL 2-based expressions and axioms in BEDSL+DE models.

Figure 7.10 shows an excerpt of a conceptual domain model, which is enriched by OWL 2-based expressions. It is a hybrid conceptual domain model and conforms to GS_{Int}.

A feature of the integration bridge is its projection of hybrid models to ontoware models. In Table 5.12 we specified the projection service, which got

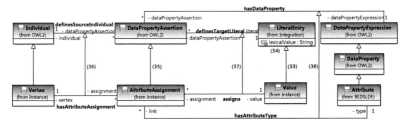

Figure 7.9. Part of GS_{Int} relevant for the instantiation **Attribute** and **AttributeAssignment**.

```
model DeviceModel {
    entity Cisco equivalentTo hasConfiguration only CiscoConfiguration{
        reference hasConfiguration : CiscoConfiguration;
    }

    entity CiscoConfiguration equivalentTo hasSlot some CiscoSlot{
        reference hasCiscoSlot : CiscoSlot;
    }

    entity CiscoSlot {
    }

    instance cisco7603 hasType Cisco {
        hasConfiguration ciscoConfiguration7603;
    }

    instance ciscoConfiguration7603 hasType CiscoConfiguration {
    }
}
```

Figure 7.10. Hybrid conceptual domain model (excerpt).

as input a hybrid model conforming to GS_{Int} and projects it to an ontoware model. Since all instantiation constructs are integrated with corresponding OWL 2 constructs, the projection service allows for interpreting ontological instances in hybrid models and projects them to individuals in the ontoware model. In addition, instantiations of entities, references, and attributes are projected to OWL 2 class assertions, object property assertions, and data property assertions, respectively. In Figure 7.11 we exemplify the projection of the hybrid conceptual domain model in Figure 7.10.

7.4 Expressions and Services for Ontological Metamodeling

Besides the explicit *hasType* relation between a domain instance and a named type, in Section 7.4.1 we also explain how to define anonymous types and expressions covering type and instance layer. In Section 7.4.2 we present a set

```
Ontology(DeviceModel

Declaration(Class(Cisco))
EquivalentClasses(Cisco ObjectAllValuesFrom(hasConfiguration CiscoConfiguration))

Declaration(Class(CiscoConfiguration))
EquivalentClasses(CiscoConfiguration ObjectSomeValuesFrom(hasSlot CiscoSlot))

Declaration(Class(CiscoSlot))

Declaration(ObjectProperty(hasCiscoSlot))

Declaration(ObjectProperty(hasConfiguration))

Declaration(Individual(cisco7603))
ClassAssertion(cisco7603 Cisco)
ObjectPropertyAssertion(hasConfiguration cisco7603 ciscoConfiguration7603)

Declaration(Individual(ciscoConfiguration7603))
ClassAssertion(ciscoConfiguration7603 CiscoConfiguration)
)
```

Figure 7.11. Ontoware model being the projection of the domain model in Figure 7.10.

of services that are used by domain modelers to validate conceptual domain models and to retrieve implicit domain information.

7.4.1 Expressions for Domain Instances and Domain Types

Domain analysis is an iterative process. Domain instances are represented in conceptual domain models and are classified by domain types. At the beginning of domain engineering, the conceptual domain models are incomplete because either instances are still not modeled or domain types and relations are missing.

Anonymous Types of Domain Instances

If the set of domain types in conceptual domain models is incomplete, domain modelers use OWL 2-based class expressions (representing anonymous types) to assert existing domain instances. In the following example the instance cisco7604 has an anonymous domain type describing those instances, which have a configuration with a Supervisor card plugged into some slot.

```
instance cisco7604 hasType hasConfiguration some (hasSlot some (hasCard some Supervisor)) {
}
```

Class Expressions for Domain Types

To restrict domain types in conceptual domain models, domain modelers use class axioms. Class axioms are used to link a domain type with a class expression, which restricts the instances of the domain type. In the following example the entity Cisco is defined as being equivalent with a class expression. It restricts all domain instances of Cisco to be linked with a configuration, which via hasSlot has a Supervisor card.

```
entity Cisco equivalentTo hasConfiguration some (CiscoConfiguration and hasSlot some (Slot and hasCard
    some Supervisor)) {
  reference hasConfiguration : CiscoConfiguration;
}
```

Expressions Covering Different Layers

Domain modelers are able to model type and instance layers within one conceptual domain model. They need to model expressions covering both layers.

In the following example the entity Supervisor, which is a domain type, is defined as being equivalent with the two instances supervisor720 and supervisor360.

```
entity Supervisor equivalentTo {supervisor720, supervisor360} {
}
```

The following instance definition gives an example of an incomplete conceptual domain model. Let us assume that the instances for the configuration and the slots are missing in the conceptual domain model. A domain modeler just describes the link of the instance cisco7603 to the instance supervisor720 as a type. The type represented as an anonymous class expression describes those instances, which are linked via the chain of hasConfiguration, hasSlot, and hasCard with the instance supervisor720.

```
instance cicso7603 hasType hasConfiguration some (hasSlot some (hasCard some {supervisor720})) {
}
```

7.4.2 Services for Domain Analysis

Domain modelers use services to validate conceptual domain models and to retrieve implicit information. These services are adopted on conceptual domain models conforming to the metamodel of the BEDSL+DE+OWL language designed in Section 7.3. All services we are going to present in the following are part of the ConceptualDomainEngineering class. All services require as an input an IntegrationBridge object, which encapsulates the integrated metamodel $GS_{BEDSL+DE+OWL}$ and which provides the projection service to project models to ontoware models.

Domain Instance Classification

During the description of the domain there are instances existing in the conceptual domain model without any domain type. Domain modelers require the automatic classification of these instances to get their possible types.

The service specified in Table 7.2 allows for determining of the domain types that a domain instance has in a conceptual domain model conforming to $GS_{BEDSL+DE+OWL}$.

Name	getDomainTypes Service
Signature	Set<EntityClass> getDomainTypes(Model m, OntologicalInstance i, IntegrationBridge b)
Pattern	S=ConceptualDomainEngineering.getDomainTypes(m, i, b)
Description	returns the set S of named domain types, which classify the domain instance i in the hybrid conceptual domain model m.

Table 7.2. getDomainTypes service.

The service uses the projection of m to an ontoware model m_o and the classification service in Table 3.9 to find all OWL classes describing some individual i_v (where i_v is the projection of the instance i). For example, the instance cisco7603 in Figure 7.3 together with the descriptions in Section 7.4.1 is classified as Cisco.

Domain Consistency Checking

Domain modelers may want to check the consistency of domain instances with regard to their domain types. This ensures a correct domain description. The domain consistency service is presented in Table 7.3.

Name	Domain Consistency Service
Signature	boolean isConsistent(Model m, IntegrationBridge b)
Pattern	r=ConceptualDomainEngineering.isConsistent(m, b)
Description	returns true if the domain instances in m are consistent with respect to their domain types.

Table 7.3. Domain consistency service.

The service uses the projection of m to an ontoware model m_o and the consistency checking service in Table 3.7 to compute the consistency of m_o. For example, the instance cisco7605 (in a closed domain) as shown below, which is directly linked via hasCard to the card supervisor720, leads to an inconsistency in a conceptual domain model, because the Cisco device cannot directly be linked with cards.

```
instance cisco7605 {
  hasCard supervisor720;
}
```

Domain Type Satisfiability Checking

Besides consistency of domain instances with regard to their types, domain modelers may also want to check the satisfiability of domain types. This ensures that domain types are instantiable.

In Table 7.4 the service for checking the satisfiability of a domain type is specified.

Name	Domain Satisfiability Service
Signature	boolean isSatisfiable(Model m, ClassExpression c, IntegrationBridge b)
Pattern	b=ConceptualDomainEngineering.isSatisfiable(m, c, b)
Description	returns true if the class expression c in m is satisfiable.

Table 7.4. Domain satisfiability service.

The service uses the projection of m to an ontoware model m_o and the satisfiability checking service in Table 3.8 for c_e in m_o (where c_e is the projection of the entity e) For example, the entity Cisco defined in the following is recognized as not being satisfiable by the service, because on the one hand it must have a CiscoConfiguration, on the other hand it cannot have such configuration.

```
entity Cisco equivalentTo (hasConfiguration only CiscoConfiguration) and not(hasConfiguration only
    CiscoConfiguration) {
  reference hasConfiguration : CiscoConfiguration;
}
```

Domain Instance Retrieval

Domain modelers may want to retrieve domain instances fulfilling a given type description. The service specified in Table 7.5 returns a set of instances, which are described by a given class expression.

Name	Domain Instance Retrieval Service
Signature	Set<OntologicalInstance> retrieveDomainInstances(Model m, ClassExpression c, IntegrationBridge b)
Pattern	S=ConceptualDomainEngineering.retrieveDomainInstances(m, c, b)
Description	returns the set of domain instances that are classified by the class expression c.

Table 7.5. Domain instance retrieval service.

The instance retrieval service uses the projection of m to an ontoware model m_o and puts all instances into the set if their projection is classified by the class expression. The following class expression used to retrieve instances returns those, which are linked via the chain of hasConfiguration, hasSlot, and hasCard with the domain instance supervisor720. For the examples given above, the retrieval service returns the instance cisco7603.

---

hasConfiguration **some** (hasSlot **some** (hasCard **some** {supervisor720}))

7.5 Related Work

In the following we compare the approaches presented in this chapter with related work. We depict related work on foundations of infrastructures for model-driven engineering. In addition we give some related work, which deals with ontological metamodeling.

Already in 2003, Atkinson and Kühne defined requirements of model-driven development infrastructures. Besides requirements for defining abstract syntax, concrete syntax and semantics within the infrastructure, they suggest to consider the dimensions of language engineering and domain engineering [AK03]. As proposed in [AK03] we provide the facility to build types and instances at the same model layer and thus allow for dynamically extending the set of domain types available for modeling.

In [LK09] a metamodeling language is presented, which allows for building ontological theories as a base for modeling languages from the philosophical point of view. The metametamodel consists of elements for individuals and universals (types) and in addition provides a textual concrete syntax. In addition to this approach, we provide formal semantics in particular for the *hasType* relation, since the metamodel elements are integrated with the OWL 2 metamodel.

In [GOS07] an ontological metamodel extension for generative architectures (OMEGA) is described as an extension to the MOF 1.4 metamodel that allows for ontological metamodeling. The core addition to the original MOF model is the introduction of concepts for *MetaElement* and *Instance*, which form the basis for all instantiations. In fact, the *hasType* relation between instances and meta-elements is implemented by a simple UML association, which does not provide any semantics to further tools.

7.6 Conclusion

In this chapter we presented an approach to support conceptual domain modeling with ontology technologies. We answered RQ 9 and RQ 10, asking for the structure of languages for conceptual domain modeling and how to combine them with ontology languages. Therefore, we first had to define which modeling languages allow for conceptual domain modeling. We presented a generic approach for extending class-based modeling languages to support the definition of types and their instances within one conceptual domain model. To support conceptual domain modeling by ontology technologies, we used the integration bridge to allow the design of conceptual domain models together with ontology-based descriptions of types and instances. Based on the formal representation of projected conceptual domain models by ontoware models, several services are provided for validating and supporting conceptual domain modeling.

Part IV

Applications

8
Domain-Specific Modeling Environments

Modeling environments play an important role in domain-specific development. These environments support the design and use of domain-specific languages.

In this chapter we report on an application of the integration bridge presented in Section 6.2. We illustrate the use of ontology technologies to describe DSLs for *network device series*. The formal semantics of OWL 2 together with reasoning services allow for addressing (1) constraint definition, (2) suggestions, and (3) debugging. Based on a scenario provided by the Polish IT company *Comarch*, we show how to design metamodels for domain-specific languages where additional constraints and semantics of the languages are formulated by integrated ontology-based annotations. We are going to answer the question:

RQ11: *How do ontology technologies support the design and use of domain-specific modeling languages?*

8.1 Chapter Context

As introduced in Section 2.2.1 and 2.2.2 all models are formally represented by a TGraph and all metamodels are formally represented by a graph schema.

8.1.1 Reused and Adopted Technologies and Approaches

The metamodeling languages considered in this chapter are used in an integrated manner together with the ontology language OWL 2. Therefore, we rely on the integration bridge introduced in Section 5.3 and its extension for linguistically instantiable models presented in Section 6.2. The integration bridge provides a mechanism to project metamodels with ontology-based annotations plus conforming instance models to one ontoware model. Metamodels are defined using the Ecore+OWL language. The language allows for defining Ecore-based metamodels, which may have ontology-based annotations as presented in Section 6.3.1. For the debugging of domain models we rely on the services for inconsistency management in Section 6.3.2.

8.1.2 Chapter Road Map

Figure 8.1 depicts the road map belonging to this chapter. In Section 8.2 we present a case study where network device series are designed by language users. They use a domain-specific language to describe a device series in a domain model. Language users rely on a DSL whose metamodel is presented in Section 8.3. To design a metamodel with integrated ontology-based restrictions and axioms, we use the Ecore+OWL metamodeling language (cf. Section 6.2.1). Given an ontoware model being the projection of metamodel and domain model we illustrate how to support domain modeling with ontology technologies in Section 8.4.

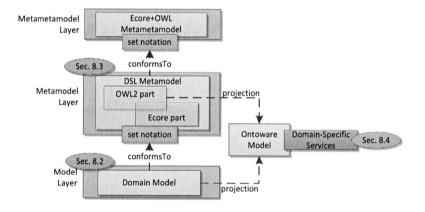

Figure 8.1. Road map of Chapter 8.

8.2 Case Study

Domain-specific languages (DSLs) are used to model and develop systems of a specific application domain. Such languages are high-level and provide abstractions and notations for better understanding and the easier modeling of applications in a special domain. A variety of different domain-specific languages are used to develop one large software system. Each DSL focuses on different problem domains and as far as possible on automatic code generation [KT07].

Domain-specific languages are designed by *DSL designers*. The developed DSL is used by the *domain experts* to build domain models describing the domain of a software system. The domain models they create are represented in a visual concrete syntax.

In the scenario we detect goals, which are related to the design and use of domain-specific languages and to the challenges presented in Section 1.1.3. Goals in this section capture the various objectives for the design and use of DSLs a modeling environment should target [vL01].

8.2.1 Scenario

Comarch[1], one of the industrial partners in the *MOST project*[2], has provided the scenario for domain-specific modeling. The company is specialized in designing, implementing and integrating IT solutions and services for *operations support system* (OSS) used by telecommunication providers [Com11]. For software development, Comarch uses model-driven methods with different kinds of domain-specific languages being deployed during the modeling process.

Comarch develops a domain-specific language to model *series of physical network devices*. For example, the *Cisco 7600 series* is a series of large network routers designed and manufactured by *Cisco Systems*[3]. Figure 8.2.1 depicts three possible routers of the Cisco 7600 series. The general structure of all devices of every series consists of a bay, which has a number of shelves. A shelf contains slots into which cards can be plugged. For example, the router *Cisco 7609* in the middle of Figure 8.2.1 has 9 slots of which all are allocated. Logically, a shelf with its possible slots and cards is stored as a configuration. In general, a series is represented by a *device type* and describes a set of network routers. A *device series* is described by a specific *configuration type*. Each configuration type requires a set of specific *card types* plugged into an appropriate slot type.

DSL designers at Comarch design a DSL to model different device types (e.g., to model the type of the Cisco 7600 series). The goal of DSL designers is to formally describe the logical structures of the configuration types. (Goal 1).

Figures 8.3 to 8.7 depict five steps of the development of the configuration type for the Cisco 7600 series. We have chosen a graphical concrete syntax, which is taken from the MOST workbench. The MOST workbench (cf. Section 10.1.4) implements the support of domain modeling with ontology technologies. The graphical syntax consists of shapes, which represent elements in domain models. These elements are instances of classes in the metamodel. The name of the class, which is instantiated, is mentioned within the model element.

---

[1] http://www.comarch.com/

[2] http://www.most-project.eu/

[3] http://www.cisco.com/

Figure 8.2. Devices of the Cisco 7600 Series [Cis04].

Firstly (step 1, Figure 8.3), the domain expert starts with an instance of the general concept DeviceType representing a device series. All devices of the Cisco 7600 series require at least one configuration. Thus he plugs in a ConfigurationType element into the device.

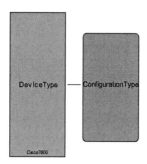

Figure 8.3. Step 1: Creating initial domain model for a new device type.

In step 2 (Figure 8.4) the domain expert adds exactly three slot types to the configuration type for the Cisco series. At this point the domain expert verifies whether the configuration satisfies the DSL restrictions. Although the domain model is incomplete, it is not inconsistent. Thus queries against it are possible asking if the domain model consists of at least one configuration with at least one slot.

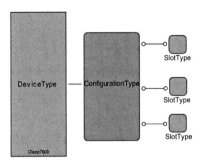

Figure 8.4. Step 2: Adding slots to the configuration.

After adding three slot types to the configuration type, the domain expert plugs in some card types to complete the end product (step 3, Figure 8.5). He inserts two **LineCards** (which represent the type of cards for port connectivity and service modules) and one **PortAdapter** (which represent the type of cards to enable services for voice, video and data transfer). At this point the domain expert wants to check the consistency of his configuration type by invoking the corresponding functionality. In the example, the domain model in step 3 (cf. Figure 8.5) is inconsistent because the mandatory processor card type is missing. The domain expert requires debugging support and needs an explanation why his model is inconsistent and how to correct it (Goal 3).

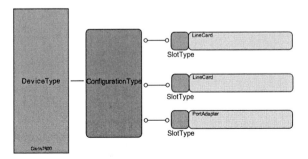

Figure 8.5. Step 3: Plugging card types into slots and checking the consistency.

In step 4 (cf. Figure 8.6) an explanation service would explain that every device type requires some **Processor** card to control the device and that one of the three card types must be replaced by it (Goal 2).

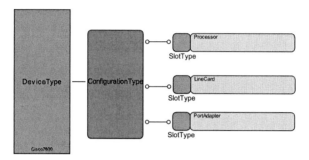

Figure 8.6. Step 4: Repairing the domain model.

The DSL defines the knowledge to which special types of cards are required and allowed by a specific configuration. Having the information that a configuration type in step 5 (cf. Figure 8.7) is connected with three slots in which some **Processor** and at least some **LineCard** or **PortAdapter** is plugged in, the refinement of the **Configuration** type to the more specific type **WANConfiguration** is recommended to the domain expert (Goal 2) by the environment. Since it was inferred that the device type has a **WANConfiguration**, in *step 5*, the recommendation service also suggests to change the type of the **Device** element to the more specific type **InternetRouter**.

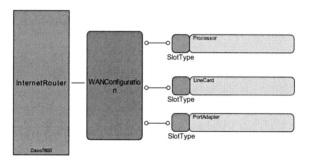

Figure 8.7. Step 5: Automatic classification of domain model elements.

8.2.2 Goals and Relations to Challenges

We concentrate on the goals derived from the scenario and relate them to the challenges presented in Section 1.1.3. The should be targeted by domain-specific modeling environments and are classified with regard to the two actors concerned: DSL designer and domain expert. First of all we will present the DSL designer's goals:

1. **Constraints and Semantics Definition:** The DSL development environment should allow for defining seamlessly integrated constraints over the DSL metamodel. DSL designers have to define formal semantics of the DSL and constraints, which elements in domain models have to fulfill. Related challenges: 1, 2

   The following goals concern the domain expert:

2. **Suggestions for suitable domain concepts:** Domain experts need suggestions for domain concepts to be used because they may not be familiar with all concepts the DSL provides. Domain experts normally commence modeling with generic concepts such as DeviceType or ConfigurationType (especially if they are first-time users of the DSL). The environment suggests the refinement of elements to the most suitable ones such as WAN-Configuration or InternetRouter (step 5). Such classifications together with explanations help novice domain experts to understand how to work with the DSL. Related challenge: 3

3. **Debugging:** Domain experts debug their domain models to find errors they may contain and to get an explanation on how to correct the model. They would like have information about any consequences of applying given domain constructs. In the scenario, domain experts want to know whether they have to replace the LineCard card type with a Processor card type (step 3). Related challenge: 3

Goal 1 exemplifies Challenge 1 and 2. To support the definition of constraints and semantics an appropriate language must be considered and bridged with languages DSL designers are familiar with. To offer suggestion and debugging services, the modeling environment for domain experts must provide appropriate services. These three goals are related to Challenge 3.

8.3 Application of Bridging Approaches

Modeling environments at Comarch are based on the tool-ready and reusable implementation of Ecore [SBPM08]. Most of the DSL metamodels at Comarch are defined by the Ecore metamodeling language [MK08, KMS09]. To support the aforementioned goals and to be compatible with existing tools, we propose to build a modeling environment, which provides an integration of the Ecore language [SBPM08] and the OWL 2 language (cf. Section 3.3.1).

DSL designers define the abstract syntax of a domain-specific language by designing a metamodel. They require a concrete syntax to model the metamodels together with embedded constraints.

8.3.1 Integration Definition

The integration of Ecore and OWL 2 is presented in Section 6.2.1. The result is an integrated metametamodel describing the abstract syntax of a language to define new language metamodels with seamlessly embedded OWL annotations.

The integrated metametamodel is presented in Figures 6.5, 6.6, and 6.7. Table 8.1 gives an overview of the constructs being integrated.

♯	Ecore	OWL 2
1.	Metamodel	Ontology
2.	Class	Class
3.	Datatype	Datatype
4.	Reference	ObjectProperty
5.	Attribute	DataProperty
6.	Enumeration	DataOneOf
7.	Literal	Literal
8.	hasSuperType	SubClassOf

Table 8.1. Integrated Ecore and OWL 2 construcs.

8.3.2 Integration Use

Given an integrated metamodeling language as built in Section 6.2.1, DSL designers are able to design hybrid metamodels.

DSL designers at Comarch rely on the languages and concrete syntaxes they are familiar with. Hence, we provide the Java-like KM3-syntax [JB06] (a concrete syntax for Ecore [SBPM08]) with an integrated OWL syntax. DSL designers are able to describe classes in DSL metamodels seamlessly integrated with OWL axioms and expressions. The grammar of the textual concrete syntax of the Ecore+OWL language is given in the Appendix A.4.

In Figure 8.8 we depict an excerpt of the metamodel of the *Physical Device DSL* (PDDSL) in concrete syntax. The metamodel is a hybrid model, which is an instance of the metamodel $GS_{EcoreOWL}$.

Using the KM3 syntax, the DSL designer defines that a DeviceType is linked with ConfigurationTypes, an InternetRouter is a specialization of DeviceType, each ConfigurationType has SlotTypes and in each SlotType different *card types* can be plugged in. All specific configuration types and card types are specializations of ConfigurationType and CardType, respectively. In Section 8.4.1 we comment on the additional axioms modeled with the integrated ontology language.

```
package PDDSL {
  class DeviceType {
    reference hasConfiguration [1−∗]: ConfigurationType;
  }

  class InternetRouter extends DeviceType, equivalentTo hasConfiguration min 1 (VoiceConfiguration or
    WANConfiguration) {
  }

  class ConfigurationType extends (hasSlot some (hasCard some Processor)){
    reference hasSlot [1−∗]: SlotType;
  }

  class VoiceConfiguration extends ConfigurationType and (hasSlot only (hasCard only (not LineCard))),
    equivalentTo hasSlot some (hasCard some VoiceInterface) {
  }

  class WANConfiguration extends ConfigurationType, equivalentTo (hasSlot min 3 SlotType) and (
    hasSlot some (hasCard some (LineCard or PortAdapter))) {
  }

  class SlotType {
    reference hasCard [0−∗]: CardType;
  }

  class CardType {
  }

  class Processor extends CardType {
  }

  class PortAdapter extends CardType and (inv(hasCard) some (inv(hasSlot) some ( ConfigurationType
    and hasSlot some (hasCard some Processor)))) {
  }

  class LineCard extends CardType {
  }

  class VoiceInterface extends CardType and (inv(hasCard) only (inv(hasSlot) only ( ConfigurationType
    and hasSlot only (hasCard only (not LineCard))))) {
  }
}
```

Figure 8.8. Metamodel of the Physical Device DSL.

Besides hybrid metamodeling the projection of a metamodel and a model is also required. We reuse the service presented in Table 6.3. It gets as input a hybrid metamodel and a domain model. The output of the projection service is an ontoware model. It represents both, the DSL metamodel with its OWL annotations and the instance model. The ontoware model is used by reasoning tools and is the basis for all services provided to designers and users.

8.4 Accomplished Goals

Now that we have presented the application of the Ecore+OWL integration bridge we will show how the goals stated in Section 8.2.2 are accomplished.

8.4.1 Constraints for Configuration Types (Goal 1)

In Figure 8.8 a DSL designer builds the metamodel of the PDDSL language using integrated Ecore+OWL metamodeling language. Besides the structure of devices, the DSL designer also defines constraints in the metamodel. Therefore, he uses the integrated OWL 2 language (an adaptation of the Manchester Style syntax [HPS09]), which is integrated with the existing KM3 syntax. In Figure 8.8 the designer states that every InternetRouter device has at least one VoiceConfiguration or WANConfiguration. A ConfigurationType is a WANConfiguration if and only if it is linked with at least three slot types in which either a LineCard or a PortAdapter card type is plugged in. A ConfigurationType is a VoiceConfiguration if and only if it has a slot in which a VoiceInterface is plugged in.

In addition, DSL designers are able to define the following restrictions over configurations and cards:

Required Card Types: All possible configuration types require that a Processor card is plugged in:

class ConfigurationType **extends** (hasSlot **some** (hasCard **some** Processor))

Disallowed Card Types: The VoiceConfiguration type disallows the use of Line-Cards:

class VoiceConfiguration **extends** ConfigurationType **and** hasSlot **only** (hasCard **only** (**not** LineCard))

Card Type Inclusion: If the card type PortAdapter is part of a configuration type then this configuration type must also implement the processor card type:

class PortAdapter **extends** CardType **and** (**inv**(hasCard) **some** (**inv**(hasSlot) **some** (
    ConfigurationType **and** hasSlot **some** (hasCard **some** LineCard))))

Card Type Exclusion: If the card type VoiceInterface is part of a configuration then LineCards are disallowed:

class VoiceInterface **extends** CardType **and** (**inv**(hasCard) **only** (**inv**(hasSlot) **only** (ConfigurationType
    and hasSlot **only** (hasCard **only** (**not** LineCard)))))

8.4.2 Formal Semantics (Goal 1)

The Ecore language has model-theoretic semantics. Ecore adopts the semantics of the integrated ontology language. Hence, elements in a PDDSL metamodel have a formal meaning. A class in the PDDSL metamodel describes a set of instances in the domain model. A reference in the PDDSL metamodel describes a set of links between instances of a corresponding type. Attributes in the metamodel describe links between instances and values in the domain model. Reasoning based on the semantics is possible after the projection of metamodel and model to one ontoware model.

8.4.3 Debugging and Suggestions (Goal 2 and 3)

To accomplish the goals for debugging and suggestions, domain experts are able to use the services for inconsistency management and suggestions as presented in Section 6.3.2.

Figure 8.9 depicts a domain model, which is incomplete because the mandatory VoiceInterface card type for the VoiceConfiguration is missing. Furthermore a LineCard is already inserted.

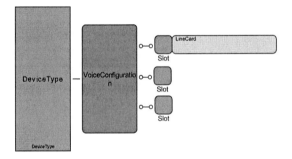

Figure 8.9. Incomplete and inconsistent domain model.

To detect inconsistencies in models, domain experts consider the *inconsistency detection* service specified in Table 6.5. For the model in Figure 8.9 the service returns false because the model is not consistent.

The reason for the model not being consistent depends on the VoiceInterface card type which excludes the LineCard (cf. the PDDSL metamodel in Figure 8.8). Although the VoiceInterface card type is not part of the current configuration, the reasoner assumes this fact, since it is required for each VoiceConfiguration. In an open world reasoners assume missing facts in models as default, which are described in metamodels. Domain experts are interested in the elements affecting the inconsistency. The *inconsistent elements* service specified in Table 6.6 returns the set {_voiceconfiguration, _slot1, _linecard}. In a development environment, these elements are highlighted in the editor to show the part of a model which is not consistent. To get suggestions for valid card types in configurations, domain experts consider the *type suggestion* service specified in Table 6.7. For example, for the instance of type LineCard the service suggests the possible type **VoiceInterface** and all other card types, which do not contradict the configuration.

8.5 Conclusion

In this chapter we presented the application of ontology technologies to design and use domain-specific languages.

Before answering RQ 11, asking for the use of ontology technologies in domain-specific modeling, we presented a scenario where network device series are designed. The creation of a domain model is achieved by DSL experts using a physical device domain-specific language (PDDSL). To design a DSL, which specifies the different valid configurations of a network device series, we use the Ecore+OWL metamodeling language. In the scenario OWL 2 helps to specify the logical restrictions for configuration types of network devices series. The integration bridge combining the Ecore language with OWL allows for projecting the DSL metamodel and conforming domain models to one ontoware model. Given such an ontoware model, language users benefit from the generic inconsistency management API, which is based on the ontoware reasoning services.

9

Joint Language and Domain Engineering

In this chapter we join the concerns of language engineering and conceptual domain engineering towards a new comprehensive approach of domain-specific development. It allows domain modelers to build domain models containing both types and instances, and it allows language designers to define language metamodels prescribing the structure of conceptual domain models. We answer the question:

RQ12: *Is there a metamodeling language that features the joint design of metamodels and conceptual domain models?*

9.1 Chapter Context

In this chapter all models are formally represented by a TGraph (cf. Section 2.2.1) and all metamodels are formally represented by a graph schema (cf. Section 2.2.2).

9.1.1 Reused and Adopted Technologies and Approaches

To achieve the capability for conceptual domain engineering, we extend the metamodels as described in Section 7.2. This extension allows for defining an explicit ontological instantiation relationship in conceptual domain models. This relationship connects ontological instances, i.e., vertices, edges, and attribute assignments, with the respective types.

9.1.2 Chapter Road Map

Figure 9.1 depicts this chapter's road map. In Section 9.2 we extend the domain models from Section 8.2. Here we consider conceptual domain models consisting of domain types and domain instances related by an ontological *hasType* relationship. Such conceptual domain models are designed by domain modelers. To prescribe the structure of conceptual domain models, prescriptive metamodels are defined, which consist of metatypes and metainstances. Conceptual domain models and the metamodel are related by the linguistic *instanceOf* relationship. In Section 9.3 we present a metamodeling language, which allows for the joint definition of metamodels and conceptual domain models and the explicit definition of a linguistic and ontological instantiation relationship. Language designers using the metamodeling language can design DSL metamodels at the metamodel layer, which is related to language engineering. Domain modelers and language users are able to create domain models containing both domain types and instances. Domain models lie at the model layer and must conform to DSL metamodels via the linguistic *instanceOf* relationship.

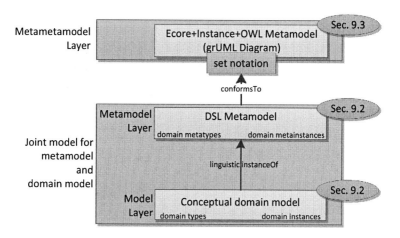

Figure 9.1. Road map of Chapter 9.

9.2 Case Study

In this section we start with an introduction of an application context, which introduces the different dimensions of metamodeling and roles used in this section. Afterwards we present a scenario where we extend the PDDSL language to provide the definition of conceptual domain models consisting of an explicit ontological instantiation relation.

In Section 8.3 we presented the design of the metamodel of PDDSL by language designers using the Ecore+OWL metamodeling language. Language users consider PDDSL to create domain models, which are composed of linguistic instances of the elements given in the metamodel.

In this case study we are going to extend the PDDSL language, since we discovered that language users want to model both, the series (e.g., the Cisco 7600 series) and in addition concrete devices of this series (e.g., the Cisco 7603). Thus, we extend PDDSL to define conceptual domain models with two ontological layers.

9.2.1 Application Context and Roles

Language designers using MDD environments require the facility to define the abstract syntax, at least one concrete syntax and the semantics of the language to be designed. From the language engineering perspective and with respect to Figure 9.2(a), linguistic instantiation supplies a linear metamodeling hierarchy [AK01]. The metametamodel is instantiated by the language designer to define the metamodel. The metamodel itself is instantiated by a language user to built domain models.

For example, the **metatype** elements and the **metainstance** elements in the metamodel are linguistic instances of the metametamodel element **class**. **type** elements and **instance** elements in the domain model are linguistic instances of the **metatype** element and **metainstance** element at the metamodel layer.

In Figure 9.2(b) the elements of Figure 9.2(a) are exemplified by concrete model elements from the domain of network devices (cf. Section 8.2.1). Here, **DeviceType** is a metatype and a possible linguistic instance of **DeviceType** is **Cisco7600**. On the right of Figure 9.2(b) we have **DeviceInstance** as a metainstance. A linguistic instance of **DeviceInstance** is **cisco7603** at the domain models layer.

At the domain model layer a domain modeler defines two ontological layers (*O2* and *O1*) within his domain model. He defines **type** elements (at *O2*), corresponding **instance** elements (at *O1*), and connects them by an ontological **hasType** relation. The relation itself is defined in the metamodel, which strongly prescribes the design of domain models (e.g., types cannot be connected to other types via **hasType**). With regard to Figure 9.2(b), **Cisco7600** is a domain type, which has a domain instance called **cisco7603** via an ontological **hasType** relation. The **hasType** relation between a **DeviceType** and a **DeviceInstance** is defined at the metamodel layer. Furthermore, a domain modeler can specialize domain types by creating **subclass** relationships, or vice versa, subsume given domain types by one super type.

We are going to present a scenario provided by Comarch. The scenario exemplifies Figure 9.2. It shows how the elements **metatype**, **metainstance**, **type**, and **instance** are defined in a metamodel and domain model and how the instantiation relations are modeled.

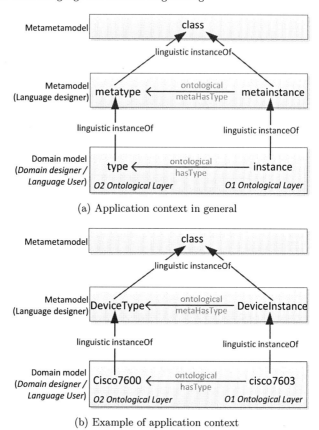

(a) Application context in general

(b) Example of application context

Figure 9.2. Linguistic and ontological metamodeling.

9.2.2 Scenario

As mentioned in Section 8.2.1, Comarch is specialized in software for telecommunication providers. Some of the tools that Comarch develops for telecommunication providers are dealing with the modeling of physical network devices. This is a domain-specific task since different configurations of network devices have to be modeled (cf. Section 8.2.1).

The following language metamodel (Figure 9.3) and domain model (Figure 9.4) are designed using a textual concrete syntax, which is based on an extended KM3 syntax [JB06].

Explicit Modeling of Ontological and Linguistic Instantiation Relationship

The domain of physical network devices as shown in Section 8.3 is described by a DSL, which provides the core metatypes such as DeviceType, ConfigurationType, SlotType and CardType with respective specializations.

Comarch language designers want to provide the facilities of conceptual domain modeling to language users and domain modelers. Thus, they have to provide a language, which allows for creating domain types and instances in domain models. Furthermore, the ontological instantiation relation must be explicitly defined.

Metatypes together with the connecting **metareferences** describe the general structure of a network device and are defined in a metamodel, which is depicted in Figure 9.3. In the same metamodel the Comarch language designer defines metainstances using the **metainstance**-keyword. Here the ontological instantiation relation is defined by the **metaHasType**-keyword.

A domain model is depicted in Figure 9.4 and consists of linguistic instances of model elements in the metamodel. Here both domain types and instances are defined using the **type**- and **instance**-keyword. Using the **instanceOf**-keyword, each domain type and domain instance is defined as a linguistic instance of a corresponding metatype and metainstance. For example, domain type Cisco7600 is a linguistic instance of DeviceType, while supervisor720 is a linguistic instance of CardInstance.

A mandatory task in the creation of domain models is the definition of an explicit *hasType* relation between instances and domain types. In the example in Figure 9.4, a domain modeler uses the **hasType**-keyword to define that the ontological instance supervisor720 has the named type CiscoCard. References such as **hasSlot** in the type definitions on the one hand represent links, which are linguistic instances of corresponding references in the metamodel, on the other they define new references for links between ontological instances.

In addition, expressions based on the ontology language OWL 2 are defined in the metamodel to prescribe the domain models (cf. Section 6.3.1) or to describe the domain (cf. Section 7.4.1). For example, in Figure 9.3 an equivalent classes axiom is used to define that each configuration type instance must be linked with at least some card via some slot.

Combination of Language Engineering and Domain Engineering

To ensure the correctness of domain models, Comarch wants to prescribe the design of each domain model. The core domain should be described by a DSL, which is used by domain modelers and language users to build domain models. So far the DSLs designed by Comarch do not allow for the creation of both types and instances in the domain model. To accomplish the prescription of the design of domain models, a Comarch language designer wants to describe DSLs in such a way as described in Figure 9.3. Here a metamodel of the

```
metatype DeviceType {
  metareference hasConfiguration [1−1]: ConfigurationType;
}


metatype ConfigurationType equivalentTo hasSlotType some (hasCardType some CardType){
  metareference hasSlot [1−∗]: SlotType;
}


metatype SlotType {
  metareference hasCard [0−∗]: CardType;
}


metatype CardType {
}


metatype Processor extends CardType {
}


metatype LineCard extends CardType {
}


metainstance DeviceInstance metaHastype DeviceType {
  metalink hasConfigurationInstance [1−∗]: ConfigurationInstance;
}


metainstance ConfigurationInstance metaHastype ConfigurationType {
  metalink hasSlotInstance [1−∗]: SlotInstance;
}


metainstance SlotInstance metaHastype SlotType {
  metalink hasCardInstance [0−∗]: CardInstance;
}


metainstance CardInstance metaHastype CardType {
}
```

Figure 9.3. Metamodel of the extended PDDSL.

extended PDDSL is depicted, which not only allows for the description of the core domain of physical network devices, it also distinguishes between domain types and instances.

Language users and domain modelers use PDDSL and create linguistic instances, which build the conceptual domain model depicted in Figure 9.4. Thus, every domain model consists of domain types (using the **type**-keyword) and corresponding instances (using the instance-keyword). Furthermore, each complete device has to follow the given structure of the order *device-configuration-slot-card* and must contain at least one card, which is prescribed by the DSL. Without a DSL that prescribes the design of domain models, a second domain modeler would be able to create domain models, which describe devices containing elements in the order *device-slot-card*. Such models of the same domain are not comparable with other domain models and not capable of being integrated.

```
type Cisco7600 instanceOf DeviceType {
  reference hasConfiguration [1−1]: Cisco7600Configuration;
}

type Cisco7600Configuration instanceOf ConfigurationType equivalentTo hasSlot some hasCard some
      Supervisor {
  reference hasSlot [1−∗]: CiscoSlot;
}

type Cisco7600Slot instanceOf SlotType {
  reference hasCard [0−∗]: CiscoCard;
}
type Cisco7600Card instanceOf CardType { }
type HotSwappableOSM instanceOf LineCard, extends Cisco7600Card { }
type Supervisor instanceOf Processor, equivalentTo oneOf(supervisor720, supervisor360) { }


instance cicso7603 instanceOf DeviceInstance{
  hasConfiguration cicso7603configuration;
}

instance cisco7604 instanceOf DeviceInstance, hasType restrictionOn hasSlot with some restrictionOn
      hasCard with some Supervisor {
}

instance cicso7603configuration instanceOf ConfigurationInstance, hasType Cisco7600Configuration{
  hasSlot slot1;
}

instance slot1 instanceOf SlotInstance, hasType Cisco7600Slot {
  hasCard supervisor360;
}
instance supervisor720 instanceOf CardInstance, hasType Cisco7600Card { }
instance supervisor360 instanceOf CardInstance, hasType Cisco7600Card { }
```

Figure 9.4. Conceptual domain model containing types and instances.

9.2.3 Goals and Relations to Challenges

Given the scenario above we identified two goals a modeling environment should target:

1. **Explicit Modeling of Ontological and Linguistic Instantiation Relationship:** To create elements in a conceptual domain model, domain modelers and language users require a (domain-specific) language whose abstract syntax is represented by a metamodel. This language should prescribe the design of conceptual domain models and provide a linguistic instantiation mechanism for the design of types and instances in domain models. In addition domain modelers require explicit modeling of an ontological instantiation relationship. It allows for assigning a conforming domain type to domain instances in the domain model.

2. **Combination of Language Engineering and Domain Engineering:** A second goal is related to the joint use of linguistic and ontological instantiation. The problem in using pure DSLs, which only allow for creating linguistic instances of elements in the metamodel, is a lack of flexibility in dynamically extending the set of domain types in domain models. Domain

modelers call for the capability to define or extend the set of domain types for modeling domain instances. This requires the simultaneous definition of types and instances in one domain model. Here an appropriate language metamodel is needed, which provides concepts to allow for defining both types and instances.

On the other hand, since pure domain engineering allows for creating arbitrary domain types, different domain models of the same domain may have different types, which do not fit together. Here some prescriptive language for domain models can be necessary to make them comparable and capable for being integrated.

The goals mentioned above are related to Challenge 4. They ask for the capability to dynamically extend the set of domain types available for modeling and this in turn requires the capability to define domain metatypes and metainstances in DSL metamodels.

9.3 Application of Bridging and Modeling Approaches

In this section we present an approach and an architecture, which provides simultaneous linguistic and ontological metamodeling.

Figure 9.5 presents a multi-layered architecture depicting the environment usable for language engineering and extended with the functionalities for domain engineering.

Core of the environment is the *Ecore+Instance+OWL 2* language, whose abstract syntax is described by an integrated metametamodel. It consists of an (extended) *Ecore metametamodel* (cf. Section 6.1.1) integrated with an *OWL 2 metamodel* (cf. the Appendix A.2). Excerpts of the metametamodel are depicted in Figure 9.6, 9.7, and 9.8.

The integrated metametamodel is used to define elements at the metamodel layer. Here the environment provides the facility for language engineering and allows for building DSL metamodels. These metamodels may contain the definition of domain metatypes and metainstances.

The DSL defined at the metamodel layer describes the core structure of a domain and is also used by a domain modeler and language user to build domain models at the model layer. Because the metamodel allows for creating domain types (using the concept **metatype**) and domain instances (using the concept **metainstance**), domain modelers and language users are able to model two ontological layers O2 and O1. Layer O2 consists of domain types and layer O1 consists of domain instances. Both ontological layers are connected by the explicit ontological *hasType* relation between domain types and instances.

The OWL 2 part of the new metamodeling language is used to define axioms and restrictions in the metamodel and domain model.

To reason on the additional semantics, especially that of the explicit *hasType*- and *instanceOf* relations, the domain model at the M1 layer with its types and instances is transformed to an ontoware model represented by the **DE Ontology** (domain engineering ontology). Its TBox describes the terminology of the domain and represents the domain types together with its constraints, while the ABox contains concrete assertions about domain instances.

In the case of language engineering and language use, the metamodel together with its metatypes and metainstances is transformed into the TBox contained by the **LE Ontology** (language engineering ontology). Each of the linguistic instances of the metamodel are transformed into the ABox.

The two ontoware models are used by reasoning tools, which provides additional services. These services for validating and explaining the metamodel can be used by the different users of the environment (cf. Sections 6.3.1 and 7.4.2).

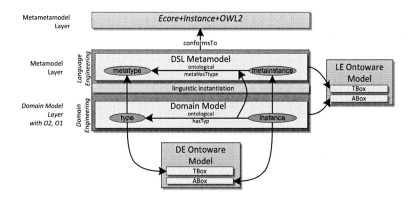

Figure 9.5. Architectural overview of the environment for linguistic and ontological metamodeling.

9.3.1 2-Dimensional Metamodeling Language

Figure 9.6 depicts an extension of the Ecore metametamodel. In particular we connect the Ecore classes Class, Reference, and Attribute with the respective classes representing their instances. Class is linked via the instantiation class HasVertexType with Vertex. Hence, we are able to define vertices as ontological instance of Ecore classes. Reference is linked with Edge and Attribute is linked with AttributeAssignment. Hence, we are able to define edges as ontological instances of references and attribute assignments as ontological instances of attributes.

The Ecore+Instance metametamodel provides all concepts for modeling (meta-)types and (meta-)instances (cf. Figure 9.7). The metametamodel dif-

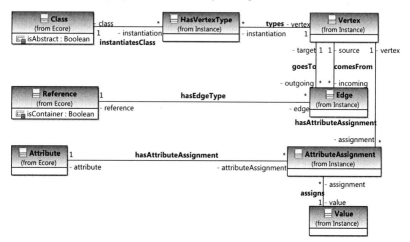

Figure 9.6. Ecore extension for instance modeling.

ferentiates between elements of the metamodel layer and those of the model layer. Metamodel elements for example are **Metatype** and **Metainstance**. Both can be connected by a **MetaHasType** relation. Model elements for example are **Type** and **Instance**, which can be connected by a **hasType** relation.

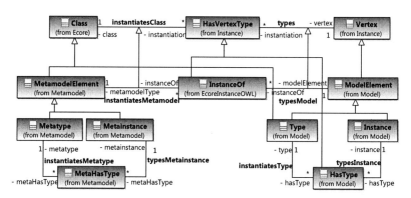

Figure 9.7. Type and instance modeling.

Besides (meta-)type and (meta-)instance definitions, the Ecore+Instance metametamodel also consists of concepts to model a **Metareference** and a **Metalink** in the metamodel layer (cf. Figure 9.8). Both can be connected with respective linguistic instances in the model layer, which are defined as a **Reference** or as a **Link**.

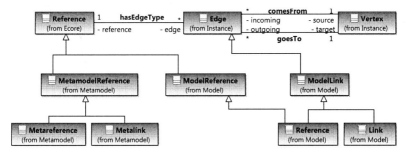

Figure 9.8. Reference and link modeling.

9.3.2 Integration with OWL

The integration of the Ecore+Instance metametamodel with the OWL 2 metamodel is accomplished as described in Section 7.3. The Ecore classes Class, Reference, and Attribute become specializations of the OWL classes Class, ObjectProperty, and DataProperty, respectively. Vertex becomes a specialization of Individual. The HasVertexType construct becomes a specialization of the OWL ClassAssertion construct. The Edge construct and the AttributeAssignment construct become specializations of OWL ObjectPropertyAssertion and DataPropertyAssertion, respectively.

9.4 Accomplished Goals

In the following we analyze the approach with respect to the goals in Section 9.2.3.

Explicit Modeling Ontological and Linguistic Instantiation Relationship (Goal 1)

To address the modeling of ontological and linguistic instantiation relationships we built a metametamodel, which allows for defining metatypes and metainstances within a language metamodel. This metamodel allows for creating types and instances in one domain model. Furthermore, the metamodel allows for explicitly designing a linguistic *instanceOf* relationship, which relates elements of two different modeling layers and an ontological *hasType* relationship, which allows for relating domain types with corresponding domain instances at the model layer.

Combination of Language Engineering and Domain Engineering (Goal 2)

To consider the combination of language engineering and domain engineering we created the Ecore+Instance+OWL 2 metametamodel that joins both concerns. Language designers using the metametamodel can design DSL meta-models at the metamodel layer, which is related to language engineering. Domain modelers and language users are able to create domain models containing both, domain types and instances. Domain models lie at the model layer and must conform to DSL metamodels via the linguistic *instanceOf* relationship.

9.5 Conclusion

In this chapter we presented an application of ontology technologies used for the combined language and domain engineering.

As an answer for RQ 12 we presented a metamodeling language, which allows for the joint definition of metamodels and conceptual domain models, and the explicit definition of a linguistic and ontological instantiation relationship.

Language designers using the metamodeling language can design DSL metamodels at the metamodel layer, which is related to language engineering. Domain modelers and language users are able to create domain models containing both domain types and instances. Domain models lie at the model layer and must conform to DSL metamodels via the linguistic *instanceOf* relationship.

Part V

Finale

10
Tool Support and Proof of Concept

In this chapter we are going to present the tool support and proof of concept of the approaches presented in this thesis.

We are going to present the tools implementing the services discussed in this thesis. We differ between implementations in *JGraLab* and in the *TwoUse toolkit*, which are realized by the author of this thesis, and the *MOST workbench*, which provides a tool for industrial modeling tasks but also concerns the approaches presented in this thesis. All implementations are presented in Section 10.1.

Besides the tool support of approaches we are going to consider the key challenges we set up in Section 1.1.3. We are going to show, which approaches presented in this thesis tackle which of the key challenges. The proof of concept evaluation is presented in Section 10.2.

10.1 Tool Support

The services presented in this thesis for the support of language designers and users are realized by tools. We depict these tools and illustrate how they are implemented.

10.1.1 Implementation Context

Figure 10.1 depicts an overview of implementations and assigns the respective frameworks and environments used to realize the approaches presented in each chapter. Furthermore, the figures in this chapter illustrating the classes providing the services are related to the chapters presenting the approaches.

The implementations with JGraLab (cf. Section 10.1.2) reach from Chapter 2 to Chapter 3. Within JGraLab the metamodels of all modelware languages (cf. Figure 10.2) and the ontoware language OWL 2 (cf. Figure 10.3) are realized. All modelware services are realized in JGraLab. The ontoware services work on OWL2 graphs. However, these services encapsulate services provided by Pellet [SPG+07]. These services are accessed using the OWL API [HB09], which is externally implemented. Basic modelware and ontoware services are provided by the *foundation layer*.

Bridges are implemented with the support of JGraLab. They are established on graph schema layer and used at the TGraph layer (cf. Figures 10.4 and 10.5). Such as the bridging services, the APIs for inconsistency management (cf. Figure 10.6) and conceptual domain modeling (cf. Figure 10.7) consider graphs and schemas as inputs and all outputs are also elements of a respective graph or schema. All services are provided by the *combination layer*.

The language engineering with the integrated metamodeling language Ecore+OWL is realized within the TwoUse toolkit (cf. Section 10.1.3). The conceptual domain modeling with ontological instantiation is realized in the MOST Workbench (cf. Section 10.1.4). In the *application layer* we show the tools considered by end users.

Since in Chapter 4 only a conceptual comparison is achieved, no implementations are available.

10.1.2 Implementations with JGraLab

The usage of TGraphs and graph schemas is supported by the *JGraLab library*[1]. JGraLab is a full Java implementation of TGraphs and schemas and offers an API for the creation, manipulation, and traversal of graphs. JGraLab is implemented at the Institute for Software Technology (Working Group Ebert) at the University of Koblenz-Landau[2].

JGraLab provides two APIs: a generic API for handling graphs without schema information and a schema-specific API for handling graphs with respect to a given graph schema. The schema-specific API is generated on the basis of a given schema. It supports the treatment of schemas and graphs in terms of vertex and edge classes, which are implemented as Java interfaces and classes. Vertices and edges are the respective objects.

Languages

Languages are represented in JGraLab by a graph schema. We differ between modelware and ontoware languages.

Modelware Languages

All modelware languages (e.g., BEDSL) are represented by their own graph schema. The graph schema in JGraLab is used to generate a schema-specific API allowing for building and traversing respective conforming TGraphs.

---

[1] http://jgralab.uni-koblenz.de/
[2] http://www.uni-koblenz-landau.de/koblenz/fb4/institute/IST/AGEbert

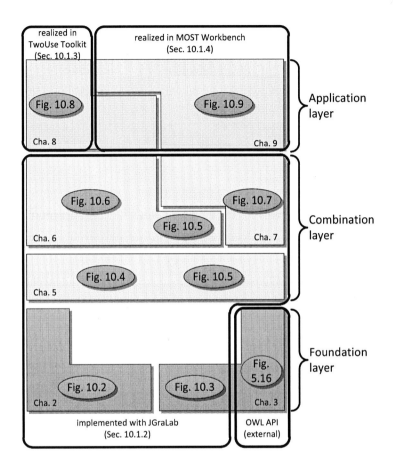

Figure 10.1. Implementation overview.

The class Modelware depicted in Figure 10.2, provides all services to create a graph for a given schema, to delete a graph, and to query a graph with a GReQL query. They are implemented as static operations.

All graph classes (e.g., BEDSL) are specializations of Graph. Graph provides the services for the manipulation of graphs for given vertex classes and edge classes. Its specializations provide schema specific services, e.g., to build entities.

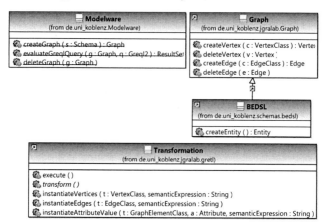

Figure 10.2. Class signatures of modelware services.

Ontoware Languages

In JGraLab the ontology language OWL 2 is represented by its own graph schema, which is considered for the generation of a schema-specific API. The API allows for building TGraphs representing an OWL 2 ontology.

The class **OWL2** depicted in Figure 10.3, represents the graph class for all TGraphs representing ontoware models. Hence, it provides services for the creation of ontologies, classes, individuals, and properties, etc.

The class **Ontoware** provides all services for ontologies. It provides all standard and non-standard reasoning services and the SPARQL query service. The services are implemented as static operations. They get an ontology as parameter.

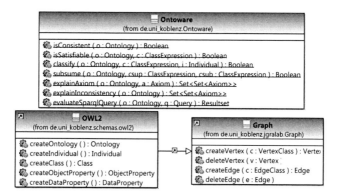

Figure 10.3. Class signatures of ontoware services.

To save ontoware models as *.owl file or to prepare ontoware models for reasoners, we use the *OWL API*. The OWL API in version $3.0.0^3$ is developed at the University of Manchester [HB09]. The API is closely aligned with the OWL 2 specification (cf. [MPSH09] and Section 3.3) and supports parsing and the rendering of ontologies written for example in OWL Functional Syntax or OWL Manchester-Syntax. It supports the treatment of ontologies in terms of object-oriented concepts, i.e., OWL classes and properties or axioms are implemented as Java classes. The use of the OWL API was illustrated in Section 5.5.1.

Services

All services for bridging, inconsistency management and domain engineering work on TGraphs. Hence, ontoware models are always invisible for language designers and users.

Bridging Services

In the following we illustrate the classes providing the services for transformation and integration bridge.

Transformation Bridge. The class BEDSL2OWL depicted in Figure 10.4 implements the transformation bridge from BEDSL models to ontoware models. It is a specialization of the GReTL class Transformation and overrides the operation transform. In transform the complete transformation is implemented using the service provided by GReTL.

The class TransformationBridge provides a transform service implemented as a static operation. It gets as input a BEDSL model and returns an ontoware model represented by an OWL2 graph. This service is provided to the user and uses the transform services in BEDSL2OWL.

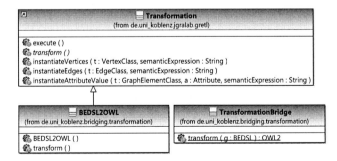

Figure 10.4. Class signature of transformation services.

---

^{3} http://owlapi.sourceforge.net/

Integration Bridge. The class implementing the integration bridge is depicted in Figure 10.5. The integration bridge is instantiated using the constructor which gets as input the two graph schemas to be integrated. In addition, the IntegrationBridge class provides the union service and all integration services.

For the use of the integration bridge, the class provides two services to load graphs. The services may be used to transform a graph to a hybrid model conforming to the integrated graph schema. Besides the load services the integration bridge provides the two projection services.

For the projection of linguistically instantiable metamodels and their instances, the bridge provides the multi-layer projection services projectGSOWL. It is implemented as a static operation and gets as input a metamodel conforming to the metametamodel EcoreOWL (in Section 6.2 implemented as a graph schema), an instance graph and the integration bridge object encapsulating the respective integration bridge.

The class Convert provides an API with services for producing a schema for an EcoreOWL graph and an adaptation service, which adapts a BEDSL graph.

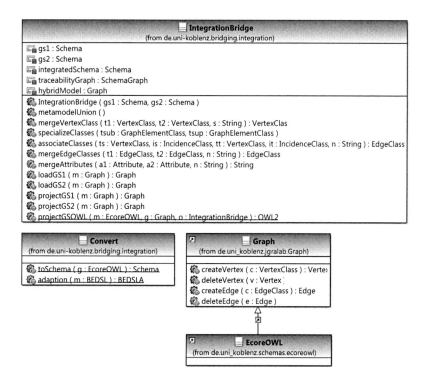

Figure 10.5. Class signature of integration bridge.

Inconsistency Management and Domain Engineering Services

The services for inconsistency management and domain engineering are also implemented in the TGraph technological space. Inputs of these services are schemas and graphs and also elements of these (i.e., vertices and edges). The outputs of these services are elements of a TGraph or a schema. Hence, users do not get in touch with ontologies.

The InconsistencyManagement class depicted in Figure 10.6 implements the services for inconsistency management. All services get as input a metamodel and a respective instance graph, as well as the integration bridge object, and are implemented as static operations.

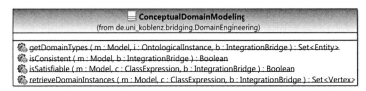

Figure 10.6. Class signature of inconsistency management services.

The DomainEngineering class depicted in Figure 10.7 implements the services for domain engineering. All services are implemented as static operation and get a conceptual domain model and the integration bridge object as input.

ConceptualDomainModeling		
(from de.uni_koblenz.bridging.DomainEngineering)		
getDomainTypes (m : Model, i : OntologicalInstance, b : IntegrationBridge) : Set<Entity>		
isConsistent (m : Model, b : IntegrationBridge) : Boolean		
isSatisfiable (m : Model, c : ClassExpression, b : IntegrationBridge) : Boolean		
retrieveDomainInstances (m : Model, c : ClassExpression, b : IntegrationBridge) : Set<Vertex>		

Figure 10.7. Class signature of domain engineering services.

Reasoning Services

All reasoning services (cf. Figure 10.3) are encapsulated by services for inconsistency management and domain engineering . They use the implementations provided by *Pellet*[4]. Pellet is an OWL 2 reasoner implemented by the US company *Clark&Parsia*[5]. Pellet supports all standard and non-standard reasoning services presented in Sections 3.4.1 and 3.4.2. In addition it provides an interface for answering queries. These queries can be formulated in SPARQL.

---

[4] http://clarkparsia.com/pellet/
[5] http://clarkparsia.com/

Pellet reasoners may be used as a Java object providing services for loading ontologies and reasoning on ontologies. The use of Pellet via the OWL API was illustrated in Section 5.5.2.

10.1.3 TwoUse Toolkit

The *TwoUse Toolkit* implemented at the WeST institute[6] is developed in the Eclipse Platform using the Eclipse Modeling Framework [SBPM08], and is freely available for download on the project website[7]. We have enriched the TwoUse toolkit with the editors for textual modeling languages.

Languages

In Figure 10.8 we see the view of a DSL designer modeling an integrated metamodel.

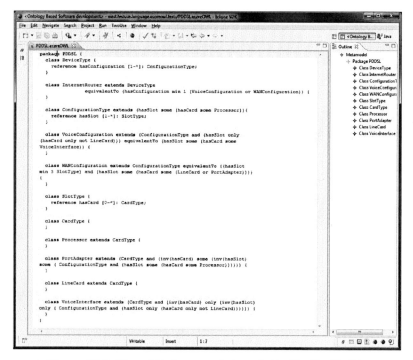

Figure 10.8. View of the language designer in the TwoUse Toolkit.

---

[6] http://west.uni-koblenz.de/
[7] http://code.google.com/p/twouse/

Integrated metamodeling is based on an integration of Ecore and OWL as explained in Section 6.2. The language designer uses the textual concrete syntax, which is the combination of the KM3 syntax and an adaptation of the OWL Manchester syntax.

For the implementation of editors for textual modeling languages we use *EMFText*[8]. EMFText is developed by the Software Technology Group of the Dresden University of Technology. It is an Eclipse plug-in that allows for defining textual concrete syntaxes for modeling languages described by an Ecore-based metamodel. After the specification of an Ecore-based language metamodel, language designers must specify the textual concrete syntax. The textual concrete syntax is defined as a set of EBNF rules, one for each class in the metamodel. Subsequently, EMFText automatically generates the language editor, which is a new Eclipse plug-in. The new editor provides features like syntax highlighting, code completion, or error reporting. Figure 10.8 depicts the editor generated for the Ecore+OWL language. For detailed information on EMFText we refer to publications [HJK+09] and its official web site: `http://www.emftext.org/`.

Bridging with JGraLab

A bidirectional bridge between the Ecore technological space and the TGraph technological space is implemented by Heckelmann [Hec10]. The bridge allows for converting models (conforming to some Ecore-based metamodel) to TGraphs and in addition it allows for converting Ecore-based metamodels to graph schemas. The current implementation additionally allows for transforming grUML-based graph schemas and TGraphs to Ecore-based metamodels and conforming models. Since the expressiveness of grUML compared to Ecore is higher, information (e.g., the type information of edge classes) either gets lost or this information has to be materialized by additional elements in Ecore-based metamodels (e.g., edge classes are transformed to separate Ecore classes with two references defining source and target).

10.1.4 MOST Workbench

Compared to the TwoUse toolkit, the MOST workbench, implemented by BOC[9], provides a framework usable for industrial domain-specific modeling tasks. Comparing the usability of both frameworks, the MOST workbench provides a graphical user interface provided to DSL users. This is currently not available in the TwoUse toolkit.

---

[8] `http://www.emftext.org/`
[9] `http://www.boc-group.com`

In Figure 10.9 we depict a screenshot of the *MOST workbench*. The workbench is developed in the ADOxx platform[10] by the company BOC, which is also industrial partner in the MOST project. The tool supports the developing of domain-specific languages, which may be coupled to different visual concrete syntaxes. A language such as the physical device domain-specific language (PDDSL) may be developed within the workbench by a DSL designer. In Figure 10.9 we see the view of a DSL user modeling concrete devices (e.g., cisco_7603) being a member of the *Cisco 7600 Routers Series*.

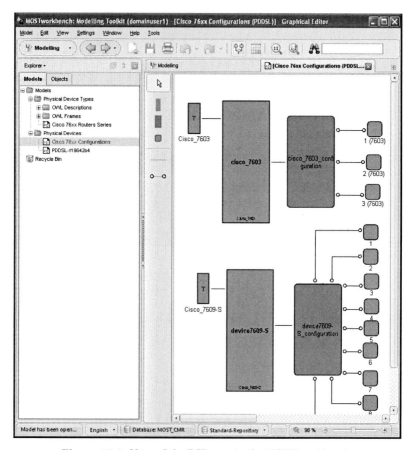

Figure 10.9. View of the DSL user in the MOST workbench.

---

[10] ADOxx® is the extensible, multi-lingual, multi-os, repository-based platform for the development of modeling tools of the BOC Group. ADOxx® is a registered trademark of the BOC Group, http://www.boc-group.com.

The integrated modeling is based on the ADOxx generic graphical modeling editor. To enable integrated modeling with OWL descriptions, languages to be integrated as well as the OWL metamodel are defined using the ADOxx M3 metametamodel (called *ADOxx Meta² Model* [BZ09]). Then the integration has been performed according to the integration approach presented in Section 5.3 [MSZ10].

The reasoning services are realized by a separate validation services component implemented by Comarch. Like the TwoUse toolkit, the reasoning component relies on Pellet. The component firstly projects models and metamodels to a format, which is readable by OWL reasoners. In addition it implements domain-specific services for inconsistency management and guidance [MSZ10].

10.2 Proof of Concept

In this section we present a proof of concept. We consider all key challenges (cf. Section 1.1.3) and mention those approaches presented in this thesis, which concern the challenges, and those applications, which exemplify the solutions.

10.2.1 Challenge 1: Bridging Technologies

Challenge 1 discusses the development of generic bridges used for the composition and the decomposition of modeling languages. Specific bridges are those combining modeling languages with ontology languages.

Approaches

All bridging approaches are presented in Chapter 5. We developed four different bridges for different purposes.

A *transformation bridge* (cf. Section 5.2) creates a respective output model according to a transformation definition and an input model. The transformation bridge usually implies some loss of information, since both languages may have different properties not all of which are transformable into the other languages. Users are restricted to the expressiveness (e.g., syntactic constructs) of the source language they are working with.

An integration of two languages using the *integration bridge* (cf. Section 5.3) results in one all-embracing new modeling language. To achieve the integration for a given mapping of concepts (which defines an intersection of both languages), integration services are used to define the new modeling language. An integrated metamodel allows language users to use the combined modeling languages in parallel. Its result is a hybrid model. Language users use for a given hybrid model projection services to derive models conforming to one of the metamodels to be combined.

A *mapping bridge* (cf. Section 5.4) allows for combining two complementary languages. Models may be developed separately by language users. Based on a mapping definition describing which constructs in metamodels can be mapped, users are able to declare mappings between elements of two different modeling languages.

An *API bridge* (cf. Section 5.5) is established by the implementation of services using the operations and services of given APIs used to traverse models, and those services of another API to build new models. On the one hand, the API bridge ensures a higher consistency of models, since the operations to create models may have well-defined pre- and post-conditions. On the other hand, the API is restricted by the set of methods and services it provides.

Applications

Applications in this thesis are mainly presented for the integration bridge since it is the most used and strongest form of bridging. In Chapter 8, we presented an application of the integration bridge. Based on the integration of the metamodeling language Ecore and the ontology language OWL 2, DSL designers are able to implement metamodels of DSLs with annotated OWL-based axioms and expressions. If DSL users need any services, the environment projects the metamodel as well as the domain model to an ontoware model.

10.2.2 Challenge 2: Formal Semantics and Correctness of Languages

Challenge 2 deals with the definition of formal semantics and the correctness of modeling languages.

Approaches

In Chapter 6 we presented the integration of the Ecore metamodeling language with OWL 2. Given the integration, language designers are able to design additional restrictions and expressions directly in the metamodel definition. In Section 6.3.1 we show that several path expressions may be designed using the integrated ontology language. These restrictions and expressions constrain user models defined by language users using the enriched metamodel. The Ecore language adopts the model-theoretic semantics of OWL 2, i.e., for a given element in an Ecore-based metamodel, its extension is described by sets of individuals, or relations between individuals, respectively.

Applications

Applications of the integration of Ecore and OWL are presented in Chapter 8. Here the PDDSL (Physical Device Domain-Specific Language) is designed defining the configurations of physical network device series. DSL designers may use the integrated ontology language to define restrictions to ensure the design of valid configurations in domain models by DSL users.

10.2.3 Challenge 3: Tooling

Challenge 3 concerns the support of designing and using modeling languages with tools.

Approaches

A basis for all tools and services supporting validation and suggestions of models are the reasoning services provided by the ontoware technological space. Services for language users are enabled after the transformation, projection, or mapping of modelware models to ontoware models. This is achieved by all bridges presented in Chapter 5.

Based on the ontoware model and the reasoning services provided by the ontoware technological space, new domain- and language specific services may be implemented. Section 6.3.2 presents strategies and services for inconsistency management. Here services provide the detection, diagnosis, and handling of inconsistencies in user models. Section 7.4.2 presents a set of services used in domain engineering for the validation of conceptual domain models.

Applications

Applications of the use of services relying on ontology technologies are presented in Section 8.4. Here the validation of (incomplete) domain models representing network device series is achieved. If models are inconsistent the respective inconsistent parts may be visualized. In addition suggestions on how to repair the models are given.

10.2.4 Challenge 4: Domain Modeling

Challenge 4 deals with the design of syntax and semantics of (domain-specific) modeling languages allowing for dynamically extending the set of domain types available for modeling.

Approaches

In Chapter 7 we presented the approaches for designing DSLs for conceptual domain modeling. We define which parts of metamodels are necessary for the definition of type and instance layer, respectively, and how they are related. For the definition of semantics the metamodel of DSLs for conceptual domain modeling is integrated with the OWL 2 metamodel. Hence, elements in the type layer represent sets of domain instances or relations of domain instances, respectively.

Applications

In Chapter 9 we presented an application of Challenge 4. We have enriched the metamodeling language Ecore, usually used for metamodel engineering, with the facility for conceptual domain engineering. Hence, language designers are able to design DSLs prescribing the structure of conceptual domain models. Domain modelers building conceptual domain models may benefit from the definition of type and instance layer within one domain model.

10.3 Conclusion

In this chapter we have illustrated the tool support for bridging software modeling with ontology technologies, and we have discussed how the challenges are tackled by the approaches presented in this thesis.

We have presented the tooling implemented with the use of JGraLab and the infrastructure provided by the TwoUse toolkit. JGraLab was used to realize the easy creation, manipulation, and traversal of TGraphs and graph schemas. To provide a simple implementation of Ecore-based metamodels with OWL-based annotations, we extended the TwoUse toolkit with respective editors. A third tool is the MOST workbench implemented for industrial domain-specific modeling tasks.

Besides tool support we discussed the challenges set up in Section 1.1.3. We showed that all are tackled by respective approaches in this thesis and are applied in Part IV of this thesis.

11

Conclusion and Outlook

In the last chapter of this thesis we conclude the complete work presenting a summarized overview and provide an outlook for future work.

11.1 Thesis Contribution

In this section we consider and answer the questions we stated in Section 1.2 and mention how they are related to the key challenges in Section 1.1.3.

Question 1: What are the particular languages and tools in the respective spaces?

Before any of the key challenges are tackled, a specification of concepts, languages, and tools is needed. In this thesis we combined a modelware and an ontoware technological space. Hence, we first analyzed these spaces.

Modelware technological spaces provide metamodeling languages to define the abstract syntax definition of a modeling language. grUML is a metamodeling language that allows for using UML class diagrams to define graph schemas representing metamodels. Metamodels are used to prescribe the structure of instance models. With respect to the tools and services, a modelware technological space provides the basic editor tools to create and manipulate models. In addition, querying tools and transformation tools are provided to retrieve facts from given instance models, or to translate models to models conforming to another modeling language.

The ontoware technological space we presented is based on OWL 2 as the language to model ontoware models (ontologies). Given an ontoware model, the ontoware technological space provides reasoning and querying tools. Reasoning tools are used to emphasize inferred knowledge in ontoware models. Querying tools are used to retrieve facts from ontoware models, where these facts may be stated explicitly in the model or may be inferred facts by reasoners.

Question 2: What are the commonalities and variations of a modelware technological space and an ontoware technological space?

For the comparison of modelware and ontoware technological spaces, we compared modeling languages provided by both spaces and the tools and services they offer. With respect to the key challenges, a comparison of spaces is needed to detect languages and services, which may help to define correctness and formal semantics of modeling languages (Challenge 2) and to support the tooling by additional services (Challenge 3). Furthermore, a comparison is needed to identify concepts which can be bridged (Challenge 1).

In particular, we compared the data modeling languages grUML and OWL 2. We identified many common concepts having similar semantics. In addition to the common concepts, OWL 2 provides a comprehensive set of class expressions and axioms used to extend the description of modeled data in ontologies. grUML is more powerful in the definition of attributes, since it allows for attributing edge classes.

Besides languages we compared the query technologies of both technological spaces. SPARQL and GReQL provide various features, which are not shared by the respective other language. In the case of querying and constraining modelware models, GReQL with its regular path expressions seems to be more applicable. Advantages of SPARQL are discovered if we add reasoning capabilities. Based on the descriptions in data models, reasoning allows for inferring new facts, which might be queried.

Question 3: What are the techniques to bridge technological spaces?

In this thesis we presented four different bridging technologies. All bridges provide services for combining two arbitrary modeling languages from different technological spaces (Challenge 1).

The transformation bridge is used to translate models according to some transformation definition. The integration bridge supports language designers to combine the metamodels of two modeling languages. Language users are able to use both languages simultaneously and to create hybrid models. The mapping bridge allows for using modeling languages separately and combining models by just declaring mappings between model elements. The API bridge provides predefined methods and services to create, modify, and save models.

Question 4: How may the formal semantics of ontology languages be used for software modeling languages?

The integration of ontology languages with metamodeling languages allows the definition of language metamodels with integrated ontology-based expressions. They define the abstract syntax of a modeling language and restrict the structure of user models.

The integration of ontology languages with modeling languages for conceptual domain modeling allows the description of domain models where the description of domain types and instances may be enriched by ontology-based expressions (Challenge 4).

The concrete syntax of modeling languages stays the same but may be extended by the definition of annotations representing ontology-based expressions.

To establish model-theoretic semantics for a given language (Challenge 2), the language is integrated with an ontology language, which specifies the semantic extensions of given model elements. The definition of semantics of modeling languages may also be achieved by a translation of models to ontoware models, which formally describe model elements according to the semantics.

Question 5: How do ontology technologies support the design and correctness of models?

The use of modeling languages may be supported by ontoware services (Challenge 3).

Based on a metamodel with ontology-based expressions and based on the formal semantics ontology languages have, several services for language users and domain modelers may be implemented. These services profit from the reasoning services freely provided by ontoware reasoning tools.

Language users benefit from services for inconsistency detection to localize problems in models, for inconsistency diagnosis to explain problems in models, and inconsistency handling to repair models.

Domain modelers use services for validating conceptual domain modeling and retrieving information from such models.

Question 6: How are integrated ontology technologies applied in domain-specific modeling?

All key challenges tackled with use of ontology languages and technologies are exemplified by a scenario for domain-specific modeling.

Metamodeling languages bridged with ontology languages allow language designers to build DSL metamodels with additional OWL 2-based expressions conceptualizing and restricting the domain to be modeled.

Integration bridges combining metamodeling languages with OWL 2 allow for the projection of the DSL metamodel and conforming domain models to one ontoware model. Given such an ontoware model, several domain-specific services to support tooling may be established based on the services provided by ontoware reasoning tools. They are used by language users for guidance and inconsistency management.

11.2 Outlook and Future Work

After we concluded this thesis we are going to present an outlook and future work. Based on the techniques and approaches developed for this thesis we set up some tasks, which should be tackled in the future.

Improvements of Bridging Technologies

One future task will be the extension of our bridging approaches. We will explore the simultaneous combination of more than two languages. Since several languages are integrated simultaneously, the respective integration information must be kept. Here we expect an extension of the traceability models. Since elements in metamodels are often annotated by constraints, e.g., written in GReQL or OCL [WK03], these also have to be integrated. We have to explore approaches that allow for merging constraints as well. Ontology technologies could help to find contradictions between these constraints because they allow for schema reasoning.

Furthermore, since metamodels are integrated, the integration bridge should also provide the capability to integrate conforming models.

The set of integration services described in Section 5.3.1 has been chosen for combining languages, which own compositional semantics, i.e., languages whose overall semantics are a combination of the partial semantics of some of the metaclasses (vertex and/or edge classes). This property allows to build the integration merely using operations on the metaclasses. By extending the set of integration services, we also plan deal with other languages.

Bridging MDE with Other Spaces

The bridges presented in this work may be used to combine ontoware spaces with modelware spaces. Nevertheless, the bridging technologies may be used to combine other technological spaces.

One space we could imagine is that for software product line engineering (SPLE) [PBL05]. Such spaces provide concepts and languages for describing commonalities as well as variations of software products being part of one family. SPLE spaces provide tools and services for validating configurations and generators to build source code for a valid configuration. The integration with a modelware technological space could enable the definition of variations and dependencies between concepts in language metamodels. Instances of these metamodels may build a concrete configuration of a software system, which is validated and translated to source code by SPLE tools.

To compare the use of ontology technologies in software modeling with technologies from other logic-based spaces, the bridging technologies may be reused. For example, the Alloy space [Jac02] providing the Alloy analyzer, which is used to validate modelware models, may be compared with our ontoware technological space.

A

Appendix

A.1 Additional Definitions for the TGraph Technological Space

A.1.1 Self-Conformance of grUML

In the following, we informally show that the grUML metaschema conforms to itself.

Therefore, we present excerpts of the grUML metaschema as graph schema in abstract syntax. Since this graph schema in abstract syntax fulfills Definition 1 it is a TGraph. Hence, we have to show that we can create a TGraph that describes the structure of the grUML metaschema and which conforms to the grUML metaschema, which in turn acts as the graph schema for the TGraph.

For the self-conformance we consider only a core of constructs ((1) vertex classes, edge classes; (2) type hierarchies; (3) attributes; (4) multiplicities).

(1) Vertex Class and Edge Class

Figure A.1 depicts a partial TGraph that describes the relation of VertexClass and EdgeClass as it is described in the grUML metaschema (cf. Figure 2.3).

Three vertices describe the vertex classes VertexClass, IncidenceClass and EdgeClass. Three further vertices describe the edge classes ComesFrom, GoesTo and EndsAt. All vertices are related to each other, where each edge class has exactly two edges to vertices representing the incidences of an edge. Further each incidence class vertex is linked to a vertex representing one end of the edge class.

The TGraph in Figure A.1 conforms to the grUML metaschema. All vertices of the graph conform to the type (represented in the vertex after ":") and to its supertypes, since all multiplicity restrictions are *locally* fulfilled and all necessary attributes are allocated by values conforming to the domain of the attributes. Further all edges in the graph conform to edge classes of the

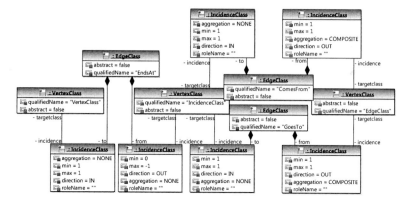

Figure A.1. grUML VertexClass- / EdgeClass-constructs in abstract syntax.

schema, since all start and end vertices conform to the corresponding vertex classes.

Locally means that we only consider those multiplicity restrictions that must be fulfilled within the scope of defining vertex classes, edge classes and incidence classes including their attributes. For example, restrictions, which ensure that each vertex class or each edge class has to belong to exactly one package, which is part of one graph schema, are not considered.

(2) Type Hierarchies

Figure A.2 depicts the TGraph, which describes the constructs to define type hierarchies of vertex classes and edge classes.

For specialization associations between vertex classes or edge classes one vertex in the TGraph of type EdgeClass is used to describe the relation between two vertex classes via two corresponding vertices of type IncidenceClass.

In both cases one vertex class and edge class can have 0 to many sub- and/or superclasses.

The TGraph in Figure A.2, representing the constructs for type hierarchies, conforms to the grUML metaschema. All vertices of the graph conform to the type and to its supertypes, since all multiplicity restrictions are fulfilled locally and all necessary attributes are allocated by values conforming to the domain of the attributes. Further all edges in the graph conform to edge classes of the schema, since all start and end vertices conform to the corresponding vertex classes.

(3) Attributes

Figure A.3 depicts the TGraph, which describes the constructs to define attributes for vertex classes and edge classes. Since the vertices, which represent

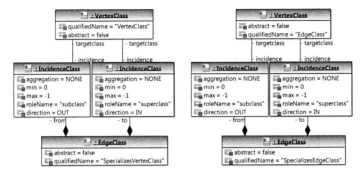

Figure A.2. grUML constructs for type hierarchy definition in abstract syntax.

vertex class and edge class, are specializations of the vertex for AttributedElementClass they are able to be connected via a vertex representing the edge class HasAttribute and two corresponding vertices for incidence classes with some vertex representing the type for attributes. Further each attribute has a domain.

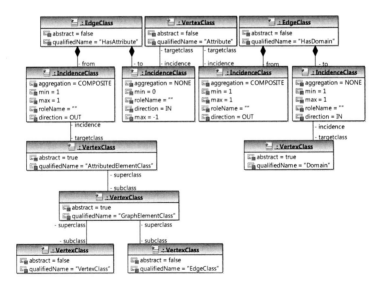

Figure A.3. grUML constructs for attribute definitions in abstract syntax.

The TGraph in Figure A.3, representing the constructs for defining attributes, conforms to the grUML metaschema. All vertices of the graph conform to the type and to its supertypes, since all multiplicity restrictions are fulfilled locally and all necessary attributes are allocated by values conforming to the domain of the attribute. Further all edges in the graph conform to edge classes of the schema, since all start and end vertices conform to the corresponding vertex classes.

(4) Multiplicities

Figure A.4 depicts the TGraph, which describes the constructs for defining multiplicities in incidence classes of one edge class. Each edge class is linked with two incidence classes, which have two attributes with domain Integer defining the min- and max-multiplicity.

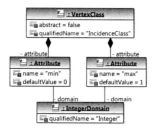

Figure A.4. grUML constructs for multiplicity definitions in abstract syntax.

The TGraph in Figure A.4, representing the constructs for defining multiplicities, conforms to the grUML metaschema. All vertices of the graph conform to the type and to its supertypes, since all multiplicity restrictions are locally fulfilled and all necessary attributes are allocated by values conforming to the domain of the attribute. Further all edges in the graph conform to edge classes of the schema, since all start and end vertices conform to the corresponding vertex classes.

A.1.2 Visualizations of Graph Schemas

Since we have graph schemas in abstract syntax form (represented as a TGraph conforming to the grUML metaschema) and in concrete syntax form (represented as a grUML diagram), in the following we are going to define a relation between both kinds of schemas. This relation is described by a *vis* function, which defines which elements of a grUML diagram are visualizations of which elements of a graph schema in abstract syntax.

We define the *vis* function in Definition 6.

Definition 6 (*Visualization of Graph Schemas*)

> The *vis* function maps elements of a graph schema in concrete syntax GS_{CS} to elements of a graph schema in abstract syntax GS_{AS}.

Visualizations of Vertex Classes. If GS_{AS} is the graph schema in abstract syntax of GS_{CS} then *vis* is an isomorphism with

$$vis : V_{GS_{CS}} \rightarrow V_{GS_{AS}}$$

and

$$\forall t \in V_{GS_{CS}} : \exists t' \in V_{GS_{AS}} : vis(t) = t'$$

where $t'.qualifiedName$ is the name of the class t in $V_{GS_{CS}}$

Visualizations of Edge Classes. If GS_{AS} is the graph schema in abstract syntax of GS_{CS} then *vis* is an isomorphism with

$$vis : E_{GS_{CS}} \rightarrow E_{GS_{AS}}$$

and

$$\forall t \in E_{GS_{CS}} : \exists t' \in E_{GS_{AS}} : vis(t) = t'$$

where $t'.qualifiedName$ is the name of the association t in $V_{GS_{CS}}$

Visualizations of Attributes. If GS_{AS} is the graph schema in abstract syntax of GS_{CS} then *vis* is an isomorphism with

$$vis : Attr_{GS_{CS}} \rightarrow Attr_{GS_{AS}}$$

and

$$\forall a \in Attr_{GS_{CS}} : \exists a' \in Attr_{GS_{AS}} : vis(a) = a'$$

where $a'.name$ is the name of the attribute a in $Attr_{GS_{CS}}$ and d with $a' \rightarrow \{HasDomain\}d$ is also the domain of a.

Correlation of Graph Schema Functions

Having a visualization relation between a graph schema GS_{AS} in abstract syntax and a graph schema GS_{CS} in concrete syntax, we can show that the results of the set notation functions (in Definition 2) of GS_{CS} correlate with the corresponding results of the set notation functions (in Definition 4) for GS_{AS}.

If t is a class or association, the vertex class or edge class in GS_{AS}, which is visualized by t, has the same attributes with the same domain:

$$\forall t \in V_{GS_{CS}} \cup E_{GS_{CS}} : \forall a \in \mathrm{dom}\; typeDefinition_{GS_{CS}}(t) :$$
$$vis(a) \in \mathrm{dom}\; typeDefinition_{GS_{AS}}(vis(t))$$
$$\wedge\, (typeDefinition_{GS_{CS}}(t))(a) = (typeDefinition_{GS_{AS}}(vis(t)))(vis(a))$$

If t_{sub} is specialized by t_{sup}, then the elements in GS_{AS}, which are visualized by t_{sub} and t_{sup}, are also related by a specialization relationship:

$$\forall\, t_{sub}, t_{sup} \in V_{GS_{CS}} \cup E_{GS_{CS}} :$$
$$t_{sub}\ isA_{GS_{CS}}\ t_{sup} \Rightarrow vis(t_{sub})\ isA_{GS_{AS}}\ vis(t_{sup})$$

If t is the association in GS_{CS}, which relates the classes t_s and t_t, then the edge class in GS_{AS}, which is visualized by the association t relates the two vertex classes, which are visualized by t_s and t_t:

$$\forall\, t \in E_{GS_{CS}} : \exists\, t_s, t_t \in V_{GS_{CS}} :$$
$$relates_{GS_{CS}}(t) = (t_s, t_t) \Rightarrow relates_{GS_{AS}}(vis(t)) = (vis(t_s), vis(t_t))$$

If t is an association, then the edge class in GS_{AS}, which is visualized by the association t, has the same multiplicities:

$$\forall\, t \in E_{GS_{CS}} : multiplicity_{GS_{CS}}(t) = multiplicity_{GS_{AS}}(vis(t))$$

A.1.3 Model-Theoretic Semantics of Graph Schemas

After we discussed in Section 2.2.2 how TGraphs conform to its graph schema, we are going to consider the relation between schemas and graphs where schemas represent the set of all possible graphs. The set of all possible graphs belonging to one graph schema is called its extensions. Since schemas consist of classes defining vertex classes, associations defining edge classes, incidences of edge classes, and attributes nested in vertex and edge classes, we describe the extension for each of them.

Representation Sets of Graph Schemas

In the following the semantic extension is assigned to each element of a graph schema by corresponding *representation* functions *repr*, which interpret graph schema elements by mapping them to subsets of vertices and edges of a given TGraph and to values as given in Definition 1.

Definition 7 (*Model-theoretic semantics of graph schemas*)

For a given graph schema GS in set notation and for a given TGraph G we define interpretation functions for vertex classes, edge classes, incidences, and attributes.

Vertex Classes and Edge Classes. The interpretation function $repr_{VC}^{G}$ assigns to each vertex class of a graph schema GS a set of vertices of a TGraph G:

$$repr_{VC}^{G} : V_{GS} \rightarrow \mathcal{P}(V)$$

The set $\overline{V} \subseteq V$ is the semantic extension of vertex class t if $repr_{VC}^{G}(t) = \overline{V}$.

The interpretation function $repr_{EC}^{G}$ assigns to each edge class of a graph schema a set of edges of a TGraph G:

$$repr_{EC}^{G} : E_{GS} \to \mathcal{P}(E)$$

The set $\overline{E} \subseteq E$ is the semantic extension of an edge class t if $repr_{EC}^{G}(t) = \overline{E}$.

Incidences. The interpretation function $repr_{Inc}^{G}$ assigns to each edge class of a graph schema a pair of functions, which define start vertex and target vertex of edges of a TGraph G:

$$repr_{Inc}^{G} : E_{GS} \to (E \to V) \times (E \to V)$$

Attributes. The interpretation function $repr_{Att}^{G}$ assigns to each attribute nested in a type of a grUML diagram a function, which defines the allocation of the attribute within a concrete vertex or edge:

$$repr_{Att}^{G} : Attr_{GS} \to (V \cup E \nrightarrow Value)$$

Given Definition 7, the semantic extensions of vertex classes and edge classes must fulfill some restrictions.

Incidence Restriction. The representation of the two incidences of an edge class is a pair of functions, which define the incidences of an edge. The edge class only represents connections of vertices from the semantic extensions of vertex classes, which are related by the given edge class:

$\forall t \in E_{GS} : repr_{Inc}^{G}(t) = (\alpha, \omega)$ with $\alpha : \overline{E} \to \overline{A}$ and $\omega : \overline{E} \to \overline{B}$ if

$$\overline{E} = repr_{EC}^{G}(t) \wedge$$
$$\overline{A} = repr_{VC}^{G}(relates(t).first) \wedge$$
$$\overline{B} = repr_{VC}^{G}(relates(t).second)$$

Thus each edge $e \in \overline{E}$ links two vertices from $\overline{A}$ and $\overline{B}$.

Attribute Restriction. The representation of an attribute is a function, which assigns vertices and edges, which contain the attribute to a set of values. The set of values must be part of the universe of all attribute values and the set of values must be equal with the domain of the attribute:

$\forall a \in Attr_{GS} : repr_{Att}^{G}(a) = f_{val}$ with $f_{val} : V \cup E \to D$ if

$$D \subseteq Value \wedge$$
$$\forall x \in V \cup E : valueSet((typeDefinition(type(x)))(a)) = D$$

Thus, all values assigned to an attribute a are in the universe of all values and the domain of a is D as defined in the schema.

Type Hierarchies. If $t_{sub} \in V_{GS} \cup E_{GS}$ is subtype of $t_{super} \in V_{GS} \cup E_{GS}$ (t_{sub} *isA** t_{super}), then every vertex or edge x with $type(x) = t_{sub}$ must additionally implement all attributes, which are nested in t_{super}. If t_{sub} and t_{super} are the vertex classes, the following condition must hold:

$$\forall\, v \in repr^G_{VC}(t_{sub}) : \forall\, a \in \mathrm{dom}\ typeDefinition(t_{super}) : a \in \mathrm{dom}\ value(v)$$

If t_{sub} and t_{super} are edge classes the following condition must hold:

$$\forall\, e \in repr^G_{EC}(t_{sub}) : \forall\, a \in \mathrm{dom}\ typeDefinition(t_{super}) : a \in \mathrm{dom}\ value(e)$$

Furthermore, each vertex v with $type(v) = t_{sub}$ must be incident with a valid number of edges conforming to the edge classes, which are incident with t_{super}:

$$\forall\, v \in repr^G_{VC}(t_{sub}) :$$

$$\quad \forall\, t \in \{t \in E_{GS} \mid relates(t).first = t_{super}\} :$$
$$\quad\quad (multiplicity(t).second).min \leq \delta^+(v,t) \leq (multiplicity(t).second).max$$
$$\quad \forall\, t \in \{t \in E_{GS} \mid relates(t).second = t_{super}\} :$$
$$\quad\quad (multiplicity(t).first).min \leq \delta^-(v,t) \leq (multiplicity(t).first).max$$

(Since t_{sub} *isA*^{0} t_{super} implies $t_{sub} = t_{super}$ all vertices must be incident with a valid number of edges conforming to the edge classes, which are incident with t_{sub}.)

Relation between *conformsTo* and *repr*

Now, concluding Section 2.2.2 and A.1.3, we have defined how a given TGraph conforms to its graph schema and which sets of TGraphs are described by a given graph schema.

We are able to relate both functions for representations and conformance for a given graph schema GS and a TGraph G. We are able to state that each vertex class of a graph schema only represents those vertices, which conform to the vertex class itself:

$$\forall\, t \in V_{GS} : \forall\, v \in repr^G_{VC}(t) : t \in conformsTo(v)$$

We can state the same for edge classes of a graph schema, which only represent those edges, which conform to the edge class itself:

$$\forall\, t \in E_{GS} : \forall\, e \in repr^G_{EC}(t) : t \in conformsTo(e)$$

Further we can state that all start and end vertices, which are represented by the two incidences of an edge class conform to vertex classes, which are incident with the edge class in the graph schema:

$$\forall\, t \in E_{GS} : repr^G_{Inc}(t) = (\alpha, \omega) \text{ with } \alpha : \overline{E} \to \overline{A}, \omega : \overline{E} \to \overline{B} :$$
$$\forall\, v_1 \in \overline{A} : relates(t).first \in conformsTo(v_1) \wedge$$
$$\forall\, v_2 \in \overline{B} : relates(t).second \in conformsTo(v_2)$$

A.1.4 Modelware Basic Services

Basic services are mainly used to create a graph and to manipulate a graph by creating or deleting vertices and edges and setting attribute values. Since graph schemas can be represented as graphs (cf. Definition 4), the services specified below allow for defining and manipulating graph schemas as well.

The service specified in Table A.1 is used to create an empty graph for a given graph schema. The service specified in Table A.2 is used to delete a graph. The services are provided by the Modelware class.

Name	Create Graph
Signature	Graph createGraph(Schema s)
Pattern	g=Modelware.createGraph(s)
Description	creates a new graph g, which conforms to s.

Table A.1. Basic service: createGraph.

Name	Delete Graph
Signature	void deleteGraph(Graph g)
Pattern	g=Modelware.deleteGraph(g)
Description	deletes the graph g.

Table A.2. Basic service: deleteGraph.

The service specified in Table A.3 creates a vertex for a given vertex class. The services in the following are provided by the graph object returned by the createGraph service specified in Table A.1.

Name	Create Vertex
Signature	Vertex createVertex(VertexClass c)
Pattern	v=g.createVertex(c)
Description	creates a new vertex v of type c in the graph g.

Table A.3. Basic service: createVertex.

The service specified in Table A.4 allows for the deletion of a vertex in a given graph.

The service specified in Table A.3 creates an edge for a given edge class. The service is provided by the graph object returned by the **createGraph** service specified in Table A.1.

The service specified in Table A.6 allows for the deletion of an edge in a given graph.

Name	Delete Vertex
Signature	void deleteVertex(Vertex v)
Pattern	g.deleteVertex(v)
Description	deletes the vertex v in the graph g.

Table A.4. Basic service: deleteVertex.

Name	Create Edge
Signature	Edge createEdge(EdgeClass c, Vertex v, Vertex w)
Pattern	e=g.createEdge(c)
Description	creates a new edge e of type c in the graph g, which goes from the vertex v to the vertex w.

Table A.5. Basic service: createEdge.

Name	Delete Edge
Signature	void deleteEdge(Vertex e)
Pattern	g.deleteEdge(e)
Description	deletes the edge e in the graph g.

Table A.6. Basic service: deleteEdge.

The service specified in Table A.7 allows for setting a given attribute to a given value.

Name	Set Attribute
Signature	void setAttribute(Attribute a, Object o)
Pattern	g.setAttribute(e)
Description	sets the attribute a in the graph g to the value described by o.

Table A.7. Basic service: setAttribute.

A.2 OWL 2 Metamodel

As mentioned in Section 3.2, $\mathcal{SROIQ}(\mathcal{D})$ is the description logic, which defines all possible constructs and semantics for OWL 2 (including datatypes and data roles). For all $\mathcal{SROIQ}(\mathcal{D})$ constructs we show how they are realized by correspondent constructs in OWL 2. We show the constructs in concrete syntax using the textual *OWL 2 Functional-Style Syntax* [MPSH09] and in abstract syntax by presenting excerpts of the metamodel GS_{OWL}.

Knowledge Bases in OWL 2

Every ontoware model describes TBox and ABox of a DL knowledge base as ontology. An ontology has an IRI and contains a set of axioms. Table A.8 shows the constructs OWL 2 provides to model an ontology.

OWL 2 / DL Construct	OWL 2 Functional-Style Syntax	DL Syntax
ontology / knowledge base	Ontology(IRI)	

Table A.8. OWL 2 construct for an initial ontology.

Figure A.5 depicts the part of GS_{OWL}, which is used to declare an ontology in an ontoware model and connects it with axioms.

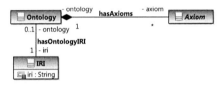

Figure A.5. OWL 2 constructs in GS_{OWL} for declaring an ontology.

Description Logic Constructs $\mathcal{S}$ in OWL 2

As shown above the description logic $\mathcal{S}$ allows for defining concepts and (transitive) roles. In addition it allows for defining the negation, the disjunction and the conjunction of several concepts, and quantifications over roles. Table A.9 describes which OWL 2 constructs realize the constructs provided by the description logic $\mathcal{S}$.

Figure A.6 depicts the part of GS_{OWL}, which is used to declare classes and object properties in an ontoware model. The declaration axiom is used to define several entities like classes and object properties and requires an IRI. An object property is declared as transitive via the given object property axiom.

Figure A.7 depicts the part of GS_{OWL}, which is used to declare quantifications in ontoware models. The *object some values* construct describes those individuals, which are linked with at least an instance of the given class expression by the given object property expression. The *object all values* construct describes those individuals, which are only linked with instances of the given class expression by the given object property expression.

Figure A.8 depicts the part of GS_{OWL}, which is used to declare boolean combinations in ontoware models. The *object complement* construct describes

OWL 2 / DL Construct	OWL 2 Functional-Style Syntax	DL Syntax
class / concept	Declaration(Class(A))	A
object property / role	Declaration(ObjectProperty(R))	R
transitive object property / transitive role	TransitiveObjectProperty(R)	$R \in \mathbf{R}_+$
object intersection / conjunction	ObjectIntersectionOf(C_1 ... C_n)	$C_1 \sqcap ... \sqcap C_2$
object union / disjunction	ObjectUnionOf(C_1 ... C_n)	$C_1 \sqcup ... \sqcap C_n$
object complement / negation	ObjectComplementOf(C)	$\neg C$
object some values / existential quantification	ObjectSomeValuesFrom(P C)	$\exists P.C$
object all values / universal quantification	ObjectAllValuesFrom(P C)	$\forall P.C$

Table A.9. OWL 2 constructs for description logic $\mathcal{S}$.

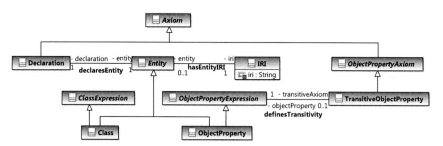

Figure A.6. OWL 2 constructs in GS_{OWL} for declaring classes and object properties.

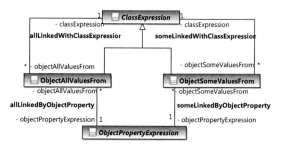

Figure A.7. OWL 2 constructs in GS_{OWL} for declaring quantifications.

the complement of one given class expression. The *object union* construct describes the union of at least two class expressions. The *object intersection* construct describes the intersection of at least two class expressions.

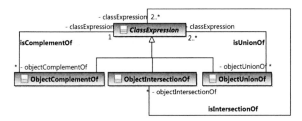

Figure A.8. OWL 2 constructs in GS_{OWL} for declaring boolean connectives.

Description Logic Constructs $\mathcal{R}$ in OWL 2

The description logic $\mathcal{R}$ allows for defining general role hierarchies and self concepts. Table A.10 describes which OWL 2 constructs realize these constructs.

OWL 2 / DL Construct	OWL 2 Functional-Style Syntax	DL Syntax
top object property / universal role	topObjectProperty	U
sub object property / generalized role inclusion	SubObjectPropertyOf(SubObjectPropertyChain(R_1 ... R_n) R)	$R_1 \circ \ldots R_n \sqsubseteq R$
object has self / self concept	ObjectHasSelf(S)	$\exists S.SELF$

Table A.10. OWL 2 constructs for description logic $\mathcal{R}$.

Figure A.9 depicts the description of *sub object property hierarchies* in GS_{OWL}. A *sub object property axiom* in an ontoware model relates exactly two object property expressions. The *sub object property chain* is a specific object property expression and allows for representing an ordered chain of object properties. Besides sub object property hierarchies Figure A.9 presents the construct for the *self concept*. It describes a class expression, which contains those individuals that are connected via a given object property to themselves.

Description Logic Constructs $\mathcal{O}$ in OWL 2

The description logic $\mathcal{O}$ allows for defining nominals, which are enumerations of individuals. Table A.11 describes which OWL 2 construct realizes nominals.

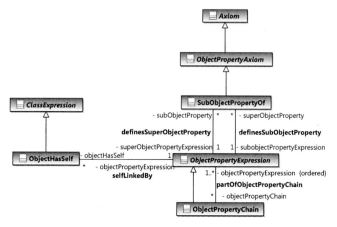

Figure A.9. OWL 2 constructs in GS_{OWL} for role hierarchies and self concepts.

OWL 2 / DL Construct	OWL 2 Functional-Style Syntax	DL Syntax
object one of / nominals	ObjectOneOf(i_1 ... i_n)	$\{i_1\} \sqcup ... \sqcup \{i_n\}$

Table A.11. OWL 2 constructs for description logic $\mathcal{O}$.

Figure A.10 depicts the description of the *object one of* construct for ontoware models. It is a class expression that represents an enumeration of at least one individual. Individuals in an ontoware model are entities, which have an IRI and must be declared.

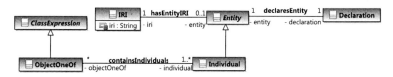

Figure A.10. OWL 2 constructs in GS_{OWL} for nominals.

Description Logic Constructs $\mathcal{I}$ in OWL 2

The description logic $\mathcal{I}$ allows for defining inverse roles. Table A.12 describes which OWL 2 construct realizes inverse roles.

Figure A.11 depicts the description of the *object inverse of* construct for ontoware models. It is an object property expression that represents the inverse of exactly one other object property expression.

OWL 2 / DL Construct	OWL 2 Functional-Style Syntax	DL Syntax
object inverse of/ inverse roles	ObjectInverseOf(R)	R^-

Table A.12. OWL 2 constructs for description logic $\mathcal{I}$.

Figure A.11. OWL 2 constructs in GS_{OWL} for inverse roles.

Description Logic Constructs $\mathcal{Q}$ in OWL 2

The description logic $\mathcal{Q}$ allows for defining quantified cardinality restrictions. Table A.13 describes which OWL 2 constructs realize these restrictions.

OWL 2 / DL Construct	OWL 2 Functional-Style Syntax	DL Syntax
object min cardinality / at least restriction	ObjectMinCardinality(n S C)	$\geq nS.C$
object max cardinality / at most restriction	ObjectMaxCardinality(n S C)	$\leq nS.C$
object exact cardinality / exact restriction	ObjectExactCardinality(n S C)	$= nS.C$

Table A.13. OWL 2 constructs for description logic $\mathcal{Q}$.

Figure A.12 depicts the description of cardinality restrictions for object properties. Each restriction is a class expression and contains an attribute to define the cardinality. Each restriction represents those individuals, which are connected by an object property expression to at least, at most, and exactly a given number of instances of a specified class expression, respectively.

Description Logic Constructs $\mathcal{D}$ in OWL 2

The description logic $\mathcal{D}$ allows for defining data roles and datatypes. Table A.14 describes which OWL 2 constructs realize datatypes, data roles and data nominals.

Figure A.13 depicts the constructs of GS_{OWL}, which allow for defining *data ranges* and *data properties* in ontoware models. Data properties are specific data property expressions. A data range is either a datatype (e.g., Integer, String, Boolean, etc.) or is realized by a *data one of* construct, which represents

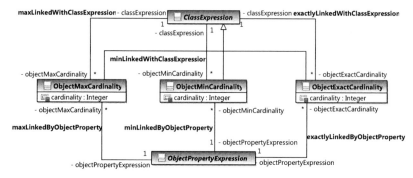

Figure A.12. OWL 2 constructs in GS_{OWL} for cardinality restrictions.

OWL 2 / DL Construct	OWL 2 Functional-Style Syntax	DL Syntax
datatype / datatype	D	D
data property / datatype role	Declaration(DataProperty(U))	U
data one of / data nominals	DataOneOf(v)	$\{v\}$
literal / data value	v	v

Table A.14. OWL 2 constructs for description logic $\mathcal{D}$ for datatypes and data roles.

an enumeration of literals (data values) valued by a lexical string. In addition, Figure A.13 presents the data property assertion construct, which allows for connecting individuals with literals via a given data property.

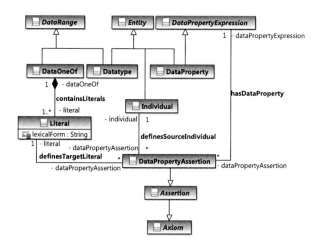

Figure A.13. OWL 2 constructs in GS_{OWL} for data ranges and data properties.

Table A.15 describes which OWL 2 constructs realize quantifications on data roles.

OWL 2 / DL Construct	OWL 2 Functional-Style Syntax	DL Syntax
data some values from / datatype existential quantification	DataSomeValuesFrom(U D)	$\exists\, U.D$
data all values from / datatype universal quantification	DataAllValuesFrom(U D)	$\forall\, U.D$

Table A.15. OWL 2 constructs for description logic $\mathcal{D}$ for data quantifications.

Figure A.14 depicts the constructs of GS_{OWL}, which allow for defining quantifications on data properties. All quantification are class expression, which describe those individuals that are connected to some data values or only are connected to data values of a given data range.

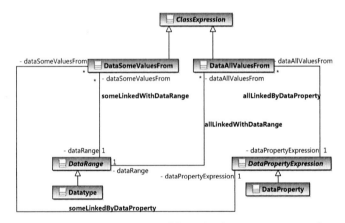

Figure A.14. OWL 2 constructs in GS_{OWL} for data property quantifications.

Table A.16 describes which OWL 2 constructs realize cardinality restrictions on data roles.

Figure A.15 depicts the description of cardinality restrictions for data properties. Each restriction is a class expression and contains an attribute to define the cardinality. Each restriction represents those individuals, which are connected by a data property expression to at least, at most, and exactly a given number of literals of a specified data range, respectively.

OWL 2 / DL Construct	OWL 2 Functional-Style Syntax	DL Syntax
data min cardinality / data at least restriction	DataMinCardinality(n U D)	$\geq nU.D$
data max cardinality / data at most restriction	DataMaxCardinality(n U D)	$\leq nU.D$
data exact cardinality / data exactly restriction	DataExactCardinality(n U D)	$= nU.D$

Table A.16. OWL 2 constructs for description logic $\mathcal{D}$ for data cardinality restrictions.

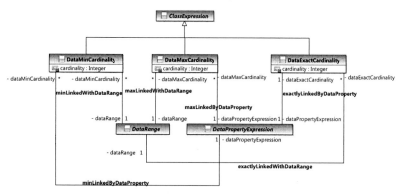

Figure A.15. OWL 2 constructs in GS_{OWL} for data property cardinality restrictions.

General Concept Inclusion Axioms and Assertions in OWL 2

As explained in Definition 5, each DL knowledge base consists of a TBox and an ABox, while the TBox consists of GCIs and the ABox consists of assertions. Table A.17 shows, which constructs OWL 2 provides to model description logics GCIs and assertions.

Figure A.16 depicts the description of GCI constructs in GS_{OWL}. Here, the *disjoint classes* axiom and the *equivalent classes* axiom are linked to at least two class expressions, where the *subclass* axiom is linked to exactly one superclass and one subclass.

Figure A.17 depicts the description of assertions in GS_{OWL}. Here, class assertions are used to define the type represented as class expression of one given individual. Object property assertions are used to assert a given object property by declaring a source and a target individual.

Auxiliary Axioms and Expressions in OWL 2

In the following, we describe some auxiliary axioms, which can be derived by combining existing constructs.

OWL 2 / DL Construct	OWL 2 Functional-Style Syntax	DL Syntax
subclass / GCI	SubClassOf(C D)	$C \sqsubseteq D$
equivalent classes / GCIs	EquivalentClasses(C_1 ... C_n)	$C_1 \equiv ... \equiv C_n$
disjoint classes / GCIs	DisjointClasses(C_1 ... C_n)	$C_i \sqcap C_j \equiv \bot$ $(1 \le i < j \le n)$
class assertion / class assertion	ClassAssertion(C c)	$c \in C$
object property assertion / role assertion	ObjectPropertyAssertion(R e d)	$(e, d) \in R$

Table A.17. OWL 2 concrete syntax for GCIs and assertions.

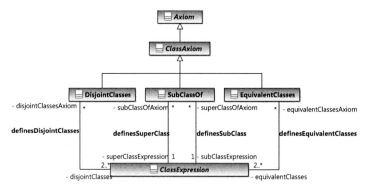

Figure A.16. OWL 2 constructs in GS_{OWL} for declaring class axioms.

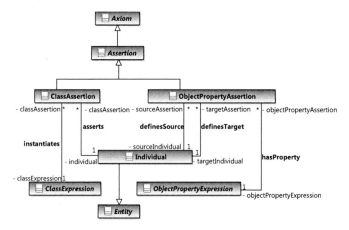

Figure A.17. OWL 2 constructs in GS_{OWL} for individual assertions.

Table A.18 describes which OWL 2 constructs realize domain and range axioms for object properties.

OWL 2 / DL Construct	OWL 2 Functional-Style Syntax	DL Syntax
object property domain / role domain	ObjectPropertyDomain(R C)	$\exists R.\top \sqsubseteq C$
object property range / role range	ObjectPropertyRange(R C)	$\top \sqsubseteq \forall R.C$

Table A.18. OWL 2 concrete syntax for domain and range of roles.

Figure A.18 depicts the constructs in GS_{OWL} for defining domain and range of an object property.

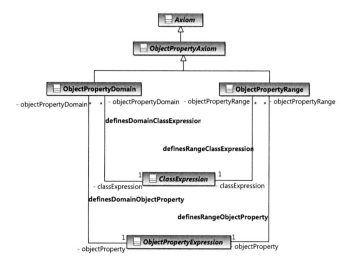

Figure A.18. OWL 2 constructs in GS_{OWL} for object property domain and range.

Table A.19 describes which OWL 2 constructs realize domain and range axioms for data properties.

OWL 2 / DL Construct	OWL 2 Functional-Style Syntax	DL Syntax
data property domain / data role domain	DatatPropertyDomain(U C)	$\exists U.\top \sqsubseteq C$
data property range / data role range	DatatPropertyRange(U D)	$\top \sqsubseteq \forall U.D$

Table A.19. OWL 2 concrete syntax for domain and range of data roles.

Figure A.19 depicts the constructs in GS_{OWL} for defining domain and range of a data property. The data property domain and range axiom define that the domain of a data property expression is a class expression and the range is a data range.

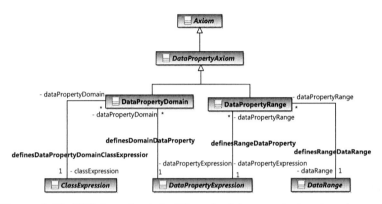

Figure A.19. OWL 2 constructs in GS_{OWL} for data property domain and range.

A.3 Bridging Technologies

A.3.1 Example of Transformation Bridge

In the following we give an example where we present eight transformation steps, one for each relation given in Table 5.2. The set of transformation steps describe how the output of a transformation service transform$_{GS_{BEDSL}}$ is produced, which conforms to GS_{OWL}. All transformation steps are formally specified in GReTL.

1. Model to Ontology

For all vertices conforming to Model in the modelware model a new vertex of type Ontology is created in the ontoware model. The ontology is connected with an IRI, which is defined by the name of the model. Figure A.20 specifies the transformation step.

2. Entity to OWL Class

For all vertices of type Entity in the modelware model a new vertex of type Class is created in the ontoware model. A declaration is created and linked with the class. The name of the entity is assigned to a correspondent IRI. At the end the declaration axiom is added to the ontology created in the first step. Figure A.21 specifies the transformation step.

---

instantiateVertices("Ontology", "**from** v:**V**{Model} **reportSet** v **end**");
instantiateVertices("IRI", "**from** v:**V**{Model} **reportSet** v **end**");
instantiateAttributeValues("IRI", "iri", "**from** v:keySet(img_Ontology) **reportMap** v, v.name **end**");
instantiateEdges("HasOntologyIRI", "**from** v: keySet(img_Ontology), w: keySet(img_IRI) **with** v=w
    reportSet v, v, w **end**");

Figure A.20. Transformation step 1: BEDSL model to OWL ontology.

---

instantiateVertices("Class", "**from** v:**V**{Entity} **reportSet** v **end**");
instantiateVertices("Declaration", "**from** v:**V**{Entity} **reportSet** v **end**");
instantiateVertices("IRI", "**from** v:**V**{Entity} **reportSet** v **end**");
instantiateAttributeValues("IRI", "iri", "**from** v:keySet(img_Class) **reportMap** v, v.name **end**");
instantiateEdges("HasEntityIRI", "**from** v:keySet(img_Class), w:keySet(img_IRI) **with** v=w **reportSet** v, v,
    w **end**");
instantiateEdges("DeclaresEntity", "**from** v:keySet(img_Declaration), w:keySet(img_Class) **with** v=w
    reportSet v, v, w **end**");
instantiateEdges("HasAxioms", "**from** v:keySet(img_Ontology), w:keySet(img_Declaration), e:**E** **with** v——
    e—>&{Entity}w **reportSet** e, v, w **end**");

Figure A.21. Transformation step 2: BEDSL entity to OWL class.

3. Datatype to Datatype

For all vertices of type **Datatype** in the modelware model a new vertex of
type **Datatype** is created in the ontoware model. The name of the data type
in the modelware model is defined by an IRI in the ontoware model. At the
end the declaration axiom is added to the ontology. Figure A.22 specifies the
transformation step.

---

instantiateVertices("Datatype", "**from** v:**V**{Datatype} **reportSet** v **end**");
instantiateVertices("Declaration", "**from** v:**V**{Datatype} **reportSet** v **end**");
instantiateVertices("IRI", "**from** v:**V**{Datatype} **reportSet** v **end**");
instantiateAttributeValues("IRI", "iri", "**from** v:keySet(img_Datatype) **reportMap** v, v.name **end**");
instantiateEdges("HasEntityIRI", "**from** v:keySet(img_Datatype), w:keySet(img_IRI) **with** v=w **reportSet** v
    , v, w **end**");
instantiateEdges("DeclaresEntity", "**from** v:keySet(img_Declaration), w:keySet(img_Datatype) **with** v=w
    reportSet v, v, w **end**");
instantiateEdges("HasAxioms", "**from** v:keySet(img_Ontology), w:keySet(img_Declaration), e:**E** **with** v——
    e—>&{Datatype}w **reportSet** e, v, w **end**");

Figure A.22. Transformation step 3: BEDSL data type to OWL data type.

4. Reference to Object Property

For all vertices of type **Reference** in the modelware model a new vertex of
type **ObjectProperty** is created in the ontoware model. The name of the object
property is defined by an IRI. In addition, two axioms defining domain and
range of the object property are created and linked with the corresponding

classes and the object property in the ontoware model. At the end the declaration axiom and the two object property axioms for domain and range are
added to the ontology. Figure A.23 specifies the transformation step.

```
instantiateVertices("ObjectProperty", "from v:V{Reference} reportSet v end");
instantiateVertices("Declaration", "from v:V{Reference} reportSet v end");
instantiateVertices("IRI", "from v:V{Reference} reportSet v end");
instantiateAttributeValues("IRI", "iri", "from v:keySet(img_ObjectProperty) reportMap v, v.name end");
instantiateEdges("HasEntityIRI", "from v:keySet(img_ObjectProperty), w:keySet(img_IRI) with v=w
    reportSet v, v, w end");
instantiateEdges("DeclaresEntity", "from v:keySet(img_Declaration), w:keySet(img_ObjectProperty) with v
    =w reportSet v, v, w end");
instantiateVertices("ObjectPropertyDomain", "from e:E{HasFeature}, v,w:V with v--e->&{Reference
    }w reportSet e end");
instantiateEdges("HasDomainObjectProperty", "from e:keySet(img_ObjectPropertyDomain), v,w:V with v
    --e->&{Reference}w reportSet e, w, end");
instantiateEdges("HasDomainClassExpression", "from e:keySet(img_ObjectPropertyDomain), v,w:V with v
    --e->&{Reference}w reportSet e, e, v end");
instantiateVertices("ObjectPropertyRange", "from e:E{PointsTo}, v,w:V with v--e->&{Entity}w
    reportSet e end");
instantiateEdges("HasRangeObjectProperty", "from e:keySet(img_ObjectPropertyRange), v,w:V with v
    --e->&{Entity}w reportSet e, e, v end");
instantiateEdges("HasRangeClassExpression", "from e:keySet(img_ObjectPropertyRange), v,w:V with v
    --e->&{Entity}w reportSet e, e, w end");
instantiateEdges("HasAxioms", "from v:keySet(img_Ontology), w:keySet(img_Declaration), e:E with v--
    e->&{Reference}w reportSet e, v, w end");
instantiateEdges("HasAxioms", "from v:keySet(img_Ontology), e:keySet(img_ObjectPropertyDomain), w:V
    with v-->--e->&{Reference}w reportSet e, v, e end");
instantiateEdges("HasAxioms", "from v:keySet(img_Ontology), e:keySet(img_ObjectPropertyRange), w:V
    with v-->-->--e->&{Entity}w reportSet e, v, e end");
```

Figure A.23. Transformation step 4: BEDSL reference to OWL object property.

5. Attribute to DataProperty

For all vertices of type **Attribute** in the modelware model a new vertex of type
DataProperty is created and declared in the ontoware model. The name of the
data property is defined by an IRI. In addition, two axioms defining domain
and range of the data property are created and linked with the corresponding
class and the data type, respectively. At the end the declaration axiom and
two data property axioms for domain and range are added to the ontology.
Figure A.24 specifies the transformation step.

6. Enumeration to DataOneOf

For all vertices of type **Enumeration** in the modelware model a new vertex of
type **DataOneOf** is created in the ontoware model. In addition, for all enumeration entries of a given enumeration a literal is created in the ontoware
model and connected with the corresponding **DataOneOf** range. Figure A.25
specifies the transformation step.

instantiateVertices("DataProperty", "from v:**V**{Attribute} **reportSet** v **end**");
instantiateVertices("Declaration", "**from** v:**V**{Attribute} **reportSet** v **end**");
instantiateVertices("IRI", "**from** v:**V**{Attribute} **reportSet** v **end**");
instantiateAttributeValues("IRI", "iri", "**from** v:keySet(img_DataProperty) **reportMap** v, v.name **end**");
instantiateEdges("HasEntityIRI", "**from** v:keySet(img_DataProperty), w:keySet(img_IRI) **with** v=w
        reportSet v, v, w **end**");
instantiateEdges("DeclaresEntity", "**from** v:keySet(img_Declaration), w:keySet(img_DataProperty) **with** v=
        w **reportSet** v, v, w **end**");
instantiateVertices("DataPropertyDomain", "**from** e:**E**{HasFeature}, v,w:**V with** v−−e−>&{Attribute}w
        reportSet e **end**");
instantiateEdges("HasDomainDataProperty", "**from** e:keySet(img_DataPropertyDomain), v,w:**V with** v−−
        e−>&{Attribute}w **reportSet** e, e, w **end**");
instantiateEdges("HasDataPropertyClassExpression", "**from** e:keySet(img_DataPropertyDomain), v,w:**V**
        with v−−e−>&{Attribute}w **reportSet** e, e, v **end**");
instantiateVertices("DataPropertyRange", "**from** e:**E**{HasAttributeDatatype}, v,w:**V with** v−−e−>&{
        Datatype}w **reportSet** e **end**");
instantiateEdges("HasRangeDataProperty", "**from** e:keySet(img_DataPropertyRange), v,w:**V with** v−−e
        −>&{Datatype}w **reportSet** e, e, v **end**");
instantiateEdges("HasDataPropertyRange", "**from** e:keySet(img_DataPropertyRange), v,w:**V with** v−−e
        −>&{Datatype}w **reportSet** e, e, w **end**");
instantiateEdges("HasAxioms", "**from** v:keySet(img_Ontology), w:keySet(img_Declaration), e:**E with** v−−
        e−>&{Attribute}w **reportSet** e, v, w **end**");
instantiateEdges("HasAxioms", "**from** v:keySet(img_Ontology), e:keySet(img_DataPropertyDomain), w:**V**
        with v−−>−−e−>&{Attribute}w **reportSet** e, v, e **end**");
instantiateEdges("HasAxioms", "**from** v:keySet(img_Ontology), e:keySet(img_DataPropertyRange), w:**V**
        with v−−>−−>−−e−>&{Entity}w **reportSet** e, v, e **end**");

Figure A.24. Transformation step 5: BEDSL attribute to OWL data property.

instantiateVertices("DataOneOf", "**from** v:**V**{Enumeration} **reportSet** v **end**");
instantiateVertices("Literal", "**from** v:**V**{EnumerationEntry} **reportSet** v **end**");
instantiateEdges("ContainsLiterals", "**from** v:keySet(img_DataOneOf), w:keySet(img_Literal) **with** v−−>
        w **reportSet** v, v, w **end**");
instantiateAttributeValues("Literal", "lexicalValue", "**from** v:keySet(img_Literal) **reportMap** v, v.value **end**
        ");

Figure A.25. Transformation step 6: BEDSL enumeration to OWL DataOneOf.

7. hasSupertype to SubClassOf-Axiom

For all edges of type hasSupertype between two Entity vertices in the modelware model a new vertex of type SubClassOf is created in the ontoware model and connected with the corresponding OWL classes, which are involved in the given specialization relationship. At the end the subclass axiom is added to the ontology. Figure A.26 specifies the transformation step.

8. hasOpposite to InverseObjectProperty-Axiom

For all edges of type hasOpposite between two references in the modelware model a vertex of type InverseObjectProperty is created in the ontoware model. It is connected with the object property representing one reference and the object property representing the opposite reference. At the end the inverse object properties axiom is added to the ontology. Figure A.27 specifies the transformation step.

```
instantiateVertices("SubClassOf", "from e:E{HasSupertype} reportSet e end");
instantiateEdges("HasSubClass", "from e:keySet(img_SubClassOf), v:keySet(img_Class), w:V with v−−e
    −>w reportSet e, e, v end");
instantiateEdges("HasSuperClass", "from e:keySet(img_SubClassOf), v:keySet(img_Class), w:V with w
    −−e−>v reportSet e, e, v end");
instantiateEdges("HasAxioms", "from v:keySet(img_Ontology), e:keySet(img_SubClassOf), w:V with v
    −−>−−e−>w reportSet e, v, e end");
```

Figure A.26. Transformation step 7: BEDSL hasSupertype to OWL SubClassOf.

```
instantiateVertices("InverseObjectProperty", "from e:E{OppositeOf} reportSet e end");
instantiateEdges("HasInversedObjectProperty", "from e:keySet(img_InverseObjectProperty), v,w:V{
    Reference} with v−−e−>w reportSet e, e, v end");
instantiateEdges("HasInverseObjectProperty", "from e:keySet(img_InverseObjectProperty), v,w:V{
    Reference} with v−−e−>w reportSet e, w end");
instantiateEdges("HasAxioms", "from v:keySet(img_Ontology), e:keySet(img_InverseObjectProperty), w:V
    with v−−>−−>−−e−>w reportSet e, v, e end");
```

Figure A.27. Transformation step 8: BEDSL hasOpposite to OWL InverseObject-
Property.

A.3.2 Example of API Bridge

In the following we are going to present the implementation of methods for
all kinds of constructs BEDSL provides. These methods get an element of the
BEDSL graph as input and use the ontology manager to add new axioms to
a given ontology.

Bridge Models

The bridgeModel method in Figure A.28 gets a BEDSL model as input and
first of all creates a new ontology. The IRI is defined according to the name
of the model. Two collections are declared to collect only those hasSuperType
edges and Feature vertices, which are locally defined in the given BEDSL
model. Subsequently the method iterates over all entities, specialization relationships, datatypes, and features in the model and invokes the corresponding
bridging methods, which are presented in the following. All bridging methods
get the ontology to be extended by additional axioms as input, the BEDSL
model element, which should be translated, and the prefix manager, which
encapsulates the prefix used to name all entities in the ontology.

Bridge Entities

The bridgeEntity method in Figure A.29 creates a new OWL class for a given
Entity vertex. The name of the OWL class is defined by the name of the entity.
A declaration axiom is added to the ontology declaring the OWL class.

```java
private void bridgeModel(Model m) {
  try {
    // Define IRI and Prefix of the ontology
    IRI iri = IRI.create("http://www.semanticsoftware.eu/"+m.get_name());
    OWLOntology ontology = manager.createOntology(iri);
    String base = "http://semanticsoftware.eu/";
    PrefixManager pm = new DefaultPrefixManager(base);

    // Create collections for HasSuperType edges and Feature vertices in the model
    Collection<HasSupertype> hasSuperTypeCollection = new ArrayList<HasSupertype>();
    Collection<Feature> featureCollection = new ArrayList<Feature>();

    // Iterate over all Entity vertices
    Iterator<ContainsModelEntity> containsEntityIterator = m.getContainsModelEntityIncidences().
      iterator();
    while(containsEntityIterator.hasNext()){
      Entity e = (Entity)containsEntityIterator.next().getOmega();
      bridgeEntity(ontology, pm, e);

      // Collect all HasSupertype edges in the model
      Iterator<HasSupertype> hasSuperTypeIterator = (e.getHasSupertypeIncidences(EdgeDirection.OUT
        ).iterator());
      while(hasSuperTypeIterator.hasNext()){
        hasSuperTypeCollection.add(hasSuperTypeIterator.next() );
      }

      // Collect all Feature vertices in the model
      Iterator<HasFeature> hasFeatureIterator = e.getHasFeatureIncidences().iterator();
      while(hasFeatureIterator.hasNext()){
        featureCollection.add((Feature)hasFeatureIterator.next().getOmega());
      }
    }

    // Iterate over all HasSupertype edges in the model
    Iterator<HasSupertype> hasSuperTypeIterator = hasSuperTypeCollection.iterator();
    while (hasSuperTypeIterator.hasNext()) {
      bridgeHasSupertype(ontology, hasSuperTypeIterator.next());
    }

    // Iterate over all Datatype vertices in the model
    Iterator<ContainsModelDatatype> containsDatatypeIterator = m.
      getContainsModelDatatypeIncidences().iterator();
    while(containsDatatypeIterator.hasNext()) {
      bridgeDatatype(ontology, pm, (Datatype)containsDatatypeIterator.next().getOmega());
    }

    // Iterate over all Features in the model
    Iterator<Feature> featureIterator = featureCollection.iterator();
    while(featureIterator.hasNext()) {
      Feature f = (Feature) featureIterator.next();
      if(f instanceof Reference)
        bridgeFeature(ontology, pm, (Reference)(f));
      if(f instanceof Attribute)
        bridgeFeature(ontology, pm, (Attribute)(f));
    }

    saveOntology(m.get_name()+".owl", ontology);

  } catch (OWLOntologyCreationException e) {
    e.printStackTrace();
  }
}
```

Figure A.28. API bridge for BEDSL models.

```
private void bridgeEntity(OWLOntology o, PrefixManager pm, Entity e) {
  OWLClass c = factory.getOWLClass(e.get_name(), pm);
  OWLDeclarationAxiom d = factory.getOWLDeclarationAxiom(c);
  manager.addAxiom(o, d);
  owlEntityMap.put(e, c);
}
```

Figure A.29. API bridge for BEDSL entities.

Bridge HasSupertype Relations

The bridgeHasSupertype method in Figure A.30 creates a subclass axiom in the ontology for a HasSupertype edge. The subclass axiom relates the OWL classes, which are created for the corresponding entities being incident with the given HasSupertype edge.

```
private void bridgeHasSupertype(OWLOntology o, HasSupertype h) {
  OWLSubClassOfAxiom sub = factory.getOWLSubClassOfAxiom((OWLClass)owlEntityMap.get(h.
      getAlpha()), (OWLClass)owlEntityMap.get(h.getOmega()));
  manager.addAxiom(o, sub);
}
```

Figure A.30. API bridge for BEDSL HasSupertype edges.

Bridge Datatypes

The bridgeDatatype method in Figure A.31 translates a BEDSL datatype into corresponding OWL constructs.

The method differs between primitive datatypes and enumerations. In the case of primitive datatypes, the method checks whether the datatype is a String, Integer, Boolean, or Double datatype by checking the name attribute. For each type a corresponding datatype in the ontology is declared. In the case of BEDSL enumerations a DataOneOf construct is created and filled with OWL literals. These literals are defined for each enumeration entry being part of the given enumeration.

Bridge Features

In Figure A.32 five different methods are implemented to bridge references and attributes in BEDSL models.

The method bridgeFeature getting a Reference as input declares a corresponding object property in the given ontology and invokes the methods bridgeHasFeature and bridgePointsTo.

The method bridgeHasFeature differs between HasFeature edges, which end at Reference vertices and also those, which end at Attribute vertices. For edges

```
private void bridgeDatatype(OWLOntology o, PrefixManager pm, Datatype d) {
  if(!(d instanceof Enumeration)){
    if(d.get_name().equalsIgnoreCase("String")){
      OWLDatatype string = factory.getOWLDatatype("xsd:string", pm);
      OWLDeclarationAxiom dec = factory.getOWLDeclarationAxiom(string);
      manager.addAxiom(o, dec);
      owlEntityMap.put(d, string);
    }
    if(d.get_name().equalsIgnoreCase("Integer")){
      OWLDatatype integer = factory.getOWLDatatype("xsd:integer", pm);
      OWLDeclarationAxiom dec = factory.getOWLDeclarationAxiom(integer);
      manager.addAxiom(o, dec);
      owlEntityMap.put(d, integer);
    }
    if(d.get_name().equalsIgnoreCase("Boolean")){
      OWLDatatype bool = factory.getOWLDatatype("xsd:boolean", pm);
      OWLDeclarationAxiom dec = factory.getOWLDeclarationAxiom(bool);
      manager.addAxiom(o, dec);
      owlEntityMap.put(d, bool);
    }
    if(d.get_name().equalsIgnoreCase("Double")){
      OWLDatatype doub = factory.getOWLDatatype("xsd:double", pm);
      OWLDeclarationAxiom dec = factory.getOWLDeclarationAxiom(doub);
      manager.addAxiom(o, dec);
      owlEntityMap.put(d, doub);
    }
  }
  else {
    Enumeration e = (Enumeration) d;
    Set<OWLLiteral> literals = new HashSet<OWLLiteral>();

    Iterator<ContainsEntry> containsEntryIterator = e.getContainsEntryIncidences().iterator();
    while(containsEntryIterator.hasNext()) {        literals.add(factory.getOWLLiteral(((EnumerationEntry
      )(containsEntryIterator.next().getOmega())).get_value()));
    }

    OWLDataOneOf dataoneof = factory.getOWLDataOneOf(literals);
    OWLDatatype dataOneOfDatatype = factory.getOWLDatatype(e.get_name(), pm);
    OWLDatatypeDefinitionAxiom def = factory.getOWLDatatypeDefinitionAxiom(dataOneOfDatatype,
      dataoneof);
    manager.addAxiom(o, def);
    owlEntityMap.put(e, dataOneOfDatatype);
  }
}
```

Figure A.31. API bridge for BEDSL data types.

of type HasFeature being incident with a Reference vertex, the method adds an object property domain axiom to the ontology. The axiom connects the class, which was created for the entity containing the feature with the object property, which in turn was created for the reference. For edges of type HasFeature being incident with an Attribute vertex the method adds a data property domain axiom to the ontology. The axiom connects the class, which was created for the entity containing the feature with the data property, which in turn was created for the attribute.

The bridgePointsTo method creates an object property range axiom. It connects the object property representing the reference in the ontology with the class representing the entity where the PointsTo edge ends.

The method bridgeFeature getting an Attribute as input declares a corresponding data property in the given ontology and invokes the methods bridge-HasFeature and bridgeHasAttributeDatatype.

The bridgeHasAttributeDatatype method creates a data property range axiom for a HasAttributeDatatype edge. The axiom connects the data property representing the Attribute vertex being incident with the given HasAttribute-Datatype edge, with the datatype in the ontology being the translation of the datatype in the BEDSL model.

```
private void bridgeFeature(OWLOntology o, PrefixManager pm, Reference r){
  OWLObjectProperty op = factory.getOWLObjectProperty(r.get_name(), pm);
  OWLDeclarationAxiom d = factory.getOWLDeclarationAxiom(op);
  manager.addAxiom(o, d);
  owlEntityMap.put(r, p);

  bridgeHasFeature(o, r.getFirstHasFeature());
  bridgePointsTo(o, r.getFirstPointsTo());
}

private void bridgeHasFeature(OWLOntology o, HasFeature e) {
  if(e.getOmega() instanceof Reference) {
    OWLObjectPropertyDomainAxiom d = factory.getOWLObjectPropertyDomainAxiom((
      OWLObjectProperty)owlEntityMap.get(e.getOmega()), (OWLClass) owlEntityMap.get(e.getAlpha())
    );
    manager.addAxiom(o, d);
  }
  if(e.getOmega() instanceof Attribute) {
    OWLDataPropertyDomainAxiom d = factory.getOWLDataPropertyDomainAxiom((OWLDataProperty)
      owlEntityMap.get(e.getOmega()), (OWLClass)owlEntityMap.get(e.getAlpha()));
    manager.addAxiom(o, d);
  }
}

private void bridgePointsTo(OWLOntology o, PointsTo e) {
  OWLObjectPropertyRangeAxiom r = factory.getOWLObjectPropertyRangeAxiom((OWLObjectProperty)
    owlEntityMap.get(e.getAlpha()), (OWLClass)owlEntityMap.get(e.getOmega()));
  manager.addAxiom(o, r);
}

private void bridgeFeature(OWLOntology o, PrefixManager pm, Attribute a){
  OWLDataProperty op = factory.getOWLDataProperty(a.get_name(), pm);
  OWLDeclarationAxiom d = factory.getOWLDeclarationAxiom(op);
  manager.addAxiom(o, d);
  owlEntityMap.put(a, op);

  bridgeHasFeature(o, a.getFirstHasFeature());
  bridgeHasAttributeDatatype(o, pm, a.getFirstHasAttributeDatatype());
}

private void bridgeHasAttributeDatatype(OWLOntology ontology, PrefixManager pm,
    HasAttributeDatatype h) {
  OWLDataPropertyRangeAxiom a = factory.getOWLDataPropertyRangeAxiom((OWLDataProperty)
    owlEntityMap.get(h.getAlpha()), (OWLDatatype)owlEntityMap.get(h.getOmega()));
  manager.addAxiom(ontology, a);
}
```

Figure A.32. API bridge for BEDSL features.

A.4 Grammar for the Ecore+OWL language

In the following, we present the grammar to design textual Ecore-based meta-models with OWL 2-based annotations:

#KM3 Grammar

package = "package" name "{" classifiers "}";

classifiers = (classifier);
classifier = class | datatype | enumeration;

class = ["abstract"] "class" name [supertypes] [classaxioms] "{" features "}";

supertypes = "extends" typelist;
typelist = {typeref', "} typeref;

features = {feature};
feature = attribute | reference;

attribute = [frontDataPropertyAxioms] "attribute" name multiplicity ":" typeref [endDataPropertyAxioms]
    ";";

reference = [frontObjectPropertyAxioms] "reference" name multiplicity iscontainer ":" typeref "oppositeOf
    " name [endObjectPropertyAxioms] ";";
multiplicity = bounds ("ordered");
bounds = "[" integer "−" integer "]" | "[" integer "− *" "]" | "[*]";
iscontainer = ("container");

datatype = "datatype" name ;

enumeration = "enumeration" name "{" literals "}";

literals = literal { ";" literal };
literal = "literal" name ;

typeref = name;

digit = "0".."9";
integer = digit {digit};

name = (letter | "_") { letter | digit | "_" } ;
letter = "a".."z" | "A".."Z" ;

KM3 Grammar Extension

classaxioms = classAxiom {"," classAxiom} ;
classAxiom = ("equivalentTo" CE | "disjointWith" CE | "subClassOf" CE | "disjointUnionOf" CE CE {CE
    }) ;
CE = (name | "not" CE | CE "and" CE { "and" CE } | CE "or" CE {"or" CE} | OPE ("some" | "only")
    CE | OPE "Self" | OPE ("min" | "max" | "exactly") integer CE | DPE ("some" | "only")
    dataRange | DPE ("min" | "max" | "exactly") integer dataRange) ;

frontObjectPropertyAxioms = frontObjectPropertyAxiom {"," frontObjectPropertyAxiom} ;
endObjectPropertyAxioms = endObjectPropertyAxiom {"," endObjectPropertyAxiom} ;
frontObjectPropertyAxiom = ("functional" | "inversefunctional" | "symmetric" | "asymmetric" | "reflexive
    " | "irreflexive" | "transitive") ;
endObjectPropertyAxiom = ("equivalentTo" OPE | "subPropertyOf" OPE | "domain" CE | "range" CE |
    "disjointWith" OPE | "inverseOf" name | "subPropertyChain" OPE "o" OPE {"o" OPE}) ;
OPE = name | "inv(" name ")" ;

frontDataPropertyAxioms = frontDataPropertyAxiom {"," frontDataPropertyAxiom} ;
endDataPropertyAxioms = endDataPropertyAxiom {"," endDataPropertyAxiom} ;
frontDataPropertyAxiom = "functional" ;

endDataPropertyAxiom = ("equivalentTo" DPE | "subPropertyOf" DPE | "domain" CE | "range"
    dataRange | "disjointWith" DPE);
DPE = name ;

dataRange = (dataConjunction "or" dataConjunction { "or" dataConjunction }) | dataConjunction;

dataConjunction = (dataPrimary "and" dataPrimary { "and" dataPrimary }) | dataPrimary ;

dataPrimary = ["not"] dataAtomic;

dataAtomic = Datatype | "{" literalList "}" | "(" dataRange ")";

Datatype = name;

literalList = name { ";" name };

List of Figures

List of Tables

References

ABGR07. Kyriakos Anastasakis, Behzad Bordbar, Geri Georg, and Indrakshi Ray. UML2Alloy: A challenging model transformation. In *Proceedings of Model Driven Engineering Languages and Systems, MoDELS 2007*, volume 4735 of *LNCS*, pages 436–450. Springer, 2007.

AH08. Dean Allemang and Jim Hendler. *Semantic Web for the Working Ontologist: Effective Modeling in RDFS and OWL*. Morgan Kaufmann, 2008.

AK01. Colin Atkinson and Thomas Kühne. The Essence of Multilevel Metamodeling. In *Proceedings of the International Conference on The Unified Modeling Language, UML*, volume 2185 of *LNCS*, pages 19–33. Springer, 2001.

AK03. Colin Atkinson and Thomas Kühne. Model-Driven Development: A Metamodeling Foundation. *IEEE Software*, 20(5):36–41, 2003.

ATL05. ATLAS Group LINA & INRIA, Nantes. *KM3: Kernel MetaMetaModel - Manual version 0.3*, 2005.

AZW06. Uwe Aßmann, Steffen Zschaler, and Gerd Wagner. Ontologies, Meta-Models, and the Model-Driven Paradigm. *Ontologies for Software Engineering and Software Technology*, pages 249–273, 2006.

Baa09. Franz Baader. Description Logics. In *Reasoning Web. Semantic Technologies for Information Systems*, volume 5689 of *LNCS*, pages 1–39. Springer, 2009.

BCG05. Daniela Berardi, Diego Calvanese, and Giuseppe De Giacomo. Reasoning on UML class diagrams. *Artificial Intelligence*, 168(1-2):70–118, 2005.

BCM+03. F. Baader, D. Calvanese, D.L. McGuinness, D. Nardi, and P.F. Patel-Schneider. *The description logic handbook: theory, implementation, and applications*. Cambridge University Press New York, 2003.

Béz06. Jean Bézivin. Model Driven Engineering: An Emerging Technological Space. In *Generative and Transformational Techniques in Software Engineering*, volume 4143 of *LNCS*, pages 36–64. Springer, 2006.

BGMR03. Jean Bézivin, Sébastien Gérard, Pierre-Alain Muller, and Laurent Rioux. MDA components: Challenges and Opportunities. In *Proceedings of Workshop on Metamodelling for MDA*, pages 23–41, 2003.

Bil08. Daniel Bildhauer. Auswertung der TGraphanfragesprache GReQL 2. Diploma Thesis, University of Koblenz-Landau, 2008.

Bil10.   Daniel Bildhauer. On the relationships between Subsetting, Redefinition and Association Specialization. In *Databases and Information Systems VI*, volume 224 of *Frontiers in Artificial Intelligence and Applications*, pages 108–121. IOSPress, 2010.

BL84.   Ronald J. Brachman and Hector J. Levesque. The tractability of subsumption in frame-based description languages. In *Proceedings of the 4th National Conference on Artificial Intelligence (AAAI-84)*, pages 34–37, 1984.

Bor96.   Alex Borgida. On the relative expressiveness of description logics and predicate logics* 1. *Artificial intelligence*, 82(1-2):353–367, 1996.

BZ09.   Andreas Bartho and Srdjan Zivkovic. Modeled software guidance/engineering processes and systems. Deliverable ICT216691/TUD/WP2-D2/D/PU/b1.00, Technial University Dresden, BOC, 2009. MOST Project, http://www.most-project.eu/.

Cis04.   Cisco Systems. Presseinformationen, March 2004. http://cebit2004.cisco.de/cis_pmap/data/de/bilder.html.

CK05.   Krzysztof Czarnecki and Chang Hwan Peter Kim. Cardinality-based feature modeling and constraints: A progress report. In *Proceedings of International Workshop on Software Factories at OOPSLA'05*, 2005.

Com11.   Comarch. Operations support systems - solutions for telecoms, April 2011. http://www.comarch.com/telecommunications/our-offer/operations-support-systems-oss-suite.

CP06.   Krzysztof Czarnecki and Krzysztof Pietroszek. Verifying feature-based model templates against well-formedness ocl constraints. In *Proceedings of the 5th international conference on Generative programming and component engineering*, pages 211–220. ACM, 2006.

Cza98.   Krzysztof Czarnecki. *Generative Programming*. PhD thesis, Department of Computer Science and Automation Technical University of Ilmenau, 1998.

DLN+96.   Francesco M. Donini, Maurizio Lenzerini, Daniele Nardi, Werner Nutt, and Andrea Schaerf. An epistemic operator for description logics. *Artificial Intelligence*, 100(1-2):225–274, 1996.

EB10.   Jürgen Ebert and Daniel Bildhauer. Reverse Engineering Using Graph Queries. In *Graph Transformations and Model-Driven Engineering*, volume 5765 of *LNCS*, pages 335–362. Springer, 2010.

Eva98.   Andy S. Evans. Reasoning with UML class diagrams. In *Proceedings of 2nd IEEE Workshop on Industrial Strength Formal Specification Techniques*, pages 102–113. IEEE Computer Society, 1998.

EW10.   Jürgen Ebert and Tobias Walter. Interoperability services for models and ontologies. In *Databases and Information Systems VI*, volume 224 of *Frontiers in Artificial Intelligence and Applications*, pages 19–36. IOS-Press, 2010.

EWD+96.   Jürgen Ebert, Andreas Winter, Peter Dahm, Angelika Franzke, and Roger Süttenbach. Graph Based Modeling and Implementation with EER / GRAL. In *Proceedings of Conceptual Modeling - ER'96*, volume 1157 of *LNCS*, pages 163–178. Springer, 1996.

Far03.   James Farrugia. Model-theoretic semantics for the web. In *WWW '03: Proceedings of the 12th international conference on World Wide Web*, pages 29–38, New York, NY, USA, 2003. ACM.

FR07.   Robert B. France and Bernhard Rumpe. Model-driven Development of
           Complex Software: A Research Roadmap. In *Proceedings of the Work-
           shop on the Future of Software Engineering (FOSE)*, pages 37–54, 2007.

FST96.   Anthony Finkelstein, George Spanoudakis, and David Till. Managing
           Interference. In *ISAW '96: Joint proceedings of the second international
           software architecture workshop (ISAW-2) and international workshop on
           multiple perspectives in software development (Viewpoints '96) on SIG-
           SOFT '96 workshops*, pages 172–174. ACM, 1996.

GFC⁺08.   Jeff Gray, Kathleen Fisher, Charles Consel, Gabor Karsai, Marjan
           Mernik, and Juha-Pekka Tolvanen. Panel - DSLs: the good, the bad,
           and the ugly. In *OOPSLA Companion '08*. ACM, 2008.

GHVD03.   Benjamin N. Grosof, Ian Horrocks, Raphael Volz, and Stefan Decker.
           Description logic programs: combining logic programs with description
           logic. In *Proceedings of the 12th International Conference on World Wide
           Web*, WWW '03, pages 48–57, New York, NY, USA, 2003. ACM.

GLR⁺02.   Anna Gerber, Michael Lawley, Kerry Raymond, Jim Steel, and Andrew
           Wood. Transformation: The missing link of MDA. In *Proceedings of
           1st International Conference on Graph Transformation*, volume 2505 of
           LNCS, pages 90–105. Springer, 2002.

GM05.   Stephan Grimm and Boris Motik. Closed World Reasoning in the Seman-
           tic Web through Epistemic Operators. In *Proceedings of the 1st OWL
           Experiences and Directions Workshop (OWLED-2005)*, volume 188 of
           CEUR Workshop Proceedings. CEUR-WS.org, 2005.

GOS07.   Ralf Gitzel, Ingo Ott, and Martin Schader. Ontological Extension to
           the MOF Metamodel as a Basis for Code Generation. *The Computer
           Journal*, 50(1):93–115, 2007.

GOS09.   Nicola Guarino, Daniel Oberle, and Steffen Staab. What Is an Ontology?
           Handbook on Ontologies, pages 1–17, 2009.

GP10.   Birte Glimm and Bijan Parsia. SPARQL 1.1 Entailment Regimes. `http:`
           `//www.w3.org/TR/2010/WD-sparql11-entailment-20100126/`, January
           2010.

Gra07.   Bernardo Cuenca Grau. OWL 2 Web Ontology Language Tractable Frag-
           ments. `http://www.w3.org/2007/OWL/wiki/Tractable_Fragments`,
           2007.

Gui05.   Giancarlo Guizzardi. *Ontological Foundations for Structural Conceptual
           Models*. PhD thesis, Centre for Telematics and Information Technology,
           Enschede, The Netherlands, 2005.

HB09.   Matthew Horridge and Sean Bechhofer. The OWL API: A Java API for
           Working with OWL 2 Ontologies. In *Proceedings of the OWL Experiences
           and Directions Workshop*, volume 529 of *CEUR Workshop Proceedings*.
           CEUR-WS.org, 2009.

HE11.   Tassilo Horn and Jürgen Ebert. The GReTL Transformation Language.
           In *Proceedings of the 4th International Conference on Model Transfor-
           mation (ICMT 2011)*, LNCS. Springer, 2011. to appear.

Hec10.   Kristina Heckelmann. Abbildung von Ecore nach grUML. Bachelor The-
           sis, University of Koblenz-Landau, 2010.

Hei09.   Florian Heidenreich. Towards systematic ensuring well-formedness of
           software product lines. In *Proceedings of the First International Work-
           shop on Feature-Oriented Software Development*, pages 69–74. ACM,
           2009.

248   References

HJK+09.   Florian Heidenreich, Jendrik Johannes, Sven Karol, Mirko Seifert, and
           Christian Wende. Derivation and Refinement of Textual Syntax for Mod-
           els. In *Proceedings of European Conference on Model-Driven Architecture
           Foundations and Applications*, volume 5562 of *LNCS*, pages 114–129.
           Springer, 2009.
HM01.   Volker Haarslev and Ralf Möller. Description of the racer system and its
           applications. In *Proceedings of Description Logics Workshop*, volume 49
           of *CEUR Workshop Proceedings*. CEUR-WS.org, 2001.
Hor05.   Ian Horrocks. OWL: A Description Logic Based Ontology Language.
           In *Logic Programming: 21st International Conference*, volume 3668 of
           LNCS, pages 1–4. Springer, 2005.
Hor08.   Ian Horrocks. Ontologies and the Semantic Web. *Communications of
           the ACM*, 51(12):58–67, 2008.
HPS04.   Ian Horrocks and Peter Patel-Schneider. Reducing OWL entailment to
           description logic satisfiability. *Web Semantics: Science, Services and
           Agents on the World Wide Web*, 1(4):345–357, 2004.
HPS09.   Matthew Horridge and Peter F. Patel-Schneider. OWL 2 Web
           Ontology Language Manchester Syntax. http://www.w3.org/TR/
           owl2-manchester-syntax, October 2009.
HS05.   Peter Haase and Ljiljana Stojanovic. Consistent Evolution of OWL On-
           tologies. In *Proceedings of Second European Semantic Web Conferenc,
           ESWC 2005*, volume 3532 of *LNCS*, pages 182–197. Springer, 2005.
HS10.   Steve Harris and Andy Seaborne. SPARQL 1.1 Query Language. http:
           //www.w3.org/TR/sparql11-query/, June 2010.
JABK08.   Frédéric Jouault, Freddy Allilaire, Jean Bézivin, and Ivan Kurtev. ATL:
           A model transformation tool. *Science of Computer Programming*, 72(1-
           2):31–39, 2008.
Jac02.   Daniel Jackson. Micromodels of Software: Lightweight Modelling and
           Analysis with Alloy, 2002.
Jac06.   Daniel Jackson. *Software Abstractions: logic, language, and analysis*. The
           MIT Press, 2006.
JB06.   Frédéric Jouault and Jean Bézivin. KM3: a DSL for Metamodel Specifi-
           cation. In *Formal Methods for Open Object-Based Distributed Systems*,
           volume 4037 of *LNCS*, pages 171–185. Springer, 2006.
Kal06.   Aditya Kalyanpur. *Debugging and Repair of OWL Ontologies*. PhD
           thesis, University of Maryland, College Park, 2006.
KBA02.   Ivan Kurtev, Jean Bézivin, and Mehmet Aksit. Technological Spaces:
           An Initial Appraisal. In *CoopIS, DOA'2002 Federated Conferences, In-
           dustrial track*, Irvine, 2002.
KBJK03.   Harald Kühn, Franz Bayer, Stefan Junginger, and Dimitris Karagiannis.
           Enterprise Model Integration. In *Proceedings of E-commerce and Web
           Technologies*, volume 2738 of *LNCS*, pages 379–392. Springer, 2003.
KKK+06.   Gerti Kappel, Elisabeth Kapsammer, Horst Kargl, Gerhard Kramler,
           Thomas Reiter, Werner Retschitzegger, Wieland Schwinger, and Manuel
           Wimmer. Lifting metamodels to ontologies: A step to the semantic inte-
           gration of modeling languages. In *Proceedings of International Confer-
           ence on Model Driven Engineering Languages and Systems(MoDELS)*,
           volume 4199 of *LNCS*, pages 528–542. Springer, 2006.

KMS09.   Marek Kasztelnik, Krzysztof Miksa, and Pawel Sabina. Case study de-
           sign. Deliverable ICT216691/CMR/WP5-D2/D/RE/b1, Comarch, 2009.
           MOST Project, http://www.most-project.eu/.

KPHS07.   A. Kalyanpur, B. Parsia, M. Horridge, and E. Sirin. Finding all justifi-
           cations of OWL DL entailments. In *Proceedings of the 6th International
           Semantic Web Conference*, volume 4825 of *LNCS*, page 267. Springer,
           2007.

KPP06.   Dimitrios S. Kolovos, Richard F. Paige, and Fiona Polack. Merging Mod-
           els with the Epsilon Merging Language (EML). In *Proceedings of Inter-
           national Conference on Model Driven Engineering Languages and Sys-
           tems(MoDELS)*, volume 4199 of *LNCS*, pages 215–229. Springer, 2006.

KPSH05.   Aditya Kalyanpur, Bijan Parsia, Evren Sirin, and James A. Hendler. De-
           bugging unsatisfiable classes in owl ontologies. *Web Semantics: Science,
           Services and Agents on the World Wide Web*, 3(4):268–293, 2005.

KS08.   Petr Kremen and Evren Sirin. SPARQL-DL Implementation Experience.
           In *Proceedings of the 4th OWL Experiences and Directions DC Work-
           shop (OWLED-DC-2008)*, volume 496 of *CEUR Workshop Proceedings*.
           CEUR-WS.org, 2008.

KT07.   Steve Kelly and Juha-Pekka Tolvanen. *Domain-Specific Modeling*. John
           Wiley & Sons, 2007.

Kur08.   Ivan Kurtev. State of the Art of QVT: A Model Transformation Lan-
           guage Standard. In *Applications of Graph Transformations with Indus-
           trial Relevance*, volume 5088 of *LNCS*, pages 377–393. Springer, 2008.

KWRS11.   Gerti Kappel, Manuel Wimmer, Werner Retschitzegger, and Wieland
           Schwinger. Leveraging Model-Based Tool Integration by Conceptual
           Modeling Techniques. In *The Evolution of Conceptual Modeling*, vol-
           ume 6520 of *LNCS*, pages 254–284. Springer, 2011.

LBM+01.   Ákos Lédeczi, Arpad Bakay, Miklos Maroti, Péter Völgyesi, Greg Nord-
           strom, Jonathan Sprinkle, and Gabor Karsai. Composing domain-specific
           design environments. *IEEE Computer*, 34(11):44–51, 2001.

LK09.   Alfons Laarman and Ivan Kurtev. Ontological Metamodeling with Ex-
           plicit Instantiation. In *Proceedings of the Conference on Software Lan-
           guage Engineering*, volume 5969 of *LNCS*, pages 174–183. Springer, 2009.

LNK+01.   Akos Ledeczi, Greg Nordstrom, Gabor Karsai, Peter Volgyesi, and Miklos
           Maroti. On metamodel composition. In *Proceedings of IEEE Interna-
           tional Conference on Control Applications*, 2001.

Mar06.   Katrin Marchewka. GReQL 2. Diploma Thesis, University of Koblenz-
           Landau, 2006.

MCF03.   Stephen J. Mellor, Anthony N. Clark, and Takao Futagami. Model-driven
           development. *IEEE software*, 20(5):14–18, 2003.

MHRS06.   Boris Motik, Ian Horrocks, Riccardo Rosati, and Ulrike Sattler. Can
           OWL and Logic Programming live together happily ever after? In *Pro-
           ceedings of the 5th International Semantic Web Conference*, volume 4273
           of *LNCS*, pages 501–514. Springer, 2006.

MK08.   Krzysztof Miksa and Marek Kasztelnik. Definition of the case study
           requirements. Deliverable ICT216691/CMR/WP5-D1/D/PU/b1, Co-
           march, 2008. MOST Project, http://www.most-project.eu/.

MM09.   Steffen Mazanek and Mark Minas. Business process models as a showcase
           for syntax-based assistance in diagram editors. In *Proceedings of Model*

Driven Engineering Languages and Systems (MoDELS), volume 5795 of *LNCS*, pages 322–336. Springer, 2009.

MMM08. Steffen Mazanek, Sonja Maier, and Mark Minas. Auto-completion for Diagram Editors based on Graph Grammars. In *Proceedings of IEEE Symposium on Visual Languages and Human-Centric Computings*, pages 242–245. IEEE, 2008.

MPSH09. Boris Motik, Peter F. Patel-Schneider, and Ian Horrocks. OWL 2 Web Ontology Language: Structural Specification and Functional-Style Syntax. http://www.w3.org/TR/owl2-syntax/, October 2009.

MS91. Manfred Schmidt-Schauß and Gert Smolka. Attributive concept descriptions with complements. *Artificial intelligence*, 48(1):1–26, 1991.

MSZ10. Krzysztof Miksa, Pawel Sabina, and Srdjan Zivkovic. First demonstrator and report on experiences. Deliverable ICT216691/CMR/WP5-D3/D/PU/b1, Comarch, 2010. MOST Project, http://www.most-project.eu/.

NE93. NIST ISEE Working Group and ECMA TC33 Task Group on the Reference Model. Reference Model for Frameworks of Software Engineering Environments, TR/55, 3rd Edition. Technical report, 1993.

NER00. Bashar Nuseibeh, Steve Easterbrook, and Alessandra Russo. Leveraging Inconsistency in Software Development. *Software Development*, 33(4):24–29, 2000.

OMG06. OMG. *Meta Object Facility (MOF) Core Specification*. Object Management Group, January 2006.

OMG07a. OMG. Ontology definition metamodel. OMG Adopted Specification OMG Document Number: ptc/2007-09-09, September 2007.

OMG07b. OMG. *Unified Modeling Language: Superstructure, version 2.1.2*. Object Management Group, November 2007.

PBL05. Klaus Pohl, Günter Böckle, and Frank Van Der Linden. *Software Product Line Engineering: Foundations, Principles, and Techniques*. Springer, 2005.

Pol10. Axel Polleres. SPARQL 1.1: New Features and Friends (OWL2, RIF). In *Web Reasoning and Rule Systems*, volume 6333 of *LNCS*, pages 23–26. Springer, 2010.

PPCR08. Colin Puleston, Bijan Parsia, James Cunningham, and Alan Rector. Integrating object-oriented and ontological representations: A case study in Java and OWL. In *Proceedings of the International Semantic Web Conference*, volume 5318 of *LNCS*, pages 130–145. Springer, 2008.

PS08. Eric Prud'hommeaux and Andy Seaborne. SPARQL Query Language for RDF. http://www.w3.org/TR/rdf-sparql-query/, January 2008.

PSM10. Peter F. Patel-Schneider and Boris Motik. OWL 2 Web Ontology Language Mapping to RDF Graphs. http://www.w3.org/TR/2009/REC-owl2-mapping-to-rdf-20091027/, October 2010.

Sat03. Ulrike Sattler. Description Logics for Ontologies. In *Conceptual Structures for Knowledge Creation and Communication*, volume 2746 of *LNAI*, pages 96–116. Springer, 2003.

SBPM08. David Steinberg, Frank Budinsky, Marcelo Paternostro, and Ed Merks. *EMF: Eclipse Modeling Framework (2nd Edition)*. Addison-Wesley, 2008.

Sch06. Douglas C. Schmidt. Guest Editor's Introduction: Model-Driven Engineering. *Computer*, 39:25–31, 2006.

SE10.   Hannes Schwarz and Jürgen Ebert. Bridging Query Languages in Se-
             mantic and Graph Technologies. In *Reasoning Web. Semantic Technolo-
             gies for Software Engineering*, volume 6325 of *LNCS*, pages 119–160.
             Springer, 2010.
SEL$^+$10.   Hannes Schwarz, Jürgen Ebert, Jens Lemcke, Tirdad Rahmani, and Srd-
             jan Zivkovic. Using Expressive Traceability Relationships for Ensuring
             Consistent Process Model Refinement. In *Proceedings of the 15th IEEE
             International Conference on Engineering of Complex Computer Systems*.
             IEEE Computer Society, 2010.
SEW10.   Hannes Schwarz, Jürgen Ebert, and Andreas Winter. Graph-based trace-
             ability: a comprehensive approach. *Software and Systems Modeling*,
             9(4):473–492, 2010.
SP07.   Evren Sirin and Bijan Parsia. SPARQL-DL: SPARQL Query for OWL-
             DL. In *Proceedings of the 3rd OWL Experiences and Directions Workshop
             (OWLED-2007)*, volume 258 of *CEUR Workshop Proceedings*. CEUR-
             WS.org, 2007.
SPG$^+$07.   Evren Sirin, Bijan Parsia, Bernardo Cuenca Grau, Aditya Kalyanpur,
             and Yarden Katz. Pellet: A practical OWL-DL Reasoner. *Web Seman-
             tics: Science, Services and Agents on the World Wide Web*, 5(2):51–53,
             2007.
ST09.   Evren Sirin and Jiao Tao. Towards integrity constraints in owl. In *Pro-
             ceedings of the Workshop on OWL: Experiences and Directions (OWLED
             2009)*, volume 529 of *CEUR Workshop Proceedings*. CEUR-WS.org,
             2009.
Süt01.   Roger Süttenbach. *Formalisierung visueller Modellierungssprachen ob-
             jektorientierter Methoden*. PhD thesis, University of Koblenz-Landau,
             2001.
SW09.   Daniel A. Sadilek and Guido Wachsmuth. Using grammarware languages
             to define operational semantics of modelled languages. In *Proceedings of
             the 47th International Conference on Objects, Components, Models and
             Patterns (TOOLS)*, volume 33 of *Lecture Notes in Business Information
             Processing*. Springer, 2009.
SWGP10.   Steffen Staab, Tobias Walter, Gerd Gröner, and Fernando Silva Parreiras.
             Model Driven Engineering with Ontology Technologies. In *Reasoning
             Web*, volume 6325 of *LNCS*, pages 62–98. Springer, 2010.
SZ01.   George Spanoudakis and Andrea Zisman. Inconsistency Management in
             Software Engineering: Survey and Open Research Issues. *Handbook of
             Software Engineering and Knowledge Engineering*, 1:329–380, 2001.
Van05.   Ragnhild Van Der Straeten. *Inconsistency Management in Model-driven
             Engineering. An Approach using Description Logics*. PhD thesis, Vrije
             Universiteit Brussel, Belgium, 2005.
vL01.   Axel van Lamsweerde. Goal-oriented requirements engineering: A guided
             tour. In *Proceedings of IEEE International Symposium on Requirements
             Engineering*, pages 249–253. IEEE Computer Society, 2001.
W3C11.   W3C. Extensible Markup Language (XML). http://www.w3.org/XML/,
             April 2011.
WE09.   Tobias Walter and Jürgen Ebert. Combining DSLs and Ontologies Using
             Metamodel Integration. In *Proceedings of IFIP Working Conference on
             Domain-Specific Languages*, volume 5658 of *LNCS*, pages 148–169, 2009.

WK03.   Jos Warmer and Anneke Kleppe. *The Object Constraint Language: Getting Your Models Ready for MDA*. Addison-Wesley, 2003.

WL99.   David M. Weiss and Chi Tau Robert Lai. *Software Product-Line Engineering: A Family-Based Software Development Process*. Addison Wesley, 1999.

WPS09.   Tobias Walter, Fernando Silva Parreiras, and Steffen Staab. OntoDSL: An Ontology-Based Framework for Domain-Specific Languages. In *Model Driven Engineering Languages and Systems, 12th International Conference, MODELS*, volume 5795 of *LNCS*, pages 408–422. Springer, 2009.

WPSE10.   Tobias Walter, Fernando Silva Parreiras, Steffen Staab, and Jürgen Ebert. Joint Language and Domain Engineering. In *Proceedings of European Conference Modelling Foundations and Applications*, volume 6138 of *LNCS*, pages 321–336. Springer, 2010.

WSN+08.   Jules White, Douglas C. Schmidt, Andrey Nechypurenko, , and Egon Wuchner. Model intelligence: an approach to modeling guidance. *UPGRADE*, 9(2):22–28, 2008.

WSR10.   Tobias Walter, Hannes Schwarz, and Yuan Ren. Establishing a Bridge from Graph-based Modeling Languages to Ontology Languages. In *Proceedings of 3rd Workshop on Transforming and Weaving Ontologies in Model Driven Engineering (TWOMDE)*, volume CEUR of *604*. CEUR-WS.org, 2010.

Index

B

Curriculum Vitae - Tobias Walter

Personal

Dipl. Inform. Tobias Walter

University of Koblenz-Landau
Universitaetsstr. 1
56070 Koblenz - Germany

Tel.: +49 261 287 2716
Fax: +49 261 287 100 2716
E-mail: walter@uni-koblenz.de
Web: http://walter.semanticsoftware.eu

Born on October 11, 1982.
German Citizen.

Education

10/2002 - 05/2008 RWTH Aachen University, Aachen, Germany
Diploma in Computer Science.

Employments

05/2008 - 08/2011 University of Koblenz-Landau, Koblenz, Germany
Research Assistant at the Institute for Software
Technology and the Institut for Web Science and
Technology.

04/2007 - 09/2007 Ericsson Eurolab GmbH, Aachen, Germany
Diploma student.

Publications

2011

Ebert, J., Walter, T.: Interoperability services for models and ontologies. In: Databases and Information Systems VI. Volume 224 of Frontiers in Artificial Intelligence and Applications, IOSPress, 19-36.

2010

Walter, T., Parreiras, F.S., Gröner, G.,Wende, C.: OWLizing: Transforming Software Models to Ontologies. In: Ontology-Driven Software Engineering. ODiSE'10, ACM (2010), 7:1-7:6.

Parreiras, F.S., Walter, T., Gröner, G.: Visualizing Ontologies with UML-like notation. In: Ontology-Driven Software Engineering. ODiSE'10, ACM (2010) 4:1-4:6

Parreiras, F.S., Walter, T., Wende, C., Thomas, E.: Bridging software languages and ontology technologies: tutorial summary. In: SPLASH/OOPSLA Companion, ACM (2010) 311-315

Parreiras, F.S., Gröner, G., Walter, T., Staab, S.: A Model-Driven Approach for Using Templates in OWL Ontologies. In: Knowledge Engineering and Management by the Masses. Volume 6317 of LNCS., Springer (2010) 350-359

Staab, S., Walter, T., Gröner, G., Parreiras, F.S.: Model Driven Engineering with Ontology Technologies. In: Reasoning Web. Volume 6325 of LNCS, Springer (2010) 62-98

Walter, T., Schwarz, H., Ren, Y.: Establishing a Bridge from Graph-based Modeling Languages to Ontology Languages. In: Proceedings of 3rd Workshop on Transforming and Weaving Ontologies in Model Driven Engineering (TWOMDE). CEUR-WS.org.

Walter, T., Parreiras, F.S., Staab, S., Ebert, J.: Joint Language and Domain Engineering. In: Proceedings of European Conference Modelling Foundations and Applications. Volume 6138 of LNCS, Springer (2010) 321-336

Miksa, K., Kasztelnik, M., Sabina, P., Walter, T.: Towards Semantic Modeling of Network Physical Devices. In: Models in Software Engineering, Workshops and Symposia at MODELS 2009. Volume 6002 of LNCS, Springer (2010) 329-343

2009

Walter, T., Parreiras, F.S., Staab, S.: OntoDSL: An Ontology-Based Framework for Domain-Specific Languages. In: Model Driven Engineering Languages and Systems, 12th International Conference, MODELS. Volume 5795 of LNCS., Springer (2009) 408-422

Walter, T.: Combining Domain-Specific Languages and Ontology Technologies. In: Proceedings of the Doctoral Symposium at MODELS 2009. Volume 2009-566 of Technical Report., School of Computing, Queen's University (2009) 34-40

Walter, T., Ebert, J.: Combining ontology-enriched Domain-Specific Languages.
In: Proceedings of 2nd Workshop on Transforming and Weaving Ontolo-
gies in Model Driven Engineering (TWOMDE). Volume CEUR of 531.,
CEUR-WS.org (2009)

Walter, T., Ebert, J.: Combining DSLs and Ontologies Using Metamodel Integration. In: Proceedings of IFIP Working Conference on Domain-Specific
Languages. Volume 5658 of LNCS, Springer (2009) 148-169

Parreiras, F.S., Saathoff, C., Walter, T., Franz, T., Staab, S.: APIs a gogo: Automatic Generation of Ontology APIs. In: Proceedings of the IEEE International Conference on Semantic Computing (ICSC), IEEE Computer
Society (2009) 342-348

2008

Mosler, C., Walter, T.: ECARES-Projekt: Kombination von graphbasierten
Redesign-Analysen. In: Proceedings of Workshop Software Reengineering.
Volume 126 of LNI., GI (2008) 149-153